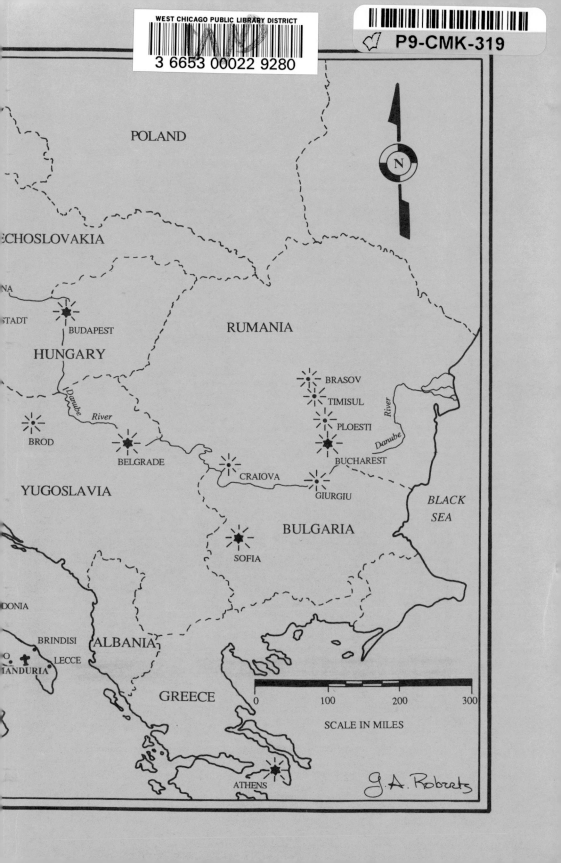

POLAND

N

ECHOSLOVAKIA

NA

STADT

BUDAPEST

HUNGARY

RUMANIA

*BRASOV

*TIMISUL

River

*PLOESTI

Danube

River

BROD

*BUCHAREST

BELGRADE

CRAIOVA

YUGOSLAVIA

*GIURGIU

BLACK
SEA

BULGARIA

*SOFIA

DONIA

BRINDISI

ALBANIA

O

LECCE

IANDURIA

GREECE

0   100   200   300

SCALE IN MILES

ATHENS

G. A. Roberts

THE WAR OF THE COTTON-TAILS

THE WAR OF THE COTTON-TAILS

MEMOIRS OF A WWII BOMBER PILOT

by WILLIAM R. CUBBINS
Lt. USAF ret.

ALGONQUIN BOOKS OF CHAPEL HILL 1989

Published by
Algonquin Books of Chapel Hill
Post Office Box 2225
Chapel Hill, North Carolina 27515-2225

a division of
Workman Publishing Company, Inc.
708 Broadway
New York, New York 10003

Library of Congress Cataloging-in-Publication Data

Cubbins, William R., 1924–
The war of the Cottontails : a bomber pilot with the Fifteenth Air
Force against Nazi Germany / by William R. Cubbins.
p.   cm.
Published in association with Workman Pub. Co., New York, New York.
ISBN 0-912697-96-2
1. Cubbins, William R., 1924–   . 2. World War, 1939–1945—Aerial
operations, American. 3. World War, 1939–1945—Personal narratives,
American. 4. United States. Army Air Forces—Biography. 5. Air
pilots, Military—United States—Biography. I. Title.
D790.C83 1989
940.54′4973—dc19
88-26227
CIP

To the memory of Sergeant Frank E. Riley, Jr., radio operator and waist-gunner of the B-24 Swashbuckler. *His was the supreme sacrifice.*

ILLUSTRATIONS

AUTHOR'S NOTE

T he story of the *Swashbuckler* and the gallant crews of the 450th Bombardment Group (Heavy), the Cottontails, and of the survivors of the other bomb and fighter groups who were incarcerated in the POW camps in Rumania is rich in the drama of human experience. Nevertheless, I resisted writing this account for these many years because the trials visited upon my men by our combat and noncombat experiences were such as to challenge the plausibility of truth. In setting down this account, I have endeavored to write in the context of my knowledge and experience as they existed at the time of these events. In those instances wherein I have written from a broader experience I have tried to make that fact known to the reader. While I have relied greatly on the memory of others in relating some of the prisoner of war experiences, the responsibility for the content and thrust of this account remains mine.

Those who assisted me in this endeavor are many. I am indebted to Pastor Robert Leach Chism—my Uncle Bob—himself a prisoner in that great war and who insisted that I tell the tale; to my wife, Lucille Martin Cubbins, who endured these years of research and writing. My special thanks goes to Mr. Harry Fletcher and other staff members of the Albert F. Simpson Historical Research Center, United States Air Force, Maxwell Air Force Base, Alabama. Without their assistance, the story would not—indeed, could not—have been written. I am particularly indebted to Sherwood Mark, a combat photographer who had the misfortune to be with us in Bucharest; to Cottontails Loren B. Heath, Jr., Samuel Stein, and Arnold Daniels, and Colonel James A. Gunn III for the loan of their treasured photos that so faithfully recorded many of the events of this account; and to British army Lieutenant Colonel J. P. Macdonald who provided the photographs of the schoolhouse and of the American and Commonwealth flyers during their captivity. Above all, I am indebted to the encouragement and assistance rendered by Robert F. Cubbins, mentor, goad, and kinsman, without whose tutelage the tale would have been unreadable. Finally, to the men of the *Swashbuckler*, whose capacity for battle and willingness to fly with me defy description by mere words.

INTRODUCTION

The origins of World War II, and our nation's objectives in that conflict—unlike our limited political objectives in Korea and Vietnam—were abundantly clear to all. Fortified by a perception of imminent danger to the nation, young men literally rushed to take up arms in freedom's name.

The early months of our entry into the war were vibrant times, times that were filled with song, the invincibility of American arms, and prospects of glorious victories over despicable enemies. "Peace" was not a conscious objective in the minds of most. Peace was the province of philosophers, and diplomats, and of mothers who feared more than we for our lives. We in the Air Force had one objective—to fly and fight. It was only after we became immersed in battle that the realities of war, of our own mortality, surfaced. Even then the probability of one's own death often took the form of a self-serving fiction: It was always *the other fellow* who would *die*.

This is not to say that we were not afraid. Fear was a constant companion, a helpmate that could galvanize us to fevered action. At other times, fear was a relentless foe that plagued us unmercifully between battles, that robbed us of character.

The quality of character that we commonly recognize as "courage" is simply the ability to rise above one's fears and do what needs to be done at the moment. As is the case with time, courage is often a fleeting thing.

Another face of courage is the love and respect that one has for comrades in battle. It is an allegiance more to one's self and others than to the "cause." That men may rise above their fears and fight in a self-sacrificial manner is not only noble, it is often the margin of victory in battle.

There are yet other aspects of the complex thing we call courage. There is the fear of failure, and of fear itself.

Fear-of-failure is a powerful impulse that can carry a man beyond his norms of physical and emotional endurance. However, fear-of-failure offers little substance of lasting value. Indeed, it alone may eventually defeat the man.

There is also the impulse to do a thing simply because it is the thing to do. If we do not emulate our peers, we become as outcasts from our closed society. The two notions seem to coalesce into the most prevalent force of all—that is, "fear of being perceived to be less than one's peers."

Fear-of-being-less-than is not a form of competition in its usual sense. It is more like a willingness to do what other men find necessary—an unspoken bond of shared responsibility. For many it is a sustaining force that bridges fear-filled moments between battles, and allows them to find comfort in "shared" danger.

One of the more notable aspects of being a prisoner of war is the manner in which emotions and responses tend to become exaggerated, to become overreactions that breed more overreaction. From the moment of capture, prisoners of war commonly perceive that the war is over for them, that they are at the mercy of their captors, that their condition is hopeless. One of the most difficult aspects of captivity to understand is that the prisoner is not *fully* at the mercy of the enemy, nor is his condition *completely* hopeless.

It is easy to make such statements in retrospect, but to recognize their validity, or even think such thoughts when one is in extreme danger, is not an easy task. While under the vulnerable circumstances of captivity, so-called normal responses of otherwise courageous men often undergo radical change. When men are stripped of their powerful weapons of war, there is a tendency to grow apart from others, to turn inward and become enveloped by a crushing aloneness. Indeed, the desire to survive can become such an overriding force, a man's response to his circumstance may vary—be less than noble—from his behavior in organized combat. Experience is clear on one point: *strong leadership and organization are crucial to many prisoners' abilities to cope with many of the life-threatening aspects of captivity.*

At the time of the events related in this account, we knew little of such things. Since then the armed services have established programs to teach men how to survive in prisoner of war camps, to escape and return from captivity. Regrettably, the success of such endeavors has been less than exemplary. We still do not know how to impart the vital elements of *attitude* and *perseverance* that give men the ability to endure and carry on despite the circumstances of their plight.

In setting down this account of combat and captivity, painful effort has been made to speak frankly and honestly. Although it represents only one point of view, experience in subsequent wars parallels these World War II data with dismaying fidelity. It is hoped that the reader will find value in this account—in our triumphs, and in our defeat.

THE WAR OF THE COTTON-TAILS

1

"YOU WILL DEPART VIA THE SOUTHERN ROUTE FOR NATAL, BRAZIL; THEN TO DAKAR, SENEGAL; THEN BY A ROUTE TO BE DESIGNATED TO MANDURIA, ITALY, FOR ASSIGNMENT TO THE 450TH BOMBARDMENT GROUP (HEAVY), FIFTEENTH AIR FORCE." The rest of the SECRET order contained the usual military jargon dealing with administrative matters.

I passed the sheaf of papers to my copilot, Lt. Frank Tarasko, and got the crew on intercom and told them our destination. After months of anxiety over wondering where we'd fight, the crew was pleased to learn that we'd be based in Italy. I doubted, however, that they'd be very happy about Manduria's location. It was midway down the heel of the Italian "boot," and there was no large city for recreation nearby. I'd worry about that later, I thought. Italy is still thousands of miles and a helluva lot of ocean and desert away, and we had just taken off from Morrison Field, West Palm Beach, Florida. The day was April 10, 1944.

The first two legs of our journey had gone well until we approached Waller Field, on the island of Trinidad. During our approach to the runway, we flew through an intense tropical shower. Shortly after we entered the deluge, number-three engine started coughing and losing power. Tarasko and our flight engineer, Sgt. Frank Lynch, applied carburetor heat to the engine, and we landed without further ado. We checked the engine after we pulled off the runway but found nothing wrong. I put the matter out of mind.

The next day, while en route to Belem, number-three acted up again. It would run fine for a while, then cough for several minutes, then run normally. After landing at Belem, Lynch and our assistant flight engineer, Sgt. Chris Dittman, worked on the engine until late into the night, but found nothing wrong. Faced with the decision of whether to remain at Belem while the carburetor was flown to Natal for bench testing and repair, or press on, I opted for the latter. I was confident that if we could get the bird off the ground at Belem we could shut down the engine, if necessary, and continue the flight on three engines. As it turned out, I'd worried needlessly. The engine performed flawlessly, and the possibility of trouble added a pinch of spice as we winged our way southward over dense jungle. I reported the carburetor problem to Natal Maintenance, and was assured that our factory-new B-24, *Swashbuckler*, would be ready for our Atlantic crossing.

After two days of preparations, and a test hop to check the ailing engine, we took off for Africa. The morning was black, and saturated by violent thunderstorms.[1] With my vision blocked by waves of rainwater washing the windshield, I made an instrument takeoff, and sweated profusely as the heavy aircraft ate up barely adequate runway in its reach for flying speed. We had just lifted off the runway and retracted our landing gear and flaps when number-three started coughing its life away. Too low to bail out, and too heavy with fuel for an assured safe landing, I battled storm turbulence, lightning, and deafening static for forty minutes to stay airborne and accomplish the impossible—find Natal airfield and put our severely overweight B-24 back on the ground. We'd abused the three good engines unmercifully in nursing the faltering ship upward to gain altitude, and I knew that they'd never last long enough for me to use the Low Frequency Radio Range to make an approach to the airfield. I had no choice but to shorten our flight pattern and use the homing station to set up the landing.

Only the sure hand of God could have put us off the end of the runway with sufficient altitude to make it to the edge of the airfield when number-three died and the overloaded bomber quit flying. We broke free of the overcast while we were still some two hundred and fifty feet above the ground. My first sight of the airfield told me that we would hit short of the runway. The landing gear held up under the spine-jarring impact, and I brought the *Swashbuckler* to a stop on the runway.

Two days later, after hanging a new carburetor on number-three and making a retraction test on our landing gear, we again launched

---

1. A present day (1980s) pilot knows better than to attempt an aircraft takeoff during such violent flying conditions.

for Dakar.[2] Five hours out from Natal, the sky darkened. Dirty stratus thickened and grew ominously black. Lightning lit storm cells like gigantic bulbs, now and then like a theater marquee flashing across the horizon. As we drew near, static electricity raised the hair on my arms and neck. The Natal weather forecaster had warned us that the permanent cold front that sits in the middle of the Atlantic was gaining strength, but the electrical potential within this front was unlike anything I had ever experienced.

The *Swashbuckler* shuddered as a giant hand flung it violently upward, nose high, and on one wing. The wheel was almost wrenched from my grasp as I struggled to get the nose down and the wings level. Purple lightning lit the rain-flooded windshield like flashes from a thousand artillery pieces. Updrafts and downdrafts jarred the ship and tossed it about with explosive violence.

Flying in furious lightning is a frightful experience. The danger of being struck by a capricious bolt is always imminent, and with unpredictable results. We'd been in the storm for no more than a few minutes when undulating sheets of blue flame formed along the leading edges of the wing and spread rearward. A sheet would build in length and depth, then large chunks of flame would break loose and fly to the rear, blown away by the aircraft's slipstream. The propellers looked like pinwheels in a fireworks display. Streams of electrical flame flowing from them broke off in large chunks and flew away to the rear, then suddenly disappeared. Sometimes the flames grew to five or six feet in length before breaking off. On several occasions large blue balls of static electricity formed on top of the wing, rolled around for a few moments, then instantly evaporated. I was thankful that none formed inside the cockpit, as they were often reported to do. By the time we were halfway through the cold front, I was soaked with perspiration and was starting to feel the weariness that follows the expenditure of excessive adrenalin. It took more than an hour altogether to get through the more severe storms. A half hour later Lt. Benoni "Ben" Green, our navigator, was again popping up into the astrodome to shoot sunlines, which he would use to compute our ground speed.

Prior to entering the front, I'd made periodic progress checks with

---

2. I was twenty years and eight days old on this date, probably the youngest pilot to ever fly the Atlantic nonstop.

him, and he'd responded each time with position fixes indicating that we were on course and would arrive at Dakar close to our predicted time. With the front behind us, we were seven hours out of Natal with roughly five hours of clear weather and vacant ocean between us and Dakar.

Several hours after we cleared the front it occurred to me that each time Green's face appeared in the astrodome, he looked more tense. Why was he making so many sun shots? Suspecting that something was wrong, I called on the interphone and told him to bring his navigation charts and log to the cockpit.

A brief glance at the chart was all I needed to see that we were in grave trouble. His star fixes—vital for setting our heading to Dakar —were much too large and irregular, and were scattered all over the chart. We had been navigating by "dead reckoning" from the outset.

"Benoni, did you check the sextant after we made that hard landing in Natal?"

The pained look on his face told me his answer before I finished the query.

"Why the hell didn't you tell me soon as you found out it was broken?"

Again, there was no answer. Whatever his reason, he'd made a potentially deadly error. The pain he'd suffered all day was not from a hangover, as I had suspected, but from unforgivable guilt. At the moment, I was caught up in my own feelings of guilt.

About two hours after taking off from Natal, our radio operator, Sgt. Frank Riley, had informed me that he believed that his Liaison Set—our long-range radio—wasn't transmitting. He could hear Natal Radio but couldn't get Natal to respond to his own transmissions. At the time, I hadn't considered the loss of the radio a serious problem. But now, without the ability to get direction-steers from Dakar Radio, we had no backup for navigation errors. My anger at Green subsided as rapidly as it had appeared. It was time for the most rational thinking that I, that all of us, could muster.

After reviewing the log and checking his calculations against forecast winds, we agreed that we were probably far to the south of our intended track. Tarasko, Lynch, and I went into a huddle to see what we could do to improve our fuel management. I decided that it would be best to maintain our heading and engine power, and let the ship drift upward to 14,000 feet. We'd use a small amount of additional fuel during the climb, but the higher altitude would allow us to sight the coast sooner, and let us receive and transmit radio signals over longer distances. The higher altitude would also allow me more time and options should I have to make an emergency landing on a beach, or ditch the ship in the ocean.

By the time we were an hour overdue at Dakar, I'd had to make yet another hard decision. The shortest distance to land lay in a heading to the right of our course. But, if we were south of course, that course change would significantly lengthen the distance to Dakar. I decided to change our heading by thirty degrees to our left—northward—and hope for the best.

Lynch had long since transferred all fuel from our auxiliaries to the main tanks, and the fuel levels in the glass sight-tubes behind me were almost out of sight. Each time Lynch went to the panel to check our fuel status, Tarasko watched the operation with resignation. He would then listen carefully as Lynch recited the figures to me. Soon, there'd be no point in watching the tubes. When the fuel ceased to be visible, we'd have just fifty gallons remaining in each of the four main tanks. From that point on it would be "fly and wait." We'd wait until ten minutes before our predicted "tanks dry" time arrived. At that point, we'd be committed to either land, ditch, or bail out.

We'd been on the new course for about fifteen minutes when Tarasko shouted, "I think I have something!"

With my eyes staring at the radio compass needle, and my ears straining, I thought that I could hear a faint signal in my headset. I couldn't identify it, but the sound was definitely Morse code, a station identifier.

Green's voice came over the interphone as I spied his head in the astrodome, his face turned toward our right wingtip. "Isn't that haze at three o'clock?"

I could barely make out a faint dinginess lying along the distant horizon.

Tarasko turned to me and said, "See that dark line at the bottom of the haze? That's land!"

It was hardly more than a pencil line at the rim of the Atlantic —the African coast! The urge to correct our heading to the right, to get land underneath the ship as soon as possible, was almost overwhelming.

I checked the instrument panel. The radio compass needle was pointing about ten degrees to the right of course. I hurriedly cross-checked the aircraft heading. It was on the mark. The compass needle had swung off the nose of the ship. I grasped the compass control switch and swung the needle ten degrees left then turned the switch back to automatic. The needle moved slowly back to its original position. Confirmed! Although I couldn't read the identifier above the engine noise, Dakar Radio was on the set with enough signal strength to let us home in on it.

Ten minutes later, the approaching coastline was in clear view and I could hear tower traffic in my headset. After making several calls on the emergency frequency, I finally got a response.

"Dakar Tower, Army Five-One-One; inbound from Natal; we have a critical fuel. I am declaring an emergency!"

"Roger, Five-One-One. Left-hand traffic; land runway Two-Seven; wind West at One-Five; altimeter is 29.80; call downwind."

"What the hell's the matter with that guy?" I shouted as I looked over at Tarasko. "To hell with him; we're going straight in!"

Minutes dragged endlessly as the coast grew in detail. The city and the airfield were now clearly visible. I leaned forward straining with my body as though that would increase our speed toward the runway. I eased the nose down to increase the mile-eating airspeed. By the time we crossed the coastline and the city, we had passed our "tanks dry" time, and I was waiting for the first engine to cough.

As we turned to the runway heading, I called the tower and told them we were on a straight-in approach for a downwind landing on runway Nine.

"Negative, Five-One-One! Land runway Two-Seven!"

"Negative tower! We're landing runway Nine. Clear the traffic!"

Just as I rolled out on final, Frank screamed, "Watch it!"

I looked up in time to see a B-24 go whizzing by in the opposite direction, its nose high and left wing rising in a hard right turn.

As we descended toward the runway, time became leaden. Expecting engines to start quitting at any moment, all I could think of was the *Swashbuckler* piled up just short of the runway. A good thing in our favor was the very thing that had us in such a bind: If we crashed, there was hardly enough fuel in the tanks to singe a marshmallow.

"Gear down! Stand by flaps!"

The ship slowed as the landing gear extended and clunked into lock.

"Half flaps!" I called.

Again the ship slowed and nosed downward as the flaps moved into position.

"One-One; you're clear to land."

"One-One, Roger." I was too busy to talk to him. I'd been conserving engine power, and when the flaps came down my airspeed had dropped so rapidly I was caught off guard. I rocked the throttles open, bit by bit, to increase, but not waste, power. We had dropped low on our approach, and I was having to "drag the landing" at low altitude: the worst thing I could possibly do under the circumstances. If an engine quits now, I thought, we're gonners! Tarasko was aware of the ragged edge we were flying and was gently trying to nudge my throttle-hand forward. Smiling to myself, I held on to the settings I had.

"Full flaps," I called as we glided over the end of the runway. I chopped the throttles and eased the nose up to landing attitude.

About two-thirds of the way down the runway I braked hard and turned onto an access taxi strip that connected the main taxiway to the runway. As I started the turn, the right outboard engine sputtered and died. The tank, fuel line, and carburetor feeding the engine were bone dry.

Taxiing toward our assigned parking spot, a warm feeling of well-being flooded through my stiff muscles. As I settled back into my seat, I suddenly realized how tense I'd become during the landing. It had been twelve hours and fifty-five minutes since we'd taken off from Natal, and I was exhausted. The sudden loss of bone-wearying tension was like being rewarded for something and not knowing why. At the moment, I didn't care.

Two days later, on takeoff from Marrakesh, Morocco, fuel siphoning from a wing tank forced us to return to Marrakesh for yet another emergency landing. Someone had cut the safety chain on one of our fuel caps and had stolen the cap during the night. Infuriated by the maintenance officer's inaction in stopping the deadly game of "musical gas caps" that had been going on for months, I had Lynch steal a cap from another B-24, and leave a note on the pilot's seat.

The next morning, still smarting over the maintenance officer's cavalier attitude, and frustrated by our seemingly endless delays, I pressed on against reason and orders to stay out of weather while flying along the North African coast. Heavy storm clouds piled against the mountainous coast forced us ever downward until we were skimming Mediterranean whitecaps to avoid entering showers and the overcast only a few feet above. We rounded a coastal promontory and found ourselves flying into a thicket of barrage balloon cables protecting Algiers harbor. I racked the ship hard to the left and nearly collided with a flight of Spitfires that had been scrambled to intercept us. The fighters joined with us and led us through a narrow gap in the coastal mountains, and on to Maison Blanche airfield.

After five days of nonstop revelry in Algiers, the weather cleared, and we departed bleary-eyed on the final leg of our journey to Manduria.

▌▌

The heel of Italy, as it appeared from our aerial perch, was an impoverished scene. As we headed inland from over the Bay of Taranto, the land flattened to a collage of dusty roads and poor villages set in the dark green of olive groves. Circling high above the airfield, I studied the base with nagging reservations. It had been carved out of a forest of olive trees. There were a sprinkling of wood and stone buildings and many tents. A hangar that didn't look to be large enough to accommodate a B-24 sat at the edge of a small parking ramp. Maintenance was being performed under the open sky, in unpaved parking areas jammed with bombers.

The single runway appeared to be nothing more than a strip of white, Italian earth. A second runway, parallel to the first, was under construction and nearing completion. The need for it was obvious. After one or two bombers lumbered down the present runway, dust blown up by churning propellers would make the takeoff of following, fuel- and bomb-laden aircraft both difficult and hazardous.

The most curious aspect of the landing area was the white paths in the tops of the olive groves at each end of the runway. While landing I noted that the paths were the bare wood of shattered treetops that had been ground away by the propellers of straining bombers struggling to become airborne. (Before our tour ended, not only would the *Swashbuckler*'s prop tips be green, there'd be fewer trees at the eastern end of the runway, as well as severe damage to our beloved bird.)

Taxiing toward the parking ramp, we tracked the "FOLLOW ME" vehicle to an empty spot and started shutting down the engines. Now that we were finally home, an uneasiness built within me. Something wasn't right and it took a moment to recognize the cause. The quiet ramp looked more like an aircraft graveyard than a center for combat operations. Normally, a bomber ramp is a beehive of activity. This one looked as though the war had taken the day off.

While we were shutting down, an officer arrived in a jeep and waited patiently for us to finish our checklists and get out of the aircraft.

Lt. John F. Wells was impressive. Staring up at me from the ramp, his fifty-mission crusher shoved back to disclose dark skin and handsome face, the guy looked as if he'd be at home on a movie set. As we shook hands, my impression changed. His somber manner didn't fit the rakish appearance.

Following introductions all around, my first question was, "What kind of outfit is this?"

His quiet, unenthusiastic reply was, "Better than some; not as good as some."

It was a strange, almost unintelligible response. Normally the question elicits such an outpouring one often regrets having asked. If his attitude could be taken as a measure, the 450th was lacking in character and spirit. He did manage to tell us that we were assigned to the 723rd, his squadron, that the officers were to go with him, and that another vehicle would be along to carry the gunners to their quarters.

Already irritated by his unenthusiastic greeting, the suggestion that I leave my crew on the ramp angered me. I didn't want them to be stuck there or to have to wander about in search of a place to live. I ignored him and kept up a conversation with the gunners until their truck arrived.

The base was as rude as it had appeared from the air. The officers' quarters turned out to be a tent set up over a wooden floor, with walls about three feet high. The canvas sides of the tent were rolled up to expose netting securely fastened to the walls and frame. The effect was akin to that of living on a screened porch. The area was well shaded by trees and was quite pleasant and airy.

Our first few days with the 450th were spent learning the disposition and routine of the base. Then came a period wherein we flew several local flights with combat pilots to prove that I could fly the *Swashbuckler* on instruments and in formation, and that Ollie King, our bombardier, could hit a target. Our most valuable time was spent in bull sessions with experienced crews. We learned much about the details of air combat by listening to them recount their experiences and the defenses of various targets. What I learned about the 450th's history changed my initially low esteem of its character and vitality as a fighting unit. But the more I learned about the Group's combat experience, the more I wished that we had been assigned elsewhere.

The Group had come into being in the spring of 1943, at Almogordo, New Mexico. Its nucleus of leadership, Col. John Stuart Mills, the commander, the squadron commanders, and other key personnel, had been pulled from other groups and sent off to the School of Applied Tactics, at Orlando, Florida. Meanwhile, aircrews and ground support personnel, almost all of whom were fresh from flying and technical schools, assembled at Almogordo and started the laborious process of becoming a viable military unit. Shortages of men, aircraft, even buildings for classrooms hampered them at every hand. However, the greater the challenge, the more cheerful and ingenious their response. On November 13, at the Saturday morning parade, what had been a growing number of individuals, now numbering 2,072 (including seventy combat crews—700 men), were declared "combat ready." None, including their leaders, had combat experience. A few days later the aircrews departed via the Southern Route as the support personnel and their equipment boarded trains for a port of embarkation.

The first aircrews arrived at Manduria during Christmas week. It was the rainy season and the base was deep in water and mud. The situation was made worse by a German air raid on the port of Bari. No one was injured, but the raid prevented the support personnel from disembarking for more than a week. In the meantime, aircrews were living in and servicing their own aircraft, and scrounging furniture and building materials for Intelligence and briefing facilities needed to prepare the crews for combat.

Christmas arrived and passed quietly in the minds and hearts of men absorbed by the tasks at hand. Finally, on January 8, the 450th and the 449th, with a combined force of thirty-four bombers, were dispatched to bomb the airfield at Mostar, Yugoslavia. As luck would have it, the target was hidden beneath clouds, and disappointed aircrews had to salvo their bombs into the Adriatic. The next six weeks produced similar results interspersed with modest successes. Their initial targets were located in Italy, southern France, and Yugoslavia, and were relatively easy. This was fortunate, in that it gave the crews and leaders time to adjust to the tensions and realities of combat, and to refine operating procedures. In time the targets became tougher—much tougher—and losses mounted.

Unknown to the crews, planners in Washington, Italy, and London had devised a major air campaign (OPERATION ARGUMENT) against some of the most heavily defended targets in Europe. All that was needed to implement the plan was good weather.

On February 22, weather in the battle area cleared and the Fifteenth joined the Eighth Air Force and the Royal Air Force Bomber Command by attacking targets in Austria and southern Germany. It was the beginning of what the bomber crews came to call "Big Week," a week in which intensive fighting saw both sides suffer severe losses in men and aircraft. In just four days, ninety-three Fifteenth Air Force bombers would go down.

The Fifteenth's opening thrust consisted of over 300 bombers and 185 fighters. However, the force was seriously weakened when 50 B-24s and 24 P-38 escorts aborted the mission because of mechanical problems. The B-17 components, the smaller group of the attacking forces of bombers, was split between three targets, with the primary force of 65 B-17s going for the Regensburg-Prufening (Germany) Messerschmitt factory.

The B-24 force was split against two targets. Aircraft of the 304th Wing, in an unrelated effort far to the south of the main action, bombed the port facilities at Sibenek, Yugoslavia. The main B-24 force of 118 bombers from the 47th Wing (the 98th, 376th, 449th, and 450th Bomb Groups), in conjunction with the B-17 strike on the Prufening factory, struck the nearby Obertraubling assembly plant. In spite of a large escort of P-38 and P-47 fighters, the bomber forces came under heavy, aggressive fighter attack. The B-24s lost 14 aircraft; the B-17s lost 5. The 4 B-24s lost by the 450th was the largest loss the Group had suffered on a single mission. Although severe damage was inflicted on the targets, the raiders had paid a heavy price; and that was only the beginning of their ordeal.

The following day, February 23, 102 B-24s bombed the Steyr (Austria) ball bearing plant. Severe damage was done to the plant but flak and 120 enemy fighters succeeded in shooting down 17 B-24s. Within two days, the B-24s had lost the equivalent of half of a Group—31 crews and their aircraft. The 450th had a two-day loss of 8 aircraft, but that was only part of the story. Many B-24s that made it home were so heavily damaged that ground crews could not repair them in time to fly the next mission.

The next day, February 24, was a black day for the 2nd Bomb Group's B-17s. Despite a coordinated strike from England by the Eighth Air Force, the Luftwaffe achieved a major defensive effort against the Fifteenth's bombers. With the B-24s stood-down for repairs, eighty-seven B-17s mounted a three-group strike against the Daimler-Puch aircraft component plant at Steyr. The force was led by fifty aircraft of the 97th and 301st groups, with the 2nd bringing up the rear.

A hundred miles from the target, the Ninety-seventh was hit by 20 enemy fighters who, despite their aggressiveness, were driven off with no losses to the bombers. Then, just prior to the Initial Point (IP),[1] the bombers were engaged by 110 German fighters who concentrated their attacks on the rear of the force. Within those few eternal minutes from the IP to the bomb release point, the Second lost 10 of its 37 aircraft. By the time the mortally stricken Group escaped its fiery hell, they'd lost 4 more. The Commander of the Ninety-seventh, realizing the desperate straits of the Second, ordered his escorting fighters to go to their aid. His gallant decision left the Ninety-seventh unprotected, but it kept the Second from suffering even more disastrous losses.[2]

The air battle lasted for more than an hour. When it was over, sixteen B-17s and three P-38s had gone down. The raiding forces (fighters and bombers) claimed thirty-five enemy fighters downed. But, the thirty-five enemy fighters downed on February 24, plus claims of fighters downed on February 22 and 23, in no way compensated for the fifty-three bombers with their 530 men lost during the three days of intense battles. Unknown to the beleaguered bomber crews, the biggest battle yet would be fought the following day, February 25—the day that the American bombers would suffer some of their heaviest losses of the war. It was also the day the 450th earned the nickname "Cottontails," and garnered the first of its two Distinguished Unit Citations, and an undeserved reputation for infamy.

On February 25, 745 heavy bombers from the Eighth Air Force in concert with 400 bombers from the Fifteenth mounted a maximum effort against targets in southern Germany, Austria, northern Italy,

---

1. The Initial Point is an easily recognizable location on the ground that serves as the terminus of the navigation route and the beginning of the bomb run.

2. Kenn C. Rust's *Fifteenth Air Force in World War II*, Historical Aviation Album, 1976 gives an excellent and concise history of Fifteenth Air Force's operations throughout the war.

and Yugoslavia. Maximum effort from the severely damaged 2nd produced only 10 B-17s, and those 10 led the B-17 force. The 450th led the B-24s. The target for both the B-17 and B-24 main forces was once again the Prufening aircraft plant at Regensburg. To the 10 crews of the 2nd Bomb Group, the prospects for the mission were grim. In a formation of 46 B-17s that would be reduced to 36 by mechanical failures before reaching the target, the 2nd was leading the entire Fifteenth Air Force.

Near Fiume, Italy, the B-17s were attacked by more than a hundred fighters. Fortunately for the 2nd, the 301st bore the brunt of the fight. Enemy fighters, periodically replaced by fresh fighters during the running battle, attacked savagely. By the time the bombers arrived at the target, the enemy had shot down eleven of the 301st's twenty-six bombers. When the ninety-minute battle was over, the 301st had lost its twelfth aircraft, and the 2nd had lost three of its ten. Four other B-17s went down at other targets, bringing the total B-17s lost to nineteen.

Not far behind the B-17s, the 450th was having its own problems. Prior to the fighter attack on the B-17s, and while still 300 miles from the target, the 450th, led by its deputy group commander, Maj. Robert R. Gideon, was hit by fifteen enemy fighters. After a short engagement, 450th gunners drove the enemy away. A few minutes later, the twenty-nine bombers were attacked by a fresh force of twenty ME-109s whose pilots were highly experienced and aggressive. Attacking from every conceivable angle, the 109s harassed the bombers unmercifully, until they lost three of their own number and ran out of ammunition. When the battle was over, the 450th's formation was still intact, but it had incurred heavy battle damage.

As was the custom, when crews weren't absorbed by their duties, Radio Berlin offered a handy source of relaxation. If one could endure Axis Sally's propaganda tirades between selections, the sounds of Glenn Miller, Harry James, the Dorseys, every big band of note, brought back memories, and in more quiet moments, moist-eyed nostalgia. To relax the crews before and after battle, pilots often tuned in Axis Sally on an aircraft radio. And so it was on the morning of February 25.

Shortly before the first group of fifteen fighters attacked, Sally had interrupted her music to acknowledge the presence of the approaching bombers.

"Come a little closer boys," she said. "We have a surprise waiting for you."

Battle-weary crews, already apprehensive about returning to the carnage they'd suffered on the previous days, had charged (loaded) their guns and waited. When the first two groups of enemy fighters attacked, the gunners were ready for battle. Then, while still some forty minutes from the target, the Luftwaffe struck with all of its force and fury. It is likely that Sally's warning was a major factor in the 450th's holding their losses to only four aircraft during the ensuing ninety-minute battle. Crews of the other groups had heard her warning and were equally prepared for battle. Hours later, Sally admonished the retreating bombers with the warning that the Luftwaffe would be waiting for them in the future.

It was a week before the 450th flew again. Bad weather gave battered groups a breather to repair battle damage to both crews and aircraft. Having lost nearly a squadron of aircraft and crews during the four days of Big Week, and with most of the rest of their aircraft battle-damaged or otherwise in need of repair, the 450th needed a rest. But escape from peril did not come.

On February 26, Sally berated "the White-Tail Liberators from Southern Italy." Why she singled out the 450th, no one knew. It wasn't because the Group bombed an orphanage, or a hospital, as crews from the other groups later came to believe. Nor did a 450th crew lower its landing gear in surrender, then proceed to shoot down the escorting enemy fighters. A likely reason was simply that the 450th's aircraft, unlike the aircraft of the other groups, bore easily identifiable white rudders. Whatever her reason Axis Sally singled out the 450th with the warning, "The Luftwaffe will be waiting for the White Tail Liberators from Southern Italy." Crews of the other bomb groups heard Sally, assumed one or more of the rumors must be true, and reveled in the prospect that they'd be exempt from fighter attacks when the Cottontails were nearby.

On February 28, Colonel Mills assembled the Group to hear commendations from the commander, Fifteenth Air Force. His reading of the Distinguished Unit Citation did little to elevate the flyers' morale. The crews had heard a rumor that Mills was threatening to put even more white paint on the tails of the aircraft. After several days of mental wound-licking, some men privately vowed to refuse to fly unless the white paint already on the tails was removed. Colonel

Mills's position in the matter was unenviable. Whatever his reasons, he left the rudders as they were and ignored Sally's threat. No crew ever carried out its threat and refused to fly.

Early March was accompanied by continuing bad weather and a need for the Fifteenth to divert its attention to the support of our ground forces at Anzio and Monte Cassino. As the weather cleared in the north, the crews turned to logistics targets that supplied German ground forces in Italy. Nevertheless, by the end of the month—after less than ninety days of combat operations—thirty-seven Cottontail crews were missing in action. This was the equivalent of two-thirds of the Group's aircraft and more than half of the original crews. Aggressive fighter attacks during the month reinforced the belief that the Cottontails had indeed been singled out for slaughter.

April arrived, bringing with it much-improved weather and enemy defenses, the beginning of an all-out effort against both the old battle area of Austria and Germany, and a new battle arena, the Balkans. Time soon disclosed that Big Week was merely the opening engagement. The gates of hell weren't flung fully open until the Fifteenth engaged the defenses of Ploesti and other Balkan targets critical to the German army and the Luftwaffe. April's schedule, just seventeen missions, cost the 450th another twenty-seven aircraft and crews. Within less than four months, the Cottontails had lost over 100 percent of their normal complement of aircraft and crews. Although many of those who went down were "green replacements," the original complement of crews had dwindled to a few. None had completed the required fifty missions, and aircrew prospects for survival were grim.

This was the 450th on April 26, the day of our arrival. Wells's perception, "Better than some; not as good as some," had been grossly misleading. By the time we flew our first mission, the history of the Cottontails had been disclosed to us in all of its brutal detail. I viewed what I'd learned with modest reservations and considered a good bit of it to be somewhat exaggerated. I couldn't have been more wrong.

III

From the moment we shook hands, I liked him. Lt. Jack Morris had completed twenty-nine of his fifty missions and was well versed in the terror and odds that a green crew like ours faced. In the few short months that he had been in combat, he'd seen the original crews dwindle to a minority among the number of replacements. Jack was reluctant to talk about it, but his crew had taken so many casualties it had been disbanded. The survivors were filling vacancies on other crews. Jack had been assigned the unenviable task of flying with replacement crews. He'd fly with a new crew until the pilot had five or six missions, then on to another crew, and so on until he completed his fifty missions. He was well aware of the extra danger attendant to flying with green crews, but he never complained.

Not one to equivocate, I made my first combat decision. I decided that the crew would probably have a better chance of surviving were I to invite him to stay with us until he finished his missions. He was pleased with my offer to pilot, and had no objections to my continuing as the crew's commander. In any event, the decision would have to be left to the squadron commander. I soon learned that he and his close friend Wells had a problem so potentially serious that flying with green crews paled in comparison. Wells and Jack believed that our squadron operations officer was setting them up to be shot down. He was scheduling them to fly Tailend Charlie far more often than the other crews. It was a grave charge, one that I was reluctant to accept; yet their occasional comments, and the remarks of other pilots, seemed well founded and wholly sincere. The bizarre conflict left me with the worry that I may have needlessly endangered my crew by inviting Jack to fly with us.

Nine days after our arrival, we were checked out and ready for combat. I had thought that when the time came for us to fly our first mission I'd have the jitters. I didn't. As copilot, many of my responsibilities for the crew passed to Jack, leaving me free to concentrate on technical aspects of the mission.

The briefing room was depressing. I couldn't decide if it was the poor lighting or the thickness of stale and fresh smoke that rasped my eyes. Seats were planks laid across bomb-fin cases. A platform at the front of the room was flanked by large curtained panels. At the center of the front wall was a small panel covered by a velvet curtain. The tension, punctuated by muffled coughing and nervous chatter, was as oppressive as the dense smoke. Counting the pilots of thirty-nine aircraft, the briefers, and the other staff, nearly a hundred people crowded the modest-sized room.

Mission orders had arrived during the night. Group Ops officers, Intelligence personnel, and the Group bombardier and navigator had plotted the attack route, details of bomb aiming points, enemy defenses, and other matters, and had prepared briefing materials while we slept. Because of security, we rarely knew our target until the briefing started.

The briefing procedure was simple and direct. The Group Intelligence officer stepped up to the velvet drape covering the small panel and jerked the drawcord.

"Gentlemen, the target today is *Ploesti!*"

Shock forced a momentary silence followed by a whisper of nervous movement and poorly muffled expletives.

I sensed Jack's body shift and thought that I detected a quiet grunt, or sigh. Turning my head to catch his reaction, I saw that Jack's eyes were riveted on the blackboard.

The exposed board contained the word "Ploesti" in large letters in yellow chalk. Beneath "Ploesti" was a schematic drawing showing the marshaling yards, oil facilities, and aiming points for the first and second attack units. I was having trouble forcing my attention away from that single word, Ploesti, and onto the drawing and the briefer's words.

While training at Colorado Springs, Col. John R. "Killer" Kane[1] had briefed us on the realities of combat. He'd assured us, "You'll never have to go back to Ploesti!"

The hell we wouldn't, I thought as I sat in the fear-filled room. This

1. Colonel John R. Kane was Commander of the 98th Bomb Group at the time of the August 1, 1943, low-level raid on Ploesti. A detailed account of that nearly suicidal mission is contained in the book, *Ploesti*, by James Dugan and Carroll Stewart, published by Random House and Bantam, 1962.

would be the fourth mission in as many weeks the Fifteenth had gone back to that oil-fired hell, and we would undoubtedly have to return many more times before the targets were destroyed.[2]

As the briefing progressed, details of the attack became clear and meaningful. We'd rendezvous with the 449th over Manduria, on course to our first turning point, San Vito D'Normannie. We would pick up escorting fighters at several points along our route, commencing at 1230 hours. Weather was "iffy." High and middle layers of stratus clouds would be a problem from the Rumanian border on. Target weather at bombing altitudes of 20,500 and 22,000 feet was highly questionable. The mission looked to be a washout, and I didn't relish the prospect of flying so deep into enemy territory and not finding the target. On the other hand, the clouds would limit the Luftwaffe's ability to attack us. All things considered, the situation didn't appear to my novice mind as bad as I had imagined. Jack said nothing and I took his silence as a favorable sign.

After the briefing we waited for King and Green, then headed for the equipment building to collect our parachutes, flak vests, and escape kits. When finished, we were loaded with personal gear, the bulk and combined weight of which were considerable. The flak vest alone weighed at least twenty pounds and looked very much like a baseball catcher's protective vest. Unlike the catcher's vest, however, it had hundreds of one-inch steel platelets sewn within its ribbing. It would be hell getting out of the thing if we had to bail out in a hurry, I reasoned. On the other hand, it looked as if it would stop shrapnel, if the pieces weren't too large.

By the time we arrived at the aircraft, our gunners and ground crew had pre-flighted the bird and had it ready to go. All Jack and I had to do was make a walk-around inspection and wonder whether the beast would be able to lift itself off the runway.

I'd not been able to pin down the reasons for my impulse to name

2. The first mission had been flown on April 5 and had cost the attacking force 13 bombers. The second and third missions, on April 15 and 24, cost the Fifteenth 11 more bombers. Our mission of May 5 saw another 19 go down. In addition to the 54 bombers lost on the August 1, 1943, low-level raid, Fifteenth Air Force lost 223 heavy bombers (24 of them were of the 450th), and 8 dive-bombing P-38 fighters of the 82nd Fighter Group. The RAF lost 15 bombers in night attacks. Three hundred heavy bombers and 8 dive-bombing fighters, plus dozens of escorting fighters, is a severe price to pay for one target complex, but the loss of Ploesti's oil (40 percent of the enemy's total resource) devastated Germany's ability to wage war.

our ship the *Swashbuckler*. Perhaps it was a moment of youthful exuberance, a less than mature attempt to express disdain for the enemy. Whatever the reason, I was disappointed with both the name and emblem painted on the nose of the ship. The overall effect turned out to be embarrassingly theatrical. The artwork had cost me thirty dollars. At least I'd had the good sense to not ask the crew to help pay the cost. Some of them were unhappy about my naming the ship without their blessing. After all, it was *their* aircraft too. Chris Dittman, our assistant engineer, had taken me to task on the matter, too late. Unknown to me—I should have asked—most of the men wanted to name the ship after Lynch's wife. I felt bad about the situation, but the deed was done and there was little to be gained by worrying.

My first sight of the *Swashbuckler* loaded with bombs brought a tense smile. I thought that we were flying heavy out of Natal, but loaded for combat the ship reminded me of a dozing hippo, and I wondered if it would refuse to fly until it gave birth to some oversized object.

The heavy load created yet another vexing problem—how to get into the ship, a heretofore simple act. The front access to the ship was through the forward bomb bay. Now, the belly was pressed so close to the ramp that we had to get down on all fours and crawl underneath to get inside. Inside, bombs crowded the bomb bay and made hauling our personal equipment up to the cockpit a laborious task. Each item had to be shoved underneath the belly, then lifted in stages from the ramp to the flight deck. Of more serious concern to me were the problems we'd have bailing out through the bomb bay if we were shot down and the bomb system malfunctioned, or we didn't have time to drop the bombs.

We had all four fans turning and were waiting for the ship preceding us in the formation to come by so we could take our place in the parade heading for the takeoff end of the runway. Our formation position was in the right box of the Second Attack Unit. Consequently, about two-thirds of the mission aircraft were ahead of us. Once we joined the stream of taxiing aircraft, the undulating line ahead of us looked like a whole herd of hippos lumbering to a waterhole.

Following brief engine checks, Jack pulled onto the end of the runway, shoved the throttles forward, and released the brakes. We were on our way.

450th BOMB GROUP'S FORMATION

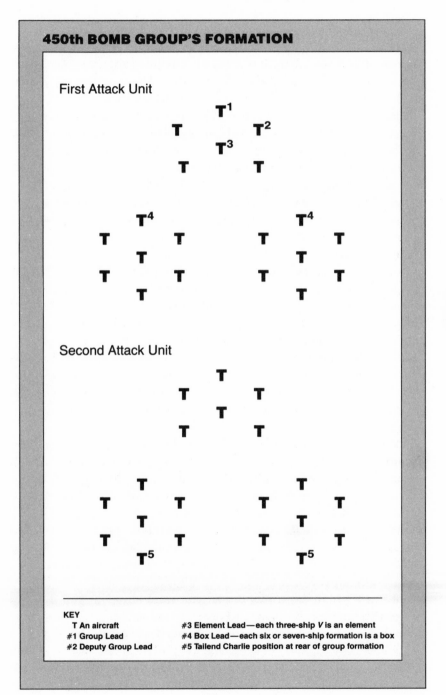

First Attack Unit

Second Attack Unit

KEY
  T An aircraft   #3 Element Lead—each three-ship *V* is an element
#1 Group Lead   #4 Box Lead—each six or seven-ship formation is a box
#2 Deputy Group Lead   #5 Tailend Charlie position at rear of group formation

The runway had been wetted-down earlier, but the prop blast of departing bombers had dried its surface. We were going to eat dust. Though not a serious hazard, the dust was thick enough to prevent us from seeing the far end of the runway and the imposing olive grove just beyond.

Acceleration was painfully slow, and there was no wind to help us with our airspeed. As we passed the "halfway" runway marker, we were committed; we had to get the bird off the ground. The less than three thousand feet of runway remaining was not enough to allow us to stop the thundering beast.

"Damn, the bird's heavy!" What with the dust and slow acceleration, it was as though we were struggling through dry molasses. Engines and props screamed their own doubt as to whether or not we'd reach flying speed before the end of the runway. The olive grove appeared in view when we had about a thousand feet of runway remaining. Jack eased the wheel rearward, the nose lifted, and the *Swashbuckler* struggled into the air. I knew from the speed of the onrushing olive grove that our propellers were about to be christened "combat green."

Staggering into the air, Jack yelled, "Gear up!"

His call came not a moment too soon. Had we clipped the trees with our gear down, we would have cut a flaming swath through the olive grove like a meteor gone berserk. Our props duly christened, we climbed slowly, circling to the left to join up with the formation taking shape in the Italian sky.

It was an invigorating morning. The assembling formation looked its purpose: a huge gaggle of warbirds gathering themselves for battle. The aircraft assembled into a combat formation of two large V's—the first and second attack units. Each V, or attack unit, was composed of three boxes of bombers with six aircraft in the lead box and seven aircraft in each of the flanking boxes. The lead box of the First Attack Unit contained the mission leader, who was flanked by two wingmen in V formation. Immediately behind and just beneath the leader was a fourth aircraft with two wingmen in V formation. To the right and left of the lead box were two similarly formed boxes of double V's, except that each of the flanking boxes had a seventh aircraft in the slot position behind and below the lead aircraft of the second V of the box.

The Second Attack Unit, with an identical formation, flew a thousand feet behind the First Attack Unit and five hundred feet higher in altitude. When fully formed, the formation looked like a mottled chevron made up of two large V's. This was the largest formation of aircraft that I had ever flown in. We were flying on the right-wing on the leader of the right box of the Second Attack Unit. I could see all of the First Attack Unit, as well as most of the aircraft in the Second Unit. It was an impressive sight.

As the formation droned over the Adriatic, when not relieving Jack of the work of flying I spent most of my time looking for the other groups of our Wing. I had to admire Jack's ability to fly close formation. He could set the aircraft in perfect position, and remain suspended there as though the ship were locked in place by an unseen arm.

We'd had very little formation flying during operational training at Colorado Springs, and it showed. I was as rough as a cob. At 22,000 feet, the heavily laden *Swashbuckler* was sloppy, and reluctant to respond to the flight controls. To make matters worse, much worse, when I would take over for Jack, I had to fly the aircraft with my right hand and work the throttles with my left hand. This was the reverse of the procedure while flying from my accustomed place, the left seat. Being uncoordinated from the right seat, I had to fly too far from the lead aircraft. This made it difficult to judge distances and detect early movement of the ship out of position. I soon discovered that the key to easy flying lay in sticking the *Swashbuckler* close to the lead ship. The slightest change in position could be detected and corrected before I had to waste too much power to get back into position. The temperature outside the aircraft was twenty degrees below zero, yet I was perspiring. I knew that after a few missions I'd become right-seat coordinated and would give a much better account of myself. At the moment, however, I wished to be elsewhere.

In contrast to our man-made thunder defiling the blue, the countryside below was peaceful. I could imagine the upturned faces, their eyes riveted on our formation, and could almost sense the fear behind strained countenances and their relief as we flew on without releasing our violent cargo. No one below was immune, especially along our withdrawal route. Sometimes a segment of the aircraft's bomb release system would malfunction and leave one or more bombs hanging inside the bomb bay. We had been briefed to drop the "hung" bombs into the Adriatic to avoid killing innocent people, but that didn't always happen. When over enemy territory, upon clearing the malfunction, as often as not bombardiers would look for opportune targets, even if it meant leaving the formation for a short while.

So far, our first mission had been just another formation flight. Although we'd already overflown enemy-occupied Yugoslavia and were well within Rumania, we hadn't run into any flak or fighters. The rapidly thickening weather could account for that. Shortly after leaving the Yugoslav coast, we'd picked up a high overcast. As we flew inland, the overcast darkened and left the sky and land shadowed in unfriendly silence. The horizon grew indistinct, looking as though it would swallow our formation and gulp it into endless darkness. One aircraft had turned back over the Adriatic because of a bad engine. Our remaining thirty-eight aircraft were pressing on, though with increasing difficulty. Already the formation was loosening because of the leader's maneuvering to avoid clouds blocking our route.

Tension built within me as I considered the spectre of his taking our huge formation into instrument flying conditions. Such action could easily result in mass carnage and a rain of bodies and torn metal as aircraft plowed into each other above the waiting earth. It is a terrifying way to die, trapped inside a disintegrating aircraft that is rolling like a wounded whale, spinning and falling through sightless clouds: oblivion. Thus far we had avoided the clouds with comfortable margins, but lessening visibility could cause us to fly into a layer of clouds without realizing the danger until it was too late.

As we approached the IP, Jack took over flying the ship. The long break had refreshed him. He eased the ship in closer and set the left props just behind and above lead's right wing. No sooner had he settled in position than the formation started a turn to the right. Simultaneously, Green's voice came over the intercom, "IP in two minutes."

Suddenly tendrils of stratus clouds streaked past us. Lead banked hard and dropped down in altitude. First Attack had disappeared beneath a layer of clouds beneath us. Flying five hundred feet lower than us, and unaware of the closeness of the clouds overhead, it had passed safely underneath the layer at our level, leaving our attack unit to fend for itself. I whipped my head around trying to see in all directions at once, to warn Jack of an impending collision with another aircraft. There was little if any chance that I'd be able to warn him in time or wrench the controls from him to avoid a collision, but I had to try.

Time strained to move forward, to hurry fate. Lead was but a fleeting shadow tearing through the dense cloud. Jack pressed our churning props to within a few feet of lead's wing which melted into the faint image of his fuselage in the obscuring mist. Had Jack not been flying so close to lead when we entered the cloud, we would have lost sight of him and been in even more desperate straits. At the moment all we could do was hold position and hope that lead didn't fly into another aircraft or formation. I had no idea where the three-ship V behind us might be—whether they were still in formation with us or had throttled back to keep from overrunning us, or had climbed when they saw us drop in altitude. When we hit the cloud, my earphones had filled with the din of frantic voices, all of them trying to talk at once. We had a breakaway procedure that everyone should be following. Communication between ships was pointless until we cleared the clouds and started to reassemble.

As suddenly as we'd entered, we broke free of clouds and into the somber gray of the morning below. There were no aircraft in sight, other than our lead ship. I had no idea where the target lay. With other bomb groups coming in on it, it would be foolhardy for us to try to find the target and make a bomb run. We were down to 18,000 feet, a nearly suicidal altitude for an attack on a target like Ploesti.

Lead started a gentle turn to the left, presumably to check for the target and determine if a bomb run were feasible. We could see nothing but countryside and a broken layer of pewtered stratus between us and where he supposed the target to be. Lead made his decision and started a right turn toward a course for home.

"Bandits! Five o'clock low," the call came crashing into my headset. The air was full of clock calls and the numbers of attacking fighters. They weren't attacking us yet; our guns remained silent.

"Keep a lookout back there!" It was Jack's voice on the intercom warning the crew.

I searched ahead and over my right shoulder for the attackers, but saw nothing. Our own fighter cover, lost from us above the clouds, was useless. We were on our own, with four hundred miles between us and home.

Jack's poke startled me. Craning my neck to see past him, I spied another Cottontail pulling into position on lead's left wing. The addition of the third ship increased our defensive firepower by 50 percent. From the sound of the persistent air battle, we might need all of the firepower we could muster. We'd been briefed to come off the target in a left turn, but we'd broken right when we hit the cloud. The retreating formations were now far to the north of our own track. I liked that. We'd be flying parallel with the retreating groups, using them as decoys against enemy fighters. Since all the attacking groups were turning left off the target, the main battle area would remain to the north. The thought struck me, Our first mission, Ploesti! No flak! No fighters!—unless we stumble into something on the way home.

I turned my Comm switch to INTERCOM.

"Ben, you know where we are?"

"Pretty much," came Green's not-too-confident reply.

"OK. Keep working on it. Don't let lead take us over any known flak. Let me know when you get us pinpointed."

"Bombardier, you on?"

"Yeah. Go ahead."

"Ollie, if we or lead can't come up with a target, we're gonna have to dump 'em in the Adriatic."

"Roger. Let you know if I spot anything."

The flight back to Manduria was uneventful. We salvoed our bombs into the Adriatic and landed at the base shortly after the main force. I was surprised to learn that our box of aircraft had caught the worst of the weather and that the rest of the formation had made it to the target. The target had been partially obscured by lower clouds, but bombardiers had been able to estimate aiming points close enough to start at least one large oil fire. The Group had picked up heavy flak and had been attacked by fighters who'd first stood off while firing cannon and rockets, then pressed their attack in a running battle that lasted twenty minutes. The remnants of our Second Attack Unit had taken the heaviest attacks. None had gone down, but between the flak and fighters twenty-one aircraft had been damaged and two crew members wounded. After learning the details of the action, I felt disappointed, but realized that we couldn't have done anything other than head for home, salvo our bombs, and wait for the next mission.

I wasn't in the mood to drink the ounce of whiskey being parceled out to each man. Ollie and I took an empty bottle from the booze table and poured our ration into it. We'd save it until we had enough for a party. At the moment, the Red Cross coffee and doughnuts being doled out at the end of the table were more appealing. It had been eleven hours since we'd eaten breakfast and all I'd had since then was the cold water I'd swigged from my canteen during the fruitless flight. I was hungry enough to eat the table. As I munched the tasteless doughnut, I made a mental note to go to the Post Exchange in Manduria and buy something to take the edge off of my hunger during future missions.

IV

Brasov, a city of 50,000, sits eighty miles north of Ploesti at the foot of the Transylvanian Alps. Our target was the marshaling yard. The RAF had bombed the refinery during the night so we expected to see smoke while still some distance from the city. The weather promised to be fine en route and at the target. Enemy fighter attacks were a certainty, but coordinated raids by other Fifteenth groups against Ploesti should hold the fighter opposition to our raid to a minimum.

We joined up with the 449th at 6,000 feet over Manduria and departed on course, picking up the 376th and 98th groups along the way. Our course took us north across the Adriatic, skirted the northern borders of Albania and Bulgaria, then went straight into the heart of Rumania. The groups striking the refineries at Ploesti were flying tracks parallel to our own, thereby giving the enemy the impression that the huge force was aimed at a single target.

The weather, as promised, was flawless all the way. With no distractions from scudding clouds, flying formation from the right seat became progressively easier, at least to the point where I was no longer embarrassed by my performance. Jack had just relieved me of the drudgery of flying. A glance at my wristwatch told me that we were only minutes from the IP.

My enjoyment of the beauty of the morning gave way to apprehension. It was as though by tightening my body and perceptions I'd be able to see better and be more responsive to the demands of the coming battle. From here on, with only minor course corrections to set the bomb run, the formation would fly straight and level until bomb release. This was the phase of the mission where we would be most vulnerable to flak and fighters. We'd bypassed several known flak installations en route and were expecting moderate to heavy flak in the target area.

K A R U M P !   K A R U M P !

I looked ahead and to each side to see what was making the soft, dull sound.

KARUMP! KARUMP! KARUMP!

The sound was much closer and the softness had become harsh, explosive.

Just as someone—I think Jack—called on the interphone, "flak!," several large puffs of black smoke with flaming centers burst to our left and slightly below us. The lead ship bobbled slightly from the explosions. All the previous questions in my mind as to what flak looks like and how it sounds were answered in a moment of tense time.

KARUMP! KARUMP! KARUMP!

Black mushrooms of smoke suddenly appeared ahead, or to one side, of the *Swashbuckler*, sometimes high, other times low. Some shells burst directly ahead and we flew right through the smoke. The first puffs we flew through made me flinch, as though we'd rammed something substantial. Embarrassed by my illogical reaction to harmless puffs of smoke, I determined to brace myself and concentrate on looking for fighters. Several times, the KARUMPs were accompanied by the sound of spattering raindrops on a metal roof. I knew that it was shrapnel penetrating the skin of the *Swashbuckler* near the flight deck. It had to be nearby or I wouldn't have heard the small sounds above our engine noise.

For some reason, the sound of the shrapnel didn't bother me. In my mind, the sounds related more to something relatively insignificant, as bee stings, rather than to grave danger. The seemingly tiny objects causing the sound might hurt but it was hard to believe that they could cause serious damage. What concerned me most was flying through the harmless smoke of shells that had burst without doing any damage. I figured that the recesses of my mind were warning me that but for a split second of timing the harmless explosions could have been direct hits or mortally wounding misses. Although I was wearing my flak jacket and had my steel helmet pulled down as far as it would go over my head, their protection gave me little comfort as I watched shell after shell exploding around us.

It seemed that the bomb run would never end. The closer we came to the release point, the more intense and accurate the flak became. It was like standing in an open field watching the black mushrooms of death suddenly appear, ever closer, blasting the heavens with lethal hail.

I didn't hear any calls from other aircraft announcing that they'd been hit, but we'd certainly picked up a number of holes. Very few shells burst near the First Attack Unit. The flak was trailing First with most of it bursting near us. I was so fascinated with the black puffs that I never saw the First Attack Unit release its bombs. Suddenly, King's voice came over the intercom, "Bombs away!," and the sudden loss of five thousand pounds of weight caused the ship to be sucked sharply upward by the lift of its wings.

Either there were more guns defending the target, or most of them were placing their shells near our box of bombers. Mushrooms popped into existence instantaneously, did their dance of destruction right in front of us, then whizzed away to our rear. Swinging into a right turn off the target, we entered the most intense area of flak. Black puffs zipped by in rapid succession as a barrage of shells exploded in front of and beneath us. The *Swashbuckler* lurched, the right wing thrown high from the force of an explosion preceeding a rain of steel pecking somewhere behind me. Number-three engine's tachometer needle started its deadly climb, confirming the screaming roar of a runaway prop.

I snapped my head around to look at the engine. It wasn't burning, and there was no trace of smoke. Shrapnel had damaged the prop governor in a manner not visible.

"Feather[1] three!" Jack's yell almost deafened me.

The prop feathering buttons are located on a panel in the ceiling, just above the junction of the pilot's and copilot's windshields. I had to reach up and forward to push the half-dollar–sized button. By the time I got it locked into place, the engine had overspeeded to three thousand RPM: two hundred RPM above the red line. Not knowing what had been damaged, I prayed that the feathering system would work. It had to work, or else the speeding engine would come apart with disastrous results. I pulled number-three throttle to idle in an attempt to help slow the engine speed, but it only increased the drag on that side of the ship and made it more difficult for Jack to fly. Pulling the throttle to idle wouldn't solve the problem with the prop,

---

1. In normal operation, the propeller blades are in a flat position relative to the direction of flight and will create enormous aerodynamic drag when an engine quits and the prop is left to windmill. Feathering means rotating the prop blades in their hubs so that the leading edges of the blades will "knife" into the onrushing air. If the feathering mechanism does not rotate the blades to the "full feathered" position, the props will still cause considerable drag.

but it might lower the manifold pressure enough to keep the engine from blowing up. If I couldn't control the engine, or get the prop to feather, we'd never make it back home. I didn't want to shut the engine down so deep in enemy territory. If I could control the RPM and use the engine, we'd get out of enemy territory sooner. If I shut it down and feathered the prop and we were attacked by fighters, the dead engine would draw them like bees to a hive. On the other hand, if the prop wouldn't feather, it would create so much aerodynamic drag we'd never get home.

Holding the feathering button in, I glued my eyes to the right tachometer and concentrated my attention, as though by power of mind I could force the speeding prop to slow. Gradually the indicator needle dropped toward the red line. The feathering system was taking hold. As engine RPM fell, the rate of feathering increased. The system was working normally.

When the engine speed dropped to 2,200, I pulled the button out to stop the action. Immediately the RPM started to increase. I glanced over at Jack and saw that he was taking quick glances at me. He saw me looking at him and nodded silent agreement with what I was trying to do, that is, control the RPM with the feathering button.

It couldn't have taken over twelve or fourteen seconds for the RPM to build up to 2,800. When the tachometer needle reached that point, I pushed the feathering button in. RPM stabilized momentarily, then started to drop. This time I let it drop to 2,000 before I pulled on the control button. Again the needle stabilized momentarily, then climbed as prop blade angle decreased. I called Jack on the intercom and told him I'd try to hold the RPM between 2,000 and 2,400.

When the trouble first started, Jack eased the ship out to the right of the formation. If we had to bail out, he wanted to insure that we didn't jump into the propellers of the aircraft behind us. Too often, in their haste to get out of their stricken ship, men jumped and immediately opened their parachutes only to drift into the paths of oncoming aircraft. It didn't take much effort to visualize the disastrous results. It is a scene that is seared in my own memory. Along with being on fire, it is the worst of in-flight emergencies.

We had escaped the flak-fields with no further damage and the crew reported no one injured. I'd been pushing and pulling the feathering button for about ten minutes and my right arm was aching from the effort. The feathering system was cycling so rapidly I couldn't release the button for more than a few seconds at a time to rest my arm between each cycle. I'd have to switch arms and give each arm a rest. Even that would eventually wear me out. In time, the strain would sap my muscles of their elasticity.

We were at least three hours from the base, and for most of our return we'd be over enemy territory. There had been a few half-hearted fighter attacks on the formation, but they had not occurred against our box. Friendly fighters I'd spotted while approaching the target had driven them away.

I reset number-three throttle to make it easier for Jack to hold rudder pressure, but the setting caused us to lose speed. The formation pulled away and lengthened its lead at a demoralizing rate. Unable to keep up, within a very short time we'd be all alone in that hostile sky, a sitting duck for enemy fighters. Our gunners were aware of this, and were straining their eyes for the first sight of bandits. Since coming off the target we'd been listening to the tight-breathed chatter of aerial engagements, and it sounded as though the formations to the north and south of us were in a running fight with the Luftwaffe.

Long before the first hour was up, the muscles of my arms tightened, causing excruciating pain from which I could find no relief. The numbness of fatigue seemed to heighten rather than lessen the pain. I was sweating profusely and was about to ask Jack for relief when he motioned for me to take control of the ship.

The relief that came with flying the aircraft was short-lived. After about fifteen minutes Jack, in turn, was perspiring and grimacing from pain. Considering the tension and pain I'd endured, I sympathized with him, but I was determined to let him operate the button until he could no longer stand it. My arms were still tight; and I knew that once I returned to the button my endurance level would progressively deteriorate. From here on, we'd have to trade duties at the wheel and button every ten minutes or so.

Flying a course that lay about twenty miles south of our briefed withdrawal route, we kept the withdrawing groups between us and German fighter bases to the north. One small dogleg took us around a known flak site and left the rest of our route clear of any known opposition.

Having passed the flak site, we started a slow letdown, trading some of our altitude for airspeed. We unsnapped our oxygen masks, but left them dangling from our helmets in case we needed them. Free of the muffling masks, Jack and I could speak to each other across the cockpit without the crew overhearing our conversation. Neither of us wanted to worry the men as we discussed various options for getting back home or to an alternate base. We decided that once we reached the Adriatic, we'd either shut the engine down or let Lynch assist with the button. In view of our experience on final approach at Natal, I was against running the engine any longer than necessary. Actually we didn't know if the prop would go to full feather, and the only way to find out was to turn off the ignition and hold the button in.

We'd been running the button marathon for better than two hours when we sighted the Yugoslav coastline. Relief came in a flood of well-being as I realized that we'd crossed so many miles of enemy territory without being bounced by fighters. The odds against our making it back alone had been weighted against us. It was a feat, a happenstance of unaccountable good fortune that didn't often grace hapless crews. Moments later Jack said, "Let's feather it."

With the sound of his words still in my ears I punched the button, killed the engine, dropped my aching arms, and sat back to watch the prop wind down to a standstill. The ordeal was over, and not a minute too soon. My upper body was thoroughly weary. My arms were fleshless pain.

We were only a few miles short of the long-awaited coast when John "J. D." Matthews—our tail-gunner—called, "Single-engine fighter coming in slow; five o'clock low!"

The manner and direction of the aircraft's approach indicated a "friendly." The gunner's rule was, "Anything that points its nose at you, shoot it!" The Luftwaffe was known to possess a number of our fighters and bombers. Therefore it made no difference if a closing aircraft were American or British. If it flew directly at you, it got hosed down with .50-calibers.

J. D. Matthews and Leon Claverie (our ball-turret gunner) tracked the fighter as the pilot, careful to not point his nose at us, slowly closed, but well to our right. Shortly, Claverie's voice came over the intercom identifying the ship as a P-51. Within moments, the little craft, a 325th Fighter Group checkered-tail, slid into position beneath our right wing.

That was a strange thing to do, I thought, as I locked eyes with the pilot. It looked as though he had crawled underneath our wing to hide. His cockpit couldn't have been over thirty feet from me. Holding his eyes, I picked up my hand mike and gave him a call. Seeing the mike held to my mouth, he gave a negative shake of his head.

I turned to Jack, told him where the Fifty-one was and that his radios were out. Jack nodded acknowledgment and shrugged his shoulders in puzzlement. I couldn't figure the situation, either. The pilot had his wing flaps partially extended so he could fly at our slow speed. Other than that, both he and his aircraft appeared to be all right. Perhaps he was offering us his protection until we were well out to sea. But the position he was holding wouldn't be of any value if we were attacked. Something had to be wrong. Perhaps he'd been in a fight and was low on fuel.

About ten minutes out from the coast, he retracted his flaps and dropped the nose of the speedy fighter. The pilot never took his eyes off me as he waved farewell and slid rapidly down from my view.

I called all gunner stations to see if anyone had him in sight. No one did. The aircraft had dropped so rapidly in altitude and out of view that I wondered if his engine had quit.

"Keep looking guys. Watch for a splash."

If he ditched, I wanted to notify Air Sea Rescue of his location. No one sighted the ship or a splash, but a dark feeling deep inside me told me that he'd gone in. Why hadn't he climbed after pulling away from us? Troubled as to his fate, we continued to search for his craft in the air and on the mild chop of the Adriatic.

The remainder of the flight home was uneventful. Despite the engine being out, Jack made a perfect landing. As we pulled into our parking space, our ground crew was smiling happily at our late return. The Group had landed some thirty minutes ahead of us, and had reported that when last seen we were falling behind with all four fans turning.

Combat missions are tough on the ground crews. They'd no sooner get to know a flight crew when that crew would return with dead or wounded, or else fail to return at all. They didn't seem to be able to work hard enough or long enough to do their part. Perhaps it was their way of apologizing for not being in a position to be shot at. If so, it was a misguided sentiment. We knew and appreciated the difficult conditions under which they labored. More often than not red-eyed from lack of rest, when a mission was expected to be a tough one they'd forego vital sleep while we were gone and wait to see if their crew would return. Their loyalties seemed divided between the aircraft and the crew that flew it. Fine men, heroic in their own manner, they often worked to exhaustion to keep us flying. Without their selfless efforts and devotion to excellence, combat would have been even more dangerous. Seldom praised, their consolation was the certain knowledge that they, too, were Cottontails.

Standing on the ramp, looking up at the flak hole in our prop hub, I asked, "Will it be ready in the morning?"

"Yessir," came our crew chief's assured reply. "It won't take long to change the governor."

With that, we boarded a waiting truck and headed for the equipment shack. Two down, and forty-eight missions to go.

I wondered how many of our remaining missions would find us in so much trouble and still end so fortunately. We had been on the brink of disaster, yet we'd come through heavy fire and inequitable odds, with no more to show for it than some tense moments and a damaged prop governor. So far our luck since leaving West Palm Beach had been miraculous—the difference between life and death. It bothered me to admit that without the factor of luck we would not have made it even this far, and that such luck couldn't hold forever.

V

The party was a bust. Shortly after entering the club, I found myself embroiled in a crap game. Two bombardiers had pooled their resources (fifteen dollars) and were on a roll. The shooter had made his fifth pass and was letting the pile of bills ride on the next point. My peerless judgment told me that the chance of his making a sixth or seventh pass was about as likely as his being able to take out all five of Ploesti's refineries on a cloudy day with one five-hundred-pounder.

I laid a hundred dollars on the table.

On his ninth pass, the last of my four hundred dollars, almost two months' pay, disappeared into the large pile of rumpled money in front of him. Disgusted with my peerless judgment, I went in search of solace.

During my check-out by Jack, my original copilot, Frank Tarasko, had been used as a filler on other crews. A natural pilot, Frank had worked very hard to become proficient during our operational training at Colorado Springs. In Italy, he'd so impressed the pilots with whom he flew that he'd just been given his own crew. Although he never flew with our crew, he still lived in our tent. I'd learned of his good fortune at dinner and had gone to the club to help him celebrate. Following my disastrous gambit at the dice table, I found him with Jack, his buddy Wells, and another pilot. They'd located a table and were well into their cups when I joined them. Frank was listing to port and starboard, at times it seemed in both directions at once.

Wells's mood was the opposite of Frank's. Normally a pillar of sobriety and quietude, Wells rarely visited the club. He preferred his own company and more private surroundings. I couldn't recall ever seeing him drink, but tonight he was a different man: an angry man.

Like us, he was scheduled to fly tomorrow. Jack and I were Tailend Charlie, left side of the Second Attack Unit. Wells was leading our box. He'd had a bitter argument with the Squadron Ops officer regarding his aircraft. He had been given a war-weary bird, one that for unknown reasons was a slow flyer. His own aircraft, *Wells Cargo*, was on the mission, but being flown by another crew. Between moments of spoken anger, he'd lapse into long periods of brooding silence. We tried jokes, tales of romantic conquests, logic, but nothing would bring him out of his gloom. Whether it was from having drunk too much, or a matter of supposed clairvoyance, Wells was convinced that the mission would be his last, and that he would die. He wanted to die in his own aircraft.

He had pleaded with the Ops officer to let him fly it. None of us could think of a logical reason for his not flying his own bird. Our agreement on that point finally made him so angry that he stood up—steadily I noted—and walked away. He was going to talk to the Ops officer "one more time." He was going to fly his own aircraft, "or else!" I didn't know what his "or else" meant, but the Ops officer wasn't going to enjoy their conversation.

After Wells's departure, Jack told me that rumor had it that we were going north in the morning, probably to Austria or Germany. Tailend Charlie over any target is fraught with limitless possibilities for disaster, but the north country held the worst prospects of all: even worse than at Ploesti. Most of the Luftwaffe's fighters, including a group of highly aggressive yellow-nose 109s, were located in the area. After hearing Jack's grim rumor I understood Wells's gloom better. I was beginning to develop my own feelings of doom and gloom. With a 3:00 A.M. wake-up call already too near, Jack and I bade goodnight to Tarasko and the other pilot and headed for bed.

The takeoff was a hair-raiser. The last aircraft to launch, we had to plow our way through thick dust left by the thirty-seven aircraft ahead of us. We were well over halfway down the strip before I saw the end of the runway and could tell that we'd get off the ground in time to clear the olive grove. My confidence had suffered ever since the briefer had yanked the curtain cord exposing large yellow letters: WIENER NEUSTADT! WOLLERSDORF AIRDROME!

The briefer had pointed out that targets in the Weiner Neustadt area had been bombed only once during the past month, so we could expect heavy fighter attacks as well as intense and accurate flak. The weather en route would be just bad enough to make the mission even more difficult. Before the briefing was half over, I knew that this was going to be an unpleasant day. Wells must have known what our target was when we talked last evening. I noted the aircraft assignment sheet with at least some satisfaction. Wells had won his argument with the Ops officer.

Join-up with the formation was rapid. We formed at 4,000 feet over the base, fell in behind the 449th, then picked up the 376th and 98th while en route to San Vito. The 376th was leading the Wing. The Cottontails were bringing up the rear. This would be a good test of the rumor that the Luftwaffe would fly by other groups to get at us. Logically the 376th should take the brunt of the battle, providing there were not enough enemy fighters to go around. Fat chance of that. More than two-hundred ME-109s and FW-190s were known to be stationed in Austria and southern Germany. Scores more were based in northern Italy and Yugoslavia, and the Ploesti fighters could easily be deployed to the battle. The enemy's defensive capabilities seemed unlimited. I was concerned that after six missions, my gunners still hadn't had a chance to fight. Other than to check their operating condition, they hadn't fired their guns in months. Austrian skies were no place to brush up on one's gunnery skills. If you weren't already skilled and honed when you got there, you might not return.

Flying Tailend Charlie was much easier than flying Wing. I found that I could pull into a position beneath element lead's propwash and stick the *Swashbuckler's* nose to within a few feet of his tail turret. I knew that Joe Ukish, our nose-gunner, wasn't enjoying my exhibition of aerial tag, which placed him eyeball-to-eyeball with lead's tail-gunner. But the closer I flew, the easier and less fatiguing to hold position.

It was not a good fighting position. I was blocking lead's ball-gunner's view to the rear, and Joe's nose turret was neutralized except from low, head-on attacks, an unlikely eventuality. Lynch, in the top turret, was also neutralized except for attacks from our rear quadrant. Since he and Joe were our primary defense against head-on attacks, once we drew near fighter territory I'd have to drop back and fly much higher.

We'd headed northeast, splitting the Adriatic neatly down the middle. Near the Yugoslav coast clouds at our altitude—20,000 feet —forced us ever eastward. With each passing mile the probability of rendezvousing with the P-38s and P-51s was diminishing. At 30,000 feet, they'd be well above the clouds and unaware that weather had forced us far off course.

We made a landfall on the Yugoslav coast at the wrong point, passed over northern Yugoslavia, and were now flying north over southern Austria. Green wasn't certain of our position, but he believed we were passing to the east of Graz, at least fifty miles east of our prescribed course. Even so, our north heading should still put us over our IP within a reasonable time, in about thirty minutes.

We were getting close, well within the expected battle zone, and I was concerned about the positions of the other groups of our Wing. The maneuvering that had been necessary to avoid the weather had wreaked havoc on the Wing formation. Instead of lining up 376th, 98th, 449th, and 450th, we were trailing the 376th by about a thousand yards, the 449th was well to our right and rear, and the 98th was not in sight. The weather was turning in our favor, however, or so I thought. One moment I was looking at a blue horizon sitting astride a carpet of silvery clouds, and then the next moment bright sparkles of light were twinkling marqueelike in front of, then within, the First Attack Unit. Jack was at the controls and had moved the ship into battle position. My wonderment as to the cause of the twinkling lights was shattered by Lynch's shout, *"Bandits! Twelve o'clock high!"*

His guns, then Ukish's, roared as they fired forward. Sighting along their tracers, I saw a spread of eight or ten fighters, almost wingtip to wingtip, flattening out from a shallow dive and boring directly into the First Attack Unit. Within moments they closed the distance, barreled through First Attack, and into and above us.

I'd never seen or envisioned anything like it. It was beautiful airmanship, a veritable flying circus. So daring were their maneuvers, so great our surprise, that I doubt that a single gunner got an effective shot at them. Lynch and Ukish fired before the fighters came into range, then had to cease firing as they flew right into our formation.

I tracked one fighter through the First Attack Unit and in between Second Attack's lead box and our own. He came racing through, throttle off with prop windmilling, a shiny yellow-nose 109 dancing on air as the pilot skillfully avoided colliding with the bombers. His rate of closure, near five hundred miles per hour, gave me only a fleeting glance as he sped by. The sunlight reflected from his face, a face that seemed to look directly at us as his oxygen mask dangled to one side. I saw him for only the briefest moment, but I was certain that he'd smiled as he sped by. I could think of only one thing: his smile had flashed the message, "I'll be back for you in a minute."

The roar of Lynch's guns brought my attention back to the front. More 20mm shells exploded in front of us, then rushed on by. The sparkles—20mm shells exploding at terminal range to prevent them from falling back to the ground undetonated—were no danger to us. It was the unseen, the unexploded avalanche of shells still tearing through the sky, that could destroy our thin-skinned bird.

Wave after wave of yellow-nose 109s, 109s with other markings, and Focke-Wulf 190s came screaming by, straight through the spaces between boxes, and through holes created by stricken aircraft pulling out of formation. In less than a minute's time, between forty and fifty enemy fighters had hit us. At least two bombers were mortally damaged during the initial passes. Low and to my right were six parachutes of men leaving a smoking B-24. I looked forward, to Wells's position. It was vacant. At the edge of my vision I spotted him dropping down and sliding to the rear of our box. *Wells Cargo* was a ball of fire with a flaming tail engulfing its fuselage, streaming by the waist-gunners and beyond, a winged meteor hurtling to destruction in lonely space. The ship was under attack by fighters that swarmed like flies on a carcass. Through trailing flames, the left waist-gunner was firing his lone machine gun at a fighter zooming up from the rear. The engineer's turret slewed around as he turned to pick up an attacker diving in from the rear. Wells was holding the aircraft straight and level to give his gunners a steady shooting platform, or else a chance to bail out—it was impossible to tell which. No chutes were in sight and the ship was going to blow at any moment. From the looks of it, it should have already exploded.

Unwilling to witness their violent deaths, I turned my head to the front. They were gallant men; fighting to their awful end. Perhaps Wells had known after all.[1]

Flak exploded all around as we flew through smoke ball after smoke ball. The gunners had us bracketed. Most of the bursts were at our

1. In 1986, at the first Cottontail reunion, I was delighted to meet Paul Farina and Dave Waterman, the engineer and navigator of *Wells Cargo*. Paul told me that six of them made it out of the burning ship. One man, believed to be the bombardier, fell with his parachute on fire. The other five landed safely, though injured, and were prisoners of war in Germany. One of them disappeared shortly after they arrived at the POW camp. At least four of them returned when the war ended. Wells refused to jump and died with his ship.

exact altitude, or just above and below. The ship was virtually dancing on sudden smoke balls that hurled unseen hail to rattle ominously against thin skin. We were being chewed up. All the while, fighters kept boring in. Some came in slowly from the rear, throttled back, noses high, lobbing 20mm shells into our formation, staying just beyond the range of our guns. Some, as they drew into range, suddenly belched black smoke, pulled up and over into a spiraling dive (to make gunners think they'd made a kill), then pulled up and fired at the formation from underneath. Others flitted about like circus acrobats, doing nip-ups and dives as their pilots jockeyed for position, pressed gun triggers, and sped away.

A muffled explosion below my feet was followed by black smoke rushing into the cockpit from behind and underneath the instrument panel. At first I thought that electrical wires were shorted and burning behind the panel, but the large volume of smoke boiling into the cockpit from beneath my rudder pedals indicated a serious fire from a different source. I hit my mike button.

"Ollie! What's going on down there? What's burning?"

No answer. I couldn't feel any heat, but the dense smoke was filling the cockpit.

"Ben! Do you read?"

Again no answer. I didn't know whether they were dead, wounded, or fighting the fire. Ukish was all right. I could see him slewing his turret, searching for fighters.

Should I get Ukish out of his turret, I wondered, or go below myself and see for myself? The flak had stopped but we were hard pressed by the fighters. Leaving the cockpit while we're under fighter attack is not a smart thing to do, I reasoned. I was about to call Jack for his thoughts when I noticed that only tendrils of smoke were coming from below now.

"Ollie! Green! One of you come in!"

"We got it out." It was Green's voice responding to my urgent call.

"What was burning?"

"The nose wheel. A shell hit it and set the tire on fire. King's wounded."

"Damn! How is he?"

"He got hit in the right knee. Ollie's on the way up there to take care of it."

I looked back over my shoulder in time to see Ollie, his face drawn, hoisting himself up to the flight deck. I unsnapped my mask and yelled at him. "You OK?"

He nodded a tense affirmative and ripped open a bandage. Seeing no blood, I assumed his wound was not life-threatening.

The sound of impacts on the ship was followed by hurried movement behind me. Turning to check on Ollie, I saw him drop from sight below the flight deck and move toward the bomb bay. My view was obscured either by light smoke or a heavy mist. Since it didn't increase in density I decided it was hydraulic fluid being misted by air blowing into the leaky bomb bay. Visions of *Wells Cargo* flitted through my mind.

Checking the hydraulic pressure gauges confirmed my conclusion. Pressure was dropping. My immediate concern was how to get out of the ship. If necessary, we could jump onto the bomb bay doors and knock them loose from the fuselage; the doors had a design weakness made for that purpose.

I kept glancing over my shoulder, looking for Ollie to return, or to see if it was necessary to go to his assistance. Shortly after he entered the bomb bay, I noticed the mist was dissipating. Moments later he appeared, teary-eyed, his face drained of color. Wounded as he was, he'd shown great courage in going into the bomb bay, without a parachute, negotiating the narrow catwalk made slippery from hydraulic fluid, and stopping the leak.

I watched him carefully as he crawled up onto the flight deck. He had just settled into a comfortable position when we were raked by cannon fire. I turned and saw that the bomb bay was again engulfed in hydraulic mist. Ollie was rifling Lynch's toolbox. With pliers in hand, he again headed for the bomb bay.

Throughout I'd been keeping Jack and the crew advised of the problem and Ollie's progress in handling it. In the meantime the rear gunners were battling for our lives.

Riley, our radio operator, and Chris were operating the waist guns and had all the targets that they could handle. J. D. Matthews in the tail turret was taking the brunt of the attack, and he'd reported his guns had jammed at the outset. Sitting with his back to the aircraft, J. D. was alone in the sky. It was as though he and his metal and glass capsule were suspended in midair, with each fighter boring in with guns blazing, firing at him alone.

None of us knew it, but Leon Claverie, our ball-turret gunner was doubled up in his turret in serious trouble. Early in the battle, perhaps during the first flak barrage, his right gun jammed. He grasped the charging handle and pulled it all the way to the rear to clear the malfunction. At that moment, a flak shell exploded beneath the ship, sending a large (it had to be quite large) piece of shrapnel through his turret. The chunk of metal struck the section of the charging handle that connected the handle to the bolt mechanism, and the handle broke loose from the bolt. Except for a numbed hand, Leon was uninjured. A smaller piece cut through his right pants leg and the electrically heated underwear lying next to his skin. Again he was uninjured, but the shrapnel cut a wire in the garment and rendered the heating system inoperative. The turret's electrical control system was also out, as were his communications. Throughout most of the battle, Leon cranked the turret manually, driving off attackers as he sent one ME-109 spiraling down in flames and possibly scored a second kill.

As the battle progressed, his situation grew more dire. His loss of communications denied him all knowledge as to what was happening inside the aircraft, and prevented him from telling us of his situation. He'd seen the smoke from the burning nose wheel and then had his turret bathed in hydraulic fluid, which clung to the plexiglass and obscured his vision. From that point on, he cranked his turret in one direction, then the other, firing short bursts from his guns to make attacking pilots think that the turret was still in action. Had they known that our belly was undefended the fighters would have made short work of the *Swashbuckler*. In the meantime, without the benefit of heated underwear, Leon was freezing in the twenty-below temperature.

The battle lasted for twenty-five minutes. We were about five minutes out from the IP when the attacks ceased and our escort arrived overhead. The P-51s set up a weaving pattern, ready to do battle. Their presence, appreciated by all, was too late for some. Looking the formation over, I counted six empty slots. Fighters and flak had severely damaged the Cottontails, and we hadn't yet reached the target.

Because of our course error, bombardiers and navigators were finding it difficult to pick up checkpoints through the broken clouds. Consequently we overflew the IP and were well into our bomb run when Group Lead discovered we were making the run on Bad Voslau

GROUP LEADS AAF IN BOMBING

During the month of August the 450th Bombardment Group led the entire 15th AAF in bombing accuracy by scoring an average of 59.4 per cent in bombs landing within 1000 feet of the target. During the month, the 15th led the 8th Air Force in efficiency and this accounting puts the 450th score among the highest in all the American Air Forces of World War II.

On August 13th the group set a new all-high record for the 15th Air Force by dropping 94 per cent of its load within 1000 feet of the target when it attacked the gun emplacements in France. Lt. Col. Howard H. Davis led the attack and Lt. Bozzo was the lead bombardier. Not content with this score Lt. Col. Robert R. Gideon led an assault on a moving target at Guirgiu, Italy, and broke the previsious score with 97.1 efficiency. Captain Rolland R. Carr was the lead bombardier on the mission which was the first attempt on the part of the 47th wing to hit a moving target

The tremendous improvements in bombing efficiency are the direct result of a change in tactics. Instead of bombing as a group or as attack units the 450th pioneered bombing by individual box units. Its success in this innovation has been so outstanding that the wing has adopted it as standard practice. With its unusally high record the 450th had raised the entire wing to the position of first in the air force.

• •

Tune To 1565 kc
The VOICE of the Cottontails

Airdrome. Our target lay eight and one-half miles south.

Intense and accurate flak was doing additional damage to the formation. Engines were knocked out and bombardiers salvoed their loads to give pilots a better chance of remaining with the formation. I was beginning to wonder if anyone would have any bombs left when we reached the target. Two damaged aircraft had salvoed their loads during the first battle. It was a proper decision; as long as they were with us, we had the benefit of their firepower, and they had a chance to save themselves and their aircraft. After the turn at what we thought was the IP, five more bomb loads were salvoed by stricken aircraft.

As we approached the target, the flak intensity was the worst I'd seen, except for the frightening scenario in view to the north, at Vienna. It didn't seem possible that anyone could experience anything worse than what was happening to us, yet the flak pall over Vienna looked infinitely more dreadful. I couldn't take my eyes from the dense smoke, lying as a dark layer of stratus cloud. Twice the cloud lit up from the orange blossoms of exploding bombers. I felt sorrow for the crews that had drawn targets in that area.

It seemed like we had been in flak for hours when we finally cleared the target and headed for home. It wasn't until we were safe from the flak that Ollie informed me that Lynch was wounded. I turned to look. Lynch was still in his turret, alive and kicking—the kicking was intended to keep Ollie from pulling him down from the turret. Ollie didn't know the nature or extent of Lynch's wound except that he had a bloody face and was yelling in pain, and refused to let Ollie near him. A squadron of P-38s had replaced the P-51s, so there was no reason Lynch couldn't come down from the turret long enough to have his wound inspected and tended. I tried talking to him on intercom. All I got in return was a shouted *"No!"* Whatever his problem, he didn't appear to be in any immediate danger, so I motioned Ollie to back off and leave him be. Ollie was in pain and had no business standing on his wounded leg to wrestle Lynch out of the turret.

Once away from the target, we became aware of Leon's plight. He hadn't checked in, nor could I contact him for a damage report. Riley and Chris checked and reported that he appeared to be alive, but they couldn't raise the turret or rotate it so they could get to the hatch and pull him inside the aircraft. I told them to use the emergency cable system to winch him in. This they did, but with great difficulty.

With the outside temperature twenty below zero, by the time they winched the turret into the aircraft and opened it Leon was in bad shape. Hurriedly they got him into his fur-lined suit and watched him as he warmed and regained presence of mind. His worst injury appeared to be badly frostbitten hands. He didn't complain, but he had to be in considerable pain.[2]

After "bombs away," I searched the skies for renewed fighter attacks but saw no trace of the enemy. All that remained was to limp back to Manduria and prepare for the ordeal of getting our bird onto the ground.

The *Swashbuckler* had suffered extensive damage. Its hydraulics were shot out; the gauges now showed no pressure in any of the systems. We'd have to crank the gear down. Our flaps were inoperative, the nose wheel tire was flat, and we had no brakes. Although the ship was light in weight, our lack of wing flaps meant we'd have to make a high-speed landing, without brakes to steer or stop us. If we ran off the runway there was no telling where we'd end up. In our condition, even though we had wounded on board we'd have to land last, to keep from blocking the runway in the event that something went wrong. Indeed, until we tried it, we couldn't even be certain that the landing gear would drop down and lock. While circling to land, I saw several ships landing ahead of us fire red flares from their Very pistols. We weren't the only craft with wounded on board.

To my surprise and relief, the gear went down and locked. We were set to land.

Jack brought the crippled ship in as slowly as he dared and touched the main wheels on the end of the runway with great care. The struts held and both tires were still inflated. He kept the nose wheel off as long as possible before setting it down. The flat tire made a loud flapping noise, but stayed on the wheel.

Our plan was to let the ship roll, and at the last minute, before we ran out of runway, the crew in back would move to the rear, causing the tail to drag for our final braking.

Either the gunners never moved to the rear, or their weight wasn't sufficient to cause the rear fuselage to set down on the runway. We

2. Leon's actions in the disabled turret were courageous. Unfortunately, his bravery was never officially recognized.

rolled, and rolled. We were going to go off the end of the runway, into the olive grove, and there was nothing we could do to prevent it. By the time we hit the overrun we were moving slow enough so that I knew we'd be all right. The aircraft would suffer, but that couldn't be helped.

I cut the engines the moment I realized that we were not going to end up in a mass of twisted metal. The props had barely ticked to a stop when we passed the end of the overrun and slowly took down several trees. Hearing a sound of hurried movement behind me, I turned to see Lynch disappear into the bomb bay, with Ollie close behind. I didn't know how the bomb bay doors had been opened, but they were, and Lynch and Ollie were scrambling out of the ship. Within moments the two of them came into view, scuffling on the ground in front of us. The scuffle ended when Ollie snatched Lynch's helmet off his head. At that moment, an ambulance braked to a stop and medics ran to the two of them.

Jack and I hurried out of the aircraft to join the crowd gathering to stare at our wounded men and our shredded bird. By the time we got there, a medic had cleaned most of the blood off of Lynch's face and was examining a tiny cut on his forehead. Another medic had Ollie sitting on the ground and was examining his wound. Before Lynch, Ollie, and Leon left in the ambulance, Lynch retrieved his helmet from the ground and handed it to me. I shook my head in disbelief. Protruding from the steel helmet, at the forehead area, was a piece of steel about the diameter of a lead pencil and about two inches in length. It had entered Lynch's turret endwise, like a bullet, penetrated the helmet, and dug into his skull. The mark on his forehead was hardly more than an eighth of an inch long, but profuse bleeding and pain had frightened him. Each time he'd tried to take off his helmet, pain and the sound of metal grating against bone had been more than he could bear. After enduring hours of pain in the turret, by the time we landed he'd lost most of his self-control. The moment Ollie snatched the helmet from his head, the pain stopped. Now, our sheepish engineer was embarrassed over his behavior, and reluctant to leave in the ambulance.

After the ambulance departed, I noticed Riley, Chris, and J. D. staring up at Riley's waist window. I walked back to them to listen in on their conversation. The topic was the large hole at the rear of Riley's window.

Shortly after we hit the first flak, Riley had turned from his gun to check on Chris. The moment he'd moved, a large piece of shrapnel had struck the rear edge of the window frame, exactly where his head had been a fraction of a second before. Had he not moved at that exact moment, his head would have been shattered. Hours later a thoroughly shaken Frank Riley was standing quietly, listening to Chris recount the details of his brush with eternity. Heretofore, Riley had been disdainful of combat, confident that he was immune to its grim possibilities. From the look of the trauma he was now showing, he, like the rest of us, would have to reassess the realities of our circumstances.

When the final count was in, the Cottontails had lost eight crews, with only thirteen of the eighty flyers known to have bailed out. Among those lost, Wells and his valiant crew were thought to be dead. Another crew returned home with one man dead. Scattered among the remainder of our crews were nine wounded, not including Lynch. Our squadron's mission report listed only King as being wounded. He was hospitalized.

The 450th had taken a beating. We'd suffered a single mission loss rate of 22 percent. Simple arithmetic, a grim clarion in this instance, told us that a few more missions like this one and there would be no more 450th. Twenty-three of our twenty-nine surviving aircraft were damaged: three, including our bird, were seriously damaged. After surveying the *Swashbuckler*, I wondered if it would ever fly again. Our three injured crew members, considering the nature of their wounds, had been lucky.

The most notable perception of the day's action was the Luftwaffe's having singled out the Cottontails. Six of our eight losses were known to have been caused by fighters. The 98th, 376th, and 449th lost one aircraft each, but to flak. Perhaps others were correct when they chided, "Having you Cottontails around is the best fighter escort there is!"

Original crew of the *Swashbuckler*. Left to right, standing: pilot W. R. Cubbins, copilot F. F. Tarasko, navigator B. S. Green, bombardier O. H. King; kneeling: crewmen F. E. Riley, Jr., C. Dittman, F. W. Lynch, L. Claverie, J. J. Ukish, J. D. Matthews.

Hangar at airfield, Manduria, Italy. Group headquarters is a lean-to at rear of building. Doorway at left leads to crew briefing room.

Bottoms Up and another Cottontail B-24 made an emergency landing at Vis. Bombs painted on *Bottoms Up* indicate eighty-five missions completed. The last of the 450th's original aircraft to arrive in Italy, *Bottoms Up* was also the last to go down, disappearing on its one-hundred-fifth mission during a raid on Wiener Neustadt.

Cottontail B-24 down on its home field at Manduria.

P. Farina; Army Air Force official photo

Crew of the ill-fated *Wells Cargo*. Left to right, standing: W. Ballantine, W. Mangrum, J. Luna, N. Lepovitch, W. Duda; kneeling: pilot J. F. Wells, copilot B. O. Baker, bombardier R. J. Kalfuss, navigator D. Waterman, flight engineer S. P. Faruna. Wells, Kalfuss, Ballantine, and Lepovitch were killed in action. Duda completed fifty missions; his replacement, F. Franz (not in photograph), was also killed in action.

A. Daniels; Army Air Force official photo

This unusual photograph, taken from above, shows two tiers of Cottontail B-24s at low-level near Manduria, preparing to land after mission.

Flying Officer Dudley C. "Pop" Egles.

L. Heath, Army Air Force official photo

L. Heath, U.S. Air Force

Cottontail B-24s over Allied Forces landing area during invasion of southern France. The formation, led by Col. R. R. Gideon, took off from Manduria at 0200 hours for the first night-formation mission ever attempted by mass bombers.

Taken at 22,000 feet, this photograph shows a Cottontail B-24 going down, with wing burning. The white object above and just to the right of the plane is the open parachute of a crewman who has just bailed out; the black spot just below to his left is a flak burst.

L. Heath, Army Air Force official photo

Cottontail B-24 formation heads for home after raid.

courtesy Lt. Col. Gunn

ME-109s making head-on pass through the 454th Bomb Group formation. Note that pilot in near plane is not wearing an oxygen mask.

L. Heath, Army Air Force official photo

Cottontail B-24s over Vienna, Austria; the flak is just beginning. Aircraft show new tail-markings.

POWs and visiting Red Cross officials, south entrance of schoolhouse, Bucharest, August 30, 1944. Among those pictured are, left to right, beginning at third from left of top row: Sgt. Ira Call (arms folded), Capt. Henry MacQueen, Flying Officer A. Poole (Royal Australian Air Force), Capt. Art Staveley, Rumanian official (wearing necktie); middle row: Rumanian officer, Capt. Anthony Polink, Sgt. S. Ferguson, Capt. E. Jackson, Capt. Ted Stanley, Capt. Floyd Robinson (with beard), Rumanian officer; bottom row: Rumanian officer, Maj. Chester Haas (with arms folded), Maj. Yeager, Lt. Col. James A. Gunn III, Rumanian official, woman Red Cross official, unidentified official (wearing necktie), Lt. Col. Bill Snaith, unidentified, Maj. Henry Harper (in dark suit), unidentified.

British Commonwealth POWs and visiting Red Cross officials, August 30, 1944: bottom row, left to right, L. Tichbourne, A. Gill, J. Coape-Smith, A. Duff, R. D. Bird, E. I. Nicholson, H. G. Paynton. Second and third rows, D. C. Egles (in undershirt), A. Kilroy, last three unidentified. Note that Duff's fingers are forming the victory symbol.

Sherwood Mark

Rumanian guard and family, Bucharest.

courtesy Lt. Col. J. P. Macdonald

POW officers' camp, schoolhouse, Estrada Sfinta Ecaterina, Bucharest.

VI

We flew again on the twenty-sixth and twenty-seventh of May—long, tiring missions over the Mediterranean, against targets at Nice and Marseilles. Inaccurate flak was a welcome relief, as was the absence of enemy fighters. Flying with a replacement ball-gunner and bombardier, I was doubly thankful for the low level of enemy reaction.

Ollie had undergone surgery to remove shrapnel from his knee, and was recuperating on the isle of Capri. Lynch had suffered no ill effects from his wound, but Leon's frostbitten hands were coated with a thick, clear plastic that immobilized his fingers. Much to his chagrin he had to be spoon-fed by Lynch and the others.

Following a day off, the Group went back into action on the twenty-ninth. We were not on the schedule, and decided to spend the day at the beach. There was just the right amount of sand, sun, and boredom to loosen our tensions a little, but supper brought me back to reality. When one eats the same food, day after day, a trip to the mess hall is almost tantamount to going on a mission. If flak has flavor, it must taste like GI chili. I knew from my first mouthful that I'd get severe indigestion.

If the food ruined my mood, the rumor I heard while eating made a shambles of the ruin. We were going back north in the morning. I could only hope that the mission would go as well as it had today. The Group had hit Wollersdorf, come through the flak with little damage, and hadn't encountered a single enemy fighter. Our sister groups, the 98th, 376th, and 449th hadn't fared as well. Each lost two aircraft and their crews.

The Intelligence briefer's sudden yank on the curtain cord sent a ripple of dismay through the crowded room. The cold dread of recognition stabbed painfully as I read the words:
WIENER NEUSTADT!

The entire B-24 fleet, fifteen heavy bomb groups, would hit indus-
trial targets in the Vienna/Wiener Neustadt area. The B-17s were
going after the marshaling yards at Zagreb, Yugoslavia. Our target
was the Ebreichsdorf carpet factory, which was producing ball bear-
ings critical to aircraft engine production. Heavy flak and fighter
defenses mounted on the day before were expected to give a repeat
performance. From the way the crews described yesterday's mission,
however, flak batteries should be out of ammunition today. I discounted
that as happy talk. I figured that German gunners had an oversupply
of ammunition and were trying to work off the surplus at every opportunity. It was the yellow-nose 109s that I was more worried about. All
the fighters that I'd seen at Wiener Neustadt were bright metal, but
the yellow-nosed 109s looked as if they'd been polished. I found that
significant. It indicated fine morale and a highly capable fighting unit.

The takeoff and join-up went well, but our rendezvous with the
449th didn't come off as planned. They were a minute late and were
flying at our rear when they should have been ahead of us. Had I
known the significance that would take over the target, I might have
been tempted to abort, as had three of our aircraft shortly after takeoff.

We picked up the 98th and 376th at San Vito D'Normanni and flew
our course, unhampered by flak or fighters, all the way to the IP.
Except for the 449th being out of position, the mission was going
well. P-51s were negotiating S's overhead to keep from outspeeding
us. If the Luftwaffe showed today, it would be a different kind of
battle than the one we'd had six days ago.

Turning at the IP, I was shocked to see the 449th trying to cut us off
and take the lead to the target. Had they kept their position,
everything would have been fine. As it was, they were driving straight
at us, at the space separating us from the First Attack Unit. Our
attack unit had no choice but to break left to avoid a sky full of crunched
bombers. The maneuver not only put us in even more intense flak,
but destroyed our run on the target. If we were to hit the target, we'd
have to maneuver in the flak for an extended time to get lined up
again. Lead did the only thing possible. He flew by the target, reversed
course, and started a bomb run in the opposite direction. All the
while, we were catching hell from German gunners.

Just when it looked as though we'd make it through the lethal hail,
the ship shuddered. Jack fought to get the right wing down. It felt
and sounded as though we'd received a direct hit. Gunners in the

rear were trying to out-shout each other over the interphone to tell us what had happened.

Jack yelled, "Feather three!"

While the propeller windmilled to a stop, I shouted the crew into silence. I couldn't understand what Riley was trying to tell me, but it sounded like he was saying that a shell had gone through number-three engine nacelle at the supercharger. The shell hadn't exploded, but it had done an enormous amount of damage to the wing. Lynch had abandoned his turret and was busily turning fuel valves. We'd already lost all of the fuel from number-three main along with a large amount out of the other right-wing tanks. There was no fire, but the damaged wing appeared to have more dihedral, looking as if it were bent upward, outboard of the dead engine. The wing could break off at any moment. The other engines were running fine.

Whether Jack had done it intentionally or the damaged wing was creating excess drag and hampering us, we'd already lost so much altitude we were well below the exploding flak. I considered the possibilitiy of our taking another hit from shells on the way up to the formation. I kept telling myself that the chance of being hit by an unexploded shell was remote, but I didn't believe it. We'd already been hit by such a shell. By the time we cleared the target, the Group was far ahead and lengthening its lead. We were alone.

Should we take a chance on the wing holding, or bail out now? The question kept running through my mind. I'd already seen two men jump from a ship in the First Attack Unit. The stricken aircraft and parachutes were no longer in sight.

Our fuel situation told me that we wouldn't make it back to Manduria. The realization that we were going down was a coldness tearing at my gut, seeping into my mind, paralyzing my thoughts. Reason demanded that we accept our fate and consider our remaining options. We were going down, and that was that. The only questions remaining were Where and How. Jack and I discussed the situation and made our decision.

Our first objective was to continue southward far enough to clear the Austrian and Hungarian borders with Yugoslavia. If we bailed out over Austria or Hungary, we were certain to be captured. If we made it to Yugoslavia we had at least a chance of being picked up by Partisans or Chetniks. The Partisans, numbering in the thounds, were our best bet.

Evasion briefings had been conspicuous by their lack of hard and useful information. Escape organizations of unknown effectiveness and size were in place, hidden within the civilian populace. The nature of the organizations and their need for secrecy prevented air crews from being given specific facts. We just had to take our chances on being picked up. Considering our alternatives, and the risks being taken by the underground, having to take our chances was not an unreasonable demand. In view of the size of the Yugoslavian resistance, we stood a fair chance of being picked up and hidden until the war was over. In any event, I was determined we'd do everything possible for ourselves before relying on others.

A crash landing was out of the question. The impact of landing on rough terrain would undoubtedly sever the wing and cause the ship to go into a violent maneuver that would probably kill us all. There remained one slim alternative—Vis.

A tiny island off the coast of Yugoslavia, Vis was being held as an amphibious operating base by Partisans, a battalion of British Commandos, and a small detachment of American Rangers. There was a short gravel runway in a mountain valley in the center of the island. The entire island was only three miles long, and the mountain-locked runway a mere thirty-five hundred feet. A detachment of British Spitfires was using the tiny airfield to make air-to-ground strikes against German forces in Yugoslavia. Other B-24 and B-17 pilots had succeeded in landing there. If our fuel held out and our landing gear worked, there was the chance that we too could set our bird on a permanent roost on Vis. It was an attractive thought, but I had little confidence that it was a realistic hope. One way or the other, the ship was in its final hours, or minutes.

Green set a course to avoid all known flak and fighter installations. All we had to do was lighten the ship so as to hold our altitude as much as possible, hope that we had sufficient fuel, hope even more that we would not be attacked by fighters, and pray.

Everything loose in the aircraft—and some things that had been attached—went overboard. Bomb shackles, flak jackets, steel helmets, ammunition, waist guns, our long-range radio, all went out of the aircraft as presents to the Austrians. If attacked by fighters, we'd bail out as rapidly as possible and hope that we'd all make it out of the aircraft.

Endless minutes strung into two impossible hours. I couldn't keep my eyes off of the damaged wing. It seemed, after an hour or so, as if it had a bit more dihedral. Perhaps my imagination, warped by the unrelenting tension, was being skewed out of reason, causing me to see things that were not. Fear can do strange things to the mind. The wing appeared to be flexing up and down more freely than it should. I watched it carefully for a while and decided that it wasn't bent upward after all.

Jack and I had been carrying on a running discussion as to our chances of landing the aircraft at Vis. Neither of us had ever seen the airstrip, and the small image of the island shown by our map indicated a difficult situation. We'd have to approach the strip with gear and flaps down, in a diving turn down the side of a mountain. For a fighter, that kind of approach would be easy; it seems to be the only way that fighter pilots know how to land. But a B-24? Negotiating an approach with a damaged wing was risky, but Jack was willing to try. That left me no choice. I'd stay. The rest of the crew would be given the choice of jumping or landing.

Having accepted the fact that we were going down and we might not make it to Vis, my mind turned to the problem of evading capture. I visualized us in the company of Tito's Partisans, effecting a long and arduous escape in much the manner I'd seen in several war movies. Soon my thoughts would bring me face-to-face with the realities of having to make a parachute jump.

Once again, fortune was with us. The coastline lay just ahead and there was still no response from the enemy. The Adriatic never looked better. We couldn't see Vis, which lay another forty miles offshore, but we were close enough to try radio contact. Jack pushed his mike button and called the tower. No answer. He tried again. Still no answer. We were wondering if our radio had been damaged by shrapnel, when the tower answered and Jack explained our situation.

After a pause, the operator responded with a heavily British "*Negative, Sir!* Jump your crew over the island."

Jack and I stared at each other.

He called the tower again and insisted on landing.

The tower operator responded, "You cawn't land, Sir! We don't 'ave any more room for aircraft on the field."

He was right about that. One side of the tiny valley was little more than a junkyard. Wrecked and seemingly flyable B-24s, B-17s, a B-25 or two, and other junked aircraft lined one side of the small runway. The other side was the fighter parking and ordnance areas. We'd have to jump.

Suprisingly, the finality of the decision did not create a hollow pit in my stomach. In the past, when thinking about the possibility that the day might come when I'd have to jump, I'd experienced a sinking feeling and a fervent hope that I'd never have to do so. Now that I was faced with reality, I had no qualms about parachuting. An impregnable wall of finality had changed fearful contemplation into acceptance of the inevitable. My main concern was getting everyone out of the aircraft.

I explained our situation to the crew, trying to sound as positive as I could. We'd make one pass over the island. They were to take up their bailout positions and stand by. The moment they heard the bailout bell, they'd jump as rapidly as possible. The rear crew would exit through the camera hatch. The front-end gang would leave through the forward bomb bay.

Jack lined the aircraft up on the imaginary center line of the island, an axis paralleling the runway. That would give us the maximum time to get everyone out. Peering down through my side window, I waited for the near coast to pass beneath us. Shortly after it slid by, I told Jack. He paused for a few moments, then toggled the alarm.

I'd unhooked my seat belt and rechecked the fit of my parachute harness while we were getting lined up for our final pass. Shortly after the bell sounded, I slid my seat to the rear and stood upright. The harness was properly tight. Waving to Jack, I ducked beneath the top turret and made my way to the bomb bay.

My mind was racing. Should I go out of the ship feet-first or head-first? Should I jump off the catwalk, or simply step into space?

My way to the bomb bay was unimpeded. Lieutenant Donnell—our replacement bombardier,—Green, and Ukish had already jumped. Suddenly I knew what I was going to do. I stooped on the edge of the catwalk, clasped my arms around my lower legs, paused a moment, and tumbled forward into space.

I wasn't prepared for the instant hurricane or the roar of my 160-mile-per-hour speed. Wind force spun me violently in a kaleido-scope of earth and sky.

"Straighten your body and count to ten," I told myself. The sound of air rushing by me had lost its roar but it was still very loud—I had decelerated to terminal velocity.[1] Straightening my body, I assumed a natural falling posture, on my back with my head low. It was exhilarating, like lying on a cushion of noisy air. All I could see was blue sky and my flying suit pressed against my legs, fluttering violently on the top side. I extended my right arm. Wind dragging my arm caused me to roll rapidly to the left. The island came into view. I was over the airfield. As the ground came into view, I pulled my arm back. Too late! My roll continued until I could again see nothing but the sky and my legs.

I didn't feel as though I was falling. The loud rush of air, the flapping of my flying suit, and the pressure of air against my back were my only sensations. The terror and tensions of the mission were forgotten, lost in a wonderful feeling of freedom. I was floating on a noisy, invisible cloud.

Again, I extended my arm for a look at the ground. I was still very high, about a mile above the airfield. There was no hurry to open the parachute. The longer I delayed pulling my rip cord, the more assurance I'd have of not drifting out over the Adriatic. I had just decided to try some manuevers when I heard a roaring sound approaching, then rapidly pass by. I jerked my head in all directions to see what it was. My first thought was that our bomber had turned in its dying moments and had nearly flown into me. Then, I saw it. A second fighter. Diving at me!

Fright paralyzed me, momentarily. I closed my eyes, doubled up, and clasped my head in my arms as though to hide from some ferocious creature. There was no time to think. The sudden thunder of the diving aircraft dominated my mind. As suddenly as it had come, the thunder was gone, leaving only the sound of the now-familiar rush of air.

I straightened my body, poked out an arm, and looked wildly about for aircraft. The noises of the two aircraft had been identical. There had been two fighters, but I could no longer see either of them. The only thing I saw was the airfield. "The ground!"

I'd forgotten the ground; that I was falling toward it. It was no longer a distant picture. The island had turned into a mass of land, and the Adriatic had disappeared.

---

1. As altitude decreases (as the jumper falls), air becomes more dense and causes increased drag on the falling jumper. Near sea-level altitude the terminal velocity of a falling jumper is 115 to 120 miles per hour.

I stuck out an arm, rolled, then stuck out the other arm. Sure enough, extending the second arm in a swan dive slowed my roll long enough for me to get a good look at the airfield and know that it was time to pull my rip cord.

Rolling once again to the back-low position, I searched frantically for the aircraft and saw nothing but blue sky. Time was running out. I had to open my chute. As I rolled face downward the ground had lost all of its picture qualities. It was moving toward me. It was moving upward faster, closer by the moment.

While reaching for the D-ring on my rip cord, I somehow turned on my back. I closed my eyes, pulled, and damned near threw my arm away. The thought that I hadn't pulled the rip cord properly was racing through my mind when the truck hit me—or so I thought at that moment.

Sudden silence was marvelous. Except for the soft sound of air strumming suspension lines and caressing the canopy above, the silence was absolute. I opened my eyes and looked at the D-ring clutched in the death grip of my right hand. I looked upward. A billowing white umbrella swayed gently, its web of slim suspension lines descending funnellike toward me, terminating at the ends of the riser straps attached to my harness. It was a beautiful sight, the canopy swaying back and forth, against a flawless blue sky.

I looked down and saw the earth, about 800 feet below, swinging back and forth. Hell! The canopy and earth aren't swinging; I am, I realized. I had to stop the oscillation. I couldn't land swinging; I could be killed or seriously injured. I was coming down on the side of a mountain at the north side of the landing strip. I looked up, grasped my risers, and pulled one pair, then the other. That reduced my swaying, but didn't stop it. I continued to work the risers until I heard a voice shouting from somewhere below me. My efforts to turn toward the voice restarted the oscillation. The voice became frantic. Tugging one riser, then the other, at the last moment, I sighted the source of the voice.

Wham! I hit the ground, flat on both feet.

Luckily, the tight fit of the harness kept my body slightly bent, an ideal posture for landing. The force of impact caused me to collapse to a fully stooped position. The moment my fanny hit my heels, I sprang up, staggered back a step, wobbled momentarily, then stood steady. The chute collapsed into olive trees above me.

The British voice, which had never ceased, was coming from behind and below me. Turning toward it, I saw that I'd landed on the edge of a rock terrace. It was at least ten feet down to the next level. Had I hit a foot or so to my left, or fallen in the wrong direction, I could easily have been killed.

The cockney voice was that of a Commando standing on the terrace below. His upstretched hand was holding a white enameled cup.

"'Ere, mait. 'Ave a spot o' tea."

I couldn't believe my eyes or ears. I'd just survived a harrowing experience and here was this fellow acting as if nothing had happened, offering me "a spot o' tea!"

"Just a minute," I said. "Let me get out of my harness." Had I not felt so suddenly jittery, I'd have laughed at the absurdity of the scene. I didn't want to offend the fellow. Neither did I want to embarrass myself by disclosing my trembling hands. I attributed the trembling to an oversupply of adrenalin released by the circumstances of the jump.

Free of the harness, I dropped to my knees and reached down and took the cup. What there was left of the tea was weak and tepid. I drank it in one swallow, thanked him, and returned the cup. He'd been right on one point. It was only a *spot* o' tea.

After gathering my chute into a loose bundle wrapped with suspension lines and riser straps, I dropped it to my benefactor. All the while, he berated me for ignoring his landing instructions. It seems that his shouting represented a complete course in parachuting, but I hadn't understood a cockneyed word he'd said. Despite my not having followed his advice, the landing couldn't have been better. As far as I knew, my only injury was a torn thumbnail which leaked a single drop of blood.

I walked along the wall until I found a point low enough to drop to his terrace. A short distance farther, we arrived at his camp. It was a sparse lean-to with a small fire dying in front of it. A white enameled teapot sat near the fire. He and his tentmate had located their camp away from the airstrip to avoid the frequent strafing attacks made by German fighters. Just beyond the tent was a foxhole.

My jump mentor insisted that I remain long enough to "Taik a full cup o' tea." While warming the brew in the pot, he said, "You're bloody lucky, mait. Jerry didn't fire at you. The ruddy bastards shot up some of your chaps!"

His revelation stunned me. Had they been German fighters diving by me?

"Did they hit anyone?"

"Cawn't say. Your chaps were too 'igh to see. Why'd they open their chutes so bloody 'igh? One chap looked like 'ee came out of the ruddy aircraft with the ruddy chute already open. Not wise, thot!" he scolded.

"Couple uh weeks back, Jerry shot up some uh your chaps bloody awful. Killed three. Cut one most in two," he said as he dragged a hand edgewise across his own midsection.

Alarm seized me. Had the fighters killed some of my crew? I wanted to get going. I hadn't noticed the road, but apparently one lay nearby. I could see a small truck making its way up the mountainside.

"When we finish tea, we'll walk to the road and 'op a lift into the village," my mentor assured me.

The ride was short and dusty. The view of the village from high on the mountain was charming. Tiled roofs hugged the steep slope to keep from tumbling onto fishing boats moored in the picturesque harbor. A scimitar of beach stretched a half-mile or more beyond the village, curving inward to a narrow inlet.

Trapped between mountainside and the water, the village clambered its way along for several hundred yards before it petered out against a sharp slope. A single cobblestone street wound its narrow way through the village. Each swerve revealed another vignette of Old World charm. Rows of shops and dwellings crowded the street like families enduring centuries of changeless time. The lorry deposited me in front of what I took to be the village inn. Jack was there, awaiting my arrival.

The first thing I noticed about him was the garrison cap shoved back from his forehead. I'll be damned, I thought, the guy had the presence of mind to grab his "fifty-mission crusher" before he jumped! The hat had survived forty-one missions and he wasn't about to part with it over some minor inconvenience—like bailing out. I admired his coolness. I never guessed that a cavalier act such as this would one day almost cost me my life.

After congratulating each other on our successful jumps, he told me that all of the crew except Frank Riley had been picked up and were on their way to the village. J. D. and Chris had landed in the

Adriatic and had been rescued by nearby fishermen. The situation on Riley was confused. One report said that he may have landed in the water, but that was not certain. We'd have to wait until the crew arrived to determine what happened to him.

Everyone seemed to be in good shape. J. D. and Chris were no worse for wear for their dunking. Green, after pulling his rip cord, had continued looking down at the chest-pack parachute and had caught a face full of suspension lines. Friction from the lines sliding against his skin had given him four line-burns. The two burn stripes on each cheek made him look as if he was peering out from behind bars.

As each man told his story, my fear grew like a poison mushroom. Riley had been the first to go through the camera hatch. In the hurried activity to get out, he'd popped his chute as he fell through the opening. The small pilot chute snagged on the edge of the hatch but deployed the canopy in a normal manner.

Lynch confirmed that Riley had a good chute. He'd exited through the bomb bay shortly before Riley, and was not far from him when the fighters made their pass. Lynch wasn't certain, but he thought that Riley had been hit by cannon or machine-gun fire. He also believed that one of the fighters had fired at him. After questioning everyone, I decided that Lynch and Riley were the only ones who'd seen the fighters. I was certain that they hadn't fired at me.

A British lieutenant who accompanied the crew from the airfield told us that Commandos and Partisans were scouring the island and its surrounding waters for our missing radio operator. The search would continue for two days, but in the end we had to conclude that Frank had landed in the water. As to whether he'd been killed by the fighters, or had drowned, we'd never know.

Chris took Riley's apparent death very hard. During the short months that we'd been together, they had become close friends. My own feelings were confused. Riley and Chris had distanced themselves from me, at times challenging me in matters of discipline. I'd overlooked most of their sallies, figuring that in time they'd come around and become as close as the rest of the crew were to me. Now it was too late. Once my mind accepted the probability that Riley was dead, I was angry at both him and myself.

He shouldn't have popped his chute so soon!

I should have been more attentive to him, made certain during our months of training that he had no unreasonable fear of jumping, that he knew the proper procedures.

Anger gave way to sorrow, then to a numbness that went beyond sorrow. I felt frustrated, defeated. Had I signaled Jack too soon, jumped the crew too early? Had I warned everyone to delay opening their chutes? I couldn't remember. An easy jump had turned into tragedy. I rationalized every aspect of the bailout. My only acceptable conclusion was that I had somehow failed him.

After briefing us on the search and his plans for further searching, the lieutenant told us that the officers would stay at the inn and the gunners would be housed in nearby buildings, until transportation could be arranged for our return to Italy. The supply ship wouldn't return for several weeks. Consequently, chances were good that we would return via Canadian torpedo boats. These were the boats that plied the Adriatic, waiting to rescue those who ditched their aircraft or had to bail out over water. He didn't know when the boats would be available. In the meantime, we could languish in any manner we wished.

The drama of the day's events and Riley's apparent death depressed me and left me in a state of exhaustion. Following supper, I bade our host goodnight and retired.

VII

I awakened at daybreak to the terrifying wail of a siren and exploding bombs. I rolled onto the floor and lay there, waiting for the next bomb to explode. When it became apparent that the raid was over, I got shakily to my feet and dressed.

After breakfast, Jack and I decided to walk across the mountain to the airfield. By road it was probably less than two miles, and the mountain was little more than a very high ridge. It was a fine morning for a walk, and going to the airstrip would be a good way to work off our jitters. The German bombs had been small and few in number; nevertheless, I'd felt totally helpless. For the first time, I wondered what it was like to be caught beneath our massive bomb drops.

Along the way, I was surprised at the number of women and young boys in Partisan uniform. All were armed with rifles or grease guns —simple, low-cost machine guns. One lad was probably no more than twelve years old. As I looked at him in wonder and respect, I couldn't help but draw a contrast between this youthful warrior and the dirty Italian boys of his age, who seemed bent only on stealing or begging from Americans. The thought angered me momentarily.

Once my anger subsided I felt guilty. The Italians were pawns who had been victimized by the Mussolini government. This youngster had a clear view of who and what the enemy was and refused to be a victim, choosing instead to fight. Studying the too-old and impassive face of the young boy, comparing him to his Italian peers, I was puzzled over the differences between them—differences of attitude, of motivation, of character.

We passed the crest of the ridge and came upon a small group of German prisoners working with picks and shovels, repairing the shoulders of the road. Their guard, a young woman, was boring them with hate-filled eyes. The grease gun, hung by a strap across her shoulder, pointed unwaveringly at the prisoners. Her countenance reflected an intention as deadly as the weapon.

As we drew near, several prisoners paused momentarily to glance our way. The woman's barked order and sudden jab of the weapon produced frantic work from the entire group. There was no question in my mind that she was looking for the slightest excuse to kill them. Not once did she take her eyes off the prisoners to look our way. I was glad to put as much distance as possible, and as soon as possible, between us. Later when I mentioned the incident to the lieutenant, he explained that it was most unusual for the Partisans to take prisoners. He didn't know why these had been taken, but he had heard a rumor that the Partisans had taken them to celebrate the end of May—today. The lieutenant believed the prisoners would be executed as part of a May Day celebration. It was a brutal story, one that I didn't enjoy. We never heard whether or not the prisoners were executed. I never saw them again; but neither did I hear any gunfire.

From the ground, the reason for the tower operator's refusal to let us land on the airstrip was even more obvious than it had been from the air. The place was a junkyard. Most of the bombers were total wrecks. Many had been bulldozed from the runway to their final resting places, and all had been stripped of serviceable equipment by the Commandos and Partisans. Looking up at the mountains surrounding the airfield, I was thankful that we'd been refused permission to land. With one engine out and a weakened wing, we might not have made it. The fire-blackened skins of a number of aircraft carcasses bore grim testimony that some had made it the hard way. I wondered how many men had died trying to land on the mountain-locked strip. We talked to several Commandos as we wandered about. They had many stories about German air raids, and various crews who'd landed on the field.

Several months before, a P-38, with one of its engines sputtering, had landed and pulled off the runway and into the fighter parking area. The pilot had tinkered with the ailing engine, refueled, and gone roaring down the runway. The engine faltered on the takeoff, but the pilot managed to pull the craft up and over the tent hospital located beyond and to one side of the runway. The aircraft exploded on the crest of a low hill beyond the hospital. A short distance farther, the hill terminates in a cliff overlooking the Adriatic. Had he made it beyond the hill, his height above the sea would probably have been enough to allow the ship to accelerate on one engine to a flyable speed.

I marveled at the spirit of the pilot and the risks he'd taken to get back to his unit. At his moment of death, he'd had the presence of mind to avoid crashing into the hospital. I wondered what thoughts he'd had at that moment.

The walk was good. Physical exertion went far to dispel the trauma of the previous day's events. However, my spirits were again plunged into darkness when the lieutenant told us that the searchers were certain that Riley had landed in the Adriatic. I thought that I had already accepted that eventuality, but his statement lent reality to the supposition and depressed me. Even so, during the next three days, I continued to hope that he would be found alive.

On the evening of our third day on Vis, the lieutenant informed us that we would be departing by PT boat early in the morning. That good news was heightened by the arrival of two officers of the Ninety-eighth Bomb Group. They were a pitiful lot. Lice-ridden, haggard, and filthy from a forty-day trek through enemy territory, they had been brought to Vis by a small group of Partisans who had them in their care throughout their arduous journey.

The pilot had a nasty gash on his forehead. The wound, angry with infection, had been sewn closed with ordinary needle and thread by the other man, the crew's bombardier. Aside from his severe state of depression, the bombardier was uninjured. Theirs was a bizarre and tragic story.

On April 23, they'd been on the big mission to Wiener Neustadt —the Schwechat ME-109 assembly plant. Their nose-gunner and another man had been killed outright during the battle. Their aircraft had been severely damaged by flak and fighters, and all those still alive, except these two, were wounded, several seriously. Flying southward over northern Yugoslavia, they were again attacked by fighters. Realizing that they would not make it back to Italy, and fearing for the lives of his critically wounded men, the pilot decided to surrender. He lowered his landing gear and let the enemy fighters join him in formation.

Meanwhile, the bombardier had removed the gunner's body from the turret. When the fighters attacked, he climbed into the turret and prepared for battle. The first thing he saw was a Messerschmitt sitting off his wingtip. Without thinking, he'd slewed the turret and fired at the enemy aircraft. He missed. The enemy broke away and set up for a new attack. Having lost his only chance to surrender, the pilot put the ship into a dive and tried to land it on the only place available, a small field. All who were still alive, except he and the bombardier, died in the crash.

The pilot related the story to us with great anger. He talked as though the man didn't exist. By his own account, the only words he'd spoken to him since they crashed were: "You sonofabitch, when we get back, I'm going to have you court-martialed!"

Later in the day, while the pilot was not in the room, the bombardier told the same story, but with great sorrow. He neither expressed nor otherwise showed any fear of the threatened trial. His sorrow was owing to the death of his comrades, for which he felt guilty. He insisted that he hadn't heard the pilot say that he was surrendering.

My sympathy was with the bombardier. His version of the account rang true. I hoped that when they returned to the Ninety-eighth, the pilot would be overruled by cooler heads.

The biggest problem I had with either of them was their constant search for lice. When they found one they'd stare at it for a while, dispose of the hateful thing, and resume the search. Both were in dire need of a bath and fumigation. I kept a respectful distance.

The boats were small—too small, I thought, for their hazardous mission. Built of plywood, they were not much more than thirty feet long. The torpedo tubes mounted on both sides of the bow were little more than adornments; there were no torpedoes in them. The twin .303-caliber Lewis guns mounted amidship, on each side, were relics from World War I. Not wanting to put down our host, I held quiet about the ancient Lewises, with their small ammo drums perched on top. I wondered what the boat crews would do if they—if we—were attacked by enemy aircraft. Because of their limited range, the Lewis guns would be ineffective against the heavier caliber guns of fighters.

We and the officers from the Ninety-eighth were shared between the two boats. At 0600 hours, our less-than-imposing flotilla put to sea from the tiny village of Komitza on the western coast of the island.

Well into the Adriatic, I looked over the boat and badgered the crew as to the craft's performance and the details of their rescue mission. I wanted to know everything about their operations; the way

Here's The Box Score For 12th, 15th AAF In '44

12th Air Force

SORTIES FLOWN

Total	193,918
By bombers	57,677
By fighters	126,009
Photo recon	4,528
Troop carrier	5,814

TONS OF BOMBS DROPPED

Total	104,313
By bombers	73,193
By fighters	31,120

ENEMY AIRCRAFT DESTROYED

Total Destroyed	597
Total (in air)	340
By bombers	46
By fighters	294
Destroyed on ground	257

LOSSES

Total	965
Bombers	252
Fighters	684
Others	29

PATIENTS EVACUATED

Total	123,589

TRACK CUTS AND ROAD BLOCKS
(including rail yards)

Total	5,814
By Bombers	1,160
By Fighters	4,654

... From May through October, the 12th AAF either destroyed or damaged ... 788 railway locomotives, 9,038 rail cars ...

BRIDGES		VEHICLES AND TRANSPORT	
Destroyed	668	Destroyed	10,155
Damaged	1,217	Damaged	8,376
SHIPS		**LOCOMOTIVES**	
Sunk	172	Destroyed	1,192
Damaged	500	Damaged	903
FACTORIES		**RAILWAY CARS**	
Destroyed	35	Destroyed	6,576
Damaged	89	Damaged	11,926
TUNNELS		**AMMUNITION AND FUEL**	
Closed	25	(Dumps destroyed)	
Damaged	64	Total	248

15th Air Force

SORTIES FLOWN

Total	159,028
By bombers	100,885
By fighters	55,398
By recon aircraft	2,754

TONS OF BOMBS DROPPED

Total	213,185
By bombers	212,220
By fighters	965

ENEMY AIRCRAFT DESTROYED

Total Destroyed	5,257
Total (in Air)	5,405
By bombers	1,750
By fighters	1,655
Destroyed on ground	1,852

LOSSES

Total	2,447
Bombers	1,674
Fighters	773

LOCOMOTIVES DESTROYED

By Fighters	743

BREAKDOWN OF BOMBS DROPPED

	Tons
On marshalling yards	65,113
On airdromes	24,613
On troops	4,955
On industrial targets	68,434
On railways	22,657
On harbors	12,856
On roads, bridges	3,233
Ground support	8,364

things had been going for us, we could one day be in need of their full services. In time I worked aft to the engine room. It was already crowded by the three Rolls Royce engines beating a thunderous roar as we clipped through moderate chop.

Anxious to be rid of the Rolls's thunder, I worked my way forward to the crowded cabin to read a book that I'd found in the engine room. I never learned how the story ended. Frequent interruptions slowed my reading to a pace matching that of the boats as they plowed their way through the choppy sea. Our voyage ended after dark on a dock at Manfredonia, Italy.

The boat crew had radioed ahead and a truck was waiting to take us to an American airfield near Foggia. It was a bumpy, dusty ride and I was weary from the long trip from Vis; but I didn't care. We were going to an airfield where we'd be fed, and could get a bath and a good night's sleep. I hadn't slept well on the island. Following the air raid, our host had told us that the nuisance raids were commonplace. I didn't consider them either a nuisance or commonplace. While on Vis, I'd noticed numerous differences in values as held by the British and myself. Their attitude toward combat was far too casual to suit me.

At the base, we went directly to a hangar-sized mess hall. The place was packed with aircrews having a grand feast. Steak! The Group commander had been notified of our impending arrival and that we were coming from Yugoslavia.

Entering through a side door, we paused in line along the wall. Spying us, the Group commander shouted his flock to silence and introduced us as "AWOLs" (persons absent without leave) who'd been *languishing* in Yugoslavia. We looked the part, in our filthy flying suits, unshaven, and ripe with fermented sweat. No one could have stood to be near us but ourselves. I felt as raunchy as we looked.

The crowd roared a welcome. To my surprise, their well-intentioned greeting and the colonel's use of the term "languishing" angered me. Aware of my illogical reaction, I wondered what had caused it. I attributed it to weariness and discomfort. In no mood for heroics, we ate our tough, greasy steaks and departed.

The trip to Bari, to Fifteenth Air Force Headquarters the next morning, didn't improve my disposition. I wanted to return to Manduria. I couldn't see any reason for the Bari trip (nor did one ever surface). I didn't know anyone at Fifteenth, and the last thing I wanted to do was become involved with "headquarters weenies."

It was another dusty ride in the back of an open truck, and I felt ill at ease as the driver left us at the entrance gate to the headquarters compound, with no instructions as to where to go or whom to see. At a loss at what to do, we filed through the gate and squatted just inside, with our backs resting against the compound wall. I felt conspicuous. Our appearance, as compared with the neatly dressed people scurrying about, made me self-conscious and resentful. The abstractness of their high-level chatter and curious glances deepened my already considerable resentment. We'd been through hell, and here these headquarters types were scurrying around, chatting about ways of creating additional hell for us.

I must be getting combat fatigue, I thought. I was certainly fatigued, and hungry. I was about to suggest we go rustle up a mess hall, when to my disbelief Frank Tarasko's smiling face rapidly closed the distance between us.

Immediately after we went down, he'd been temporarily transferred to Fifteenth headquarters. He knew that we'd gone down but until now he hadn't known whether we were alive or otherwise. Seeing us squatting against the wall had been a shock. During lunch I regaled him with the details of our misfortune and told him of Riley's death. He assured us that he'd arrange for us to be flown back to Manduria. He'd informed us early on that we were listed as Missing in Action, so I asked him to notify the proper people of our return. I wanted to head off the Missing in Action telegrams that I knew would be sent to our families. If it was too late for that, I wanted follow-up telegrams sent right away so our families would know that we'd returned.[1] To make sure, I was given permission to send a telegram through Red Cross channels.

The situation at Manduria was abominable, but no more so than we must have looked to others. My gunners had lost most of their clothing and other possessions to scavengers. Over the next several days I made my views on the matter known in loud and precise terms to every senior officer I could find. The officers' belongings had been gathered by Tarasko for shipment to our families. I got back everything except my hoard of cigarettes. I suspected our Italian houseboy, Roberto, but I had no proof.

Our return created confusion at every level of command. There were conflicting views as to what should be done about us. Should we be returned to the States, or to combat? Policy required those who'd gone down in enemy territory to be removed from combat. The belief was that if one returned to enemy territory and was captured, he would be considered a spy and summarily executed. The argument was ridiculous. Vis was firmly under Allied control. There was no question about that. The headquarters response to that was: "Maybe the Germans have your name."

Five days after our return from Vis we were scheduled for a mission. I felt relieved that the decision had been made. However, when I

1. Sending the telegram was an unfortunate mistake. It read:

DISREGARD ANY MESSAGE CONCERNING ME AM WELL WILL WRITE

It arrived at my home on June 7. I had no way of knowing, but the official Missing in Action telegram didn't arrive until June 18. It read:

THE SECRETARY OF WAR DESIRES ME TO EXPRESS HIS DEEP REGRET THAT YOUR SON SECOND LIEUTENANT WILLIAM R CUBBINS HAS BEEN BEEN MISSING IN ACTION SINCE THIRTY MAY IN NORTH AFRICAN AREA IF FURTHER DETAILS OR OTHER INFORMATION ARE RECEIVED YOU WILL BE PROMPTLY NOTIFIED

On June 24 my family received yet another notice in the form of a letter from the War Department. The letter confirmed that I was missing, and explained what the term "missing in action" meant. At that point my family was in utter confusion and despair.

WESTERN UNION

QA45

CDU31   INTL=CD SANSORIGINE VIA RCA 20 6

NLT MRS FANNIE D CUBBINS=

1263 DRIVER MFS=

DISREGARD ANY MESSAGE CONCERNING ME AM WELL WILL WRITE LOVE=

RICHARD CUBBINS.

MRS F D C
BW 736A MAILED

heard the rumor "We'll be going north in the morning," most of my feeling of relief evaporated.

That evening in the club, a dramatic scenaio unfolded. One of the original Cottontail pilots was being consoled by Jack and several others. The man was near tears. He'd flown over forty missions, and was questioning his own fitness for combat. His friends knew that he'd had a particularly tough combat tour and sympathized with him. However, I think we were all shocked when he suddenly blurted out, "I can't take it anymore. If tomorrow's target is near Switzerland, we're going to get ourselves interned."

My second shock occurred when, after a moment's pause, all those in attendance agreed with him. I'd never heard the subject broached before, but after flying only thirteen missions, I could see how the man's attitude could occur. Various members of the group suggested that he reconsider. They well knew how his action would be viewed. As the discussion progressed, I became convinced that the man was not a coward, but he obviously feared being branded as one. He was simply fatigued, combat-fatigued. And as is usually the case with fatigue under conditions of great stress, fear had seized him in its debilitating grasp. By the time I left for my tent, I felt that the Group medical staff had erred by not pulling the crew off combat duty, at least temporarily.

When the briefer exposed the name of our target, I knew the Group would be shy at least one crew by the end of the day. We were going to

MUNICH!

Jack was stone quiet. I just shook my head from side to side. I didn't know what to think, except that the mission could be a really bad one. As the briefing details unfolded, I learned about a different kind of "bad"; and I didn't like it any more than I liked the traditional kind.

Our target was the Oberpaffenhoffen airdrome. We could expect heavy flak and fighter opposition. That was the "old" kind of bad. The weather would be clear at bombing altitude, but there was a strong chance that lower clouds would be piled up against the Alps and would obscure our target. Our secondary target was the city of Munich. If we had to hit Munich, lead bombardiers would use radar to pick out their aiming points in the city. There were enough designated aiming points to cause great destruction in the city. We were going to follow England's lead in the war and "terror bomb." That was the "new bad," and I didn't like it.

Heretofore I'd never thought of our raids as being against people. We bombed targets. I'd never liked the obvious side effect, but neither had I tried to fool myself. I'd accepted the certainty that civilians would be killed by our raids against military targets. But to bomb them intentionally—the idea was reprehensible. That was the sort of thing the Nazis did in Holland, at Coventry; the list is long. But this wasn't a game we were playing. We could well die on this, or the next, mission. With that rationale reinforcing my will, I directed my thinking to mission details.

The manner in which the mission developed was strange. We'd already overflown Austria and were turning just south of Regensburg, at least forty-five minutes into heavily defended airspace, and there hadn't been a shot fired. It was uncanny, as if the enemy had taken a day off from the war.

Oberpaffenhoffen was covered by a solid deck of clouds. Unable to see the target, we headed south for Munich. Flying on top of the clouds with the Alps rising high above them, the scene was spectacular, the war a million miles away. Approaching Munich, we still had nine-tenths cloud cover beneath us.

We'd started our bomb run and there was still no flak or fighters. The 376th was leading. We followed, with the 98th, then the 449th bringing up the rear. The 376th released its bombs before the first flak was sighted. It was sporadic at first, as though the gunners didn't want to disclose the location of the city beneath the clouds. The initial bursts exploded well below the 376th. The flak became more intense as the bursts climbed upward to meet the formations. Shortly after we dropped our bombs, bursting shells climbed into our formation, but stayed away from our aircraft. We escaped unscathed. However, another of our aircraft suffered the ultimate misfortune. The ship exploded over the target in a fireball from a direct hit. Expecting the Luftwaffe to exact its revenge at any moment, we were again surprised by their total absence.

The flight home was relaxed and enjoyable. While flying down the coast of northern Italy, one of our aircraft left the formation and headed for a target on our secondary list. The ship's bombs hadn't released over Munich. After leaving the target, the bombardier cleared the malfunction. The pilot, a fellow I'd checked out only a few weeks ago, was determined not to waste his bombs on fish. Watching him pull out of the formation, I figured that I or someone else would be checking out his replacement in the near future. About twenty minutes after we landed, he came nonchalantly in, as though nothing out of the ordinary had happened. It had, of course. He'd left a very large oil fire blazing in northern Italy.

During the mission debriefing, I learned that we'd lost a second airplane. Near Siegenburg, one of our aircraft, apparently under control, was seen disappearing into the clouds. Prior to its disappearance, three open parachutes were counted. Siegenburg is hundreds of miles from Switzerland.

After landing at Manduria, I learned that the distraught pilot and his crew were missing. Determining which of the two missing crews had blown up and which was missing would have been a simple matter. All I had to do was check the formation plot or the Missing Crew Report. I didn't. I didn't want to know.

The next morning, I learned that headquarters still hadn't made up its bureaucratic mind about us. Having just flown a mission, the irony of their "official indecision" infuriated me. Nevertheless, we had no choice but to wait.

VIII

Shortly after the Munich mission Ollie returned from Capri with lucid descriptions of the swimsuits worn by Italian girls. It was "Rest and Recuperation" just listening to his dissertations on the attributes of bikinis at rest and in motion. Although he was back on the crew, he hadn't been cleared for combat.

Time became a relentless foe. Lower casualties during the month meant fewer replacement crews and aircraft, and left us with little to do. I was embarrassed at having to sit on the ground while others were flying combat. Our only escape was to get away from the base. We asked for a three-day pass and got it. On a fine, sunny morning, Ollie, Jack, and I hitched a ride on a supply truck and headed for Bari.

Bari, a hot, bustling city, was overrun with soldiers, pimps, and prostitutes. We soon tired of noisy crowds and sought the quiet of shady streets in a nearby neighborhood. Had it not been for a delightful stroll along the waterfront and a few hours spent sailing about the harbor, our trip would have been a bust. Our last night was marked by a humorous but moving conversation with a pilot from one of the northern groups.

I had become separated from Ollie and Jack and had gone into the bar of the Miramar Hotel to kill time. The Miramar was Bari's equivalent of Broadway and Forty-second Street. If one remained there long enough, he'd see everyone he'd ever known. Or so the story went.

The room was crowded with flyers and others bent on drinking and laughing the war away. Making my way through the crowd, I found a seat at the bar and ordered a drink. I had just taken a sip when someone jostled against my back. An American lieutenant was holding onto the edge of the bar and striving mightily to climb up onto the stool. On his third try, with my assistance, he finally made it.

"Bartinnr! Gimme uh dring! Whiskey watr!"

Had his elbows not been leaning on the bar, he'd have collapsed onto the floor. He nearly did when he lifted his left elbow and turned toward me. I placed a hand on his shoulder and steadied him while his eyes stabilized.

"Wher yuh frum fella?"

"Four-fiftieth." He was having difficulty focusing his eyes, and my reply startled him so, he almost lost the other elbow off the bar.

"You don shay! You por bashtrds. Wha kinda outfit is th four-fit . . . ?"

He almost lost it again. I steadied him and echoed John Wells's words, "Better'n some; not as good as some."

"You por bashtrds!"

The bartender sat the drink on the bar and gave me a look of reproval. Reinforced with a gulp of whiskey and water, most of which dribbled down his chin, he spoke again.

"Shay fella, wur you at Veeanna las' month?"

"No. I was on two of the missions to Wiener Neustadt."

I didn't want to tell him we'd been shot down. He might not have been able to handle it. As it was, when I said the magic words, Wiener Neustadt, I had to grab him to keep him from falling from the stool.

"You por bashtrds! I shaw you down ther. I wudn go to Weenr Nooshtdt for all th'tea in China. All uh cud see wus that blak cloud an you por bashtrds blowin' up!"

By the time he'd forced the statement out of his mind and onto his whiskey-thickened tongue, his eyes had misted from the struggle he was having with his emotions. He was looking directly at me but seeing only the things in his mind. He then sort of collapsed back to the bar and sat quietly, struggling to hold his head upright.

I was grateful when Jack arrived and rescued me. The lieutenant was less than two swallows from being sick, or spinning-in into a heap on the floor, and I didn't want to be anywhere near him. I was wearing my only uniform.

Our conversation hadn't been a complete loss. His description of the view of Wiener Neustadt from his vantage over Vienna was identical to my view of Vienna from Weiner Neustadt. I hadn't the courage to tell him that. It was best to let him think that others had had it worse than he.

A month had passed since we parachuted onto Vis, and our only mission since then had been the milk run to Munich. The waiting had, in many ways, been worse than flying missions. Consequently, when we returned from Bari and learned that we would be allowed to complete our missions, I felt as if I'd been cured of a chronic disease.

When we entered the briefing room the crews were busily chatting about the mission ordnance—fragmentation bombs. For the first time since our arrival at Manduria, they were more concerned about the bombs than the target.

Frag bombs—small bombs bundled in clusters—create a lot of debris in the air when the cluster units come apart and release their bombs. The clusters had been known to open prematurely, creating hazards to other aircraft. Worse yet, the arming propellers spin off their shafts and arm the bombs shortly after they're released. The spectre of an aircraft being hit by enemy fire, pulling up and salvoing hundreds of armed frag bombs onto the formation can't be ignored. It could mean mass carnage, an aerial junkyard.

The crews quieted as the briefer reached for the curtain cord: ZAGREB AIRDROME!

Zagreb lay in northwestern Yugoslavia. It was a hot area for fighters, but that was our mission: destroy the fighters on the ground. It sounded easy except for one detail: enemy fighters aren't in the habit of sitting on airdromes while high-flying bombers rain frag bombs on them.

The weather at Zagreb was forecast to be marginal, maybe bad enough to hold the fighters on the ground. It could also keep us from acquiring the target; but it wouldn't prevent flak gunners from working off their inventory of shells. It's one thing to trail bombs into a city, one aircraft load at a time, as the British had been doing for years. It is quite another thing to drop waves of hundreds of bombs on civilians and their homes. Our raid on Munich had signaled a new bombing policy, and the enemy was expected to respond in force at every hand.

Heading inland from the coast, the formation maneuvered for room to climb above layers of clouds. More and more the mission looked to be a bust. We were leading the Wing with the 376th, 98th, and 449th trailing. Flying Tailend Charlie, I searched the skies to our rear during turns, but didn't see any of the other groups. By the time we reached 25,000 feet, we were pressed to keep up with the formation. The ship was slow and sloppy. It wouldn't hold wings-level, and the nose kept swinging from side to side as though it were hunting for an invisible groove in which to fly.

Leveling off at 25,500 feet, we accelerated to a more comfortable speed. Even so, the beast was like a boat with a loose rudder. I was glad we were flying Tailend Charlie. Holding a wing position would have been exhausting. Indeed, the wing-men were finding it all but impossible to hold position. The antics of all the aircraft were almost humorous. A pilot would get his ship stabilized for a few moments, then drop a wing and wobble around like a wounded goose. There was just enough turbulence to cause all our wings, already bowed upward, to move up and down like huge birds struggling to stay aloft.

We were trailing the formation by a hundred yards when the target came into view. We'd been flying on top of solid clouds, but now there was a large hole in the undercast and I could see part of the airdrome underneath the far edge. I wondered whether the lead bombardiers could see the patch of target long enough to aim our bombs. The answer came within moments.

We'd sighted the target while over the IP. As soon as the leader set the bomb course, he took the formation into a shallow dive. I couldn't believe it. Lead was looking for a cloud-free altitude or, the thought hit me, he was going to try to dive-bomb with a formation of four-engine bombers. The stunt had no chance of succeeding.

My main worry was the 376th. Were they still with us? Were they still at high altitude? Would they drop their bombs on us? A glance at my airspeed indicator discounted that possibility. We were indicating 200 miles per hour. That should keep us well ahead of the 376th; but it wasn't keeping us in position. The formation was about two hundred yards ahead and pulling away.

We were almost at the target when the flak started. I couldn't see it, but muffled explosions to our rear announced its presence. Our high speed and rapidly changing altitude had thrown the early rounds off-target, but as we continued the dive, scattered bursts appeared below us.

Immediately after we leveled off for bomb release, the air exploded. A barrage, so inaccurate that it trailed Second Attack Unit by two hundred yards, shredded our ship.

Number-four was hit and smoking. Number-two's gauges were doing their death dance, but the engine was still running. I punched four's feathering button and held my breath. My eyes locked on the smoking engine, expecting it to burst into flames at any moment. It didn't. The prop wound down to full feather and the engine quit smoking.

Ollie salvoed our bombs shortly after we were hit. But with one engine gone and a second engine going, our chances of getting home faded; so did the formation pulling steadily away from us. We were at 14,000 feet and there wasn't enough power in our remaining engines to climb to a higher altitude. It was all we could do to hold what we had. Once we lost number-two, we wouldn't be able to do even that; and it was a very long way home.

Vis was probably out. We knew from the morning briefing that the weather over central Yugoslavia was worse than it was here. We'd never be able to locate ourselves over the tiny island with enough accuracy to parachute onto it. Still there was hope. We'd hold course and fly as long as we could. Our track would take us to within forty miles of the island. If the weather improved in that direction, we'd alter course and make our second jump. If not, we'd continue on course to its terminus, one of the numerous airfields near Foggia, our northernmost bases. We'd be over Yugoslavia most of the first half of the flight, then over the Adriatic for the last and most questionable half. The next step was to lighten the ship.

Once again, everything that was loose or could be torn loose went overboard. Flak jackets, helmets, bomb shackles, radios, guns, ammunition: we even considered chopping the ball turret loose and dropping it. Number-two was sputtering along but not well enough to be of much help. Lynch and I worked the controls to get as much power as possible out of the engine. We were losing altitude far too rapidly and I was concerned about our two good engines. Running them at climb power in the warm air of low altitude was causing them to heat up, and there wasn't anything I could do except stare at the gauges and hope they'd continue to run.

Vis was no longer an option, nor was number-two. The dying engine ran out of oil and I shut it down before it caught fire. Several minutes later, according to Green, we broke the coast. We couldn't see it because of the clouds, but far ahead a thin line of blue peeked from beneath the undercast. We still had the Adriatic between us and the Promontorio del Gargano—the spur of the Italian boot—the nearest friendly territory.

Limiting our remaining engines to climb power cost us altitude, but we didn't dare run them harder. They had to be conserved. We had 10,000 feet of altitude, which we could trade for airspeed and pray that we'd run out of Adriatic before we ran out of altitude. At the moment, our chances of doing so appeared remote. We were losing altitude at an alarming rate, and there were ninety miles of water and at least thirty miles of Italian hill country to cross before we got to Foggia and Foggia Main airfield.

The sight of the sea stretching to beyond the horizon was accompanied by pangs of remorse. I shouldn't have been so negative about the PT boat rescue operation.

I longed for a radio so I could call the boats and give them our position and heading. As it was, all we could do was hope they hadn't all returned to port, that they were nearby, cruising along our track.

Halfway across the Adriatic, we cleared the undercast. Where are they? I asked myself over and over. There was no sign of the boats. The sea was vacant.

Why shouldn't it be? I thought. Considering the poor weather over enemy territory, and the lateness of the hour, there was no reason for the boats to be on station.

By the time we were down to 5,000 feet, it appeared the sea was going to win the race. I felt sorry for our new radio operator, Frank "Dave" Davis. He'd joined the crew after our return from Vis and had asked if he could continue with us until he finished his missions. We had been delighted to have the friendly South Carolinian. Dave was an original Cottontail. He'd been with us on the Munich raid and had given no indication of being worried about going to such a tough target. Dave had been to all the tough ones and could still manage a quiet sense of humor. I doubted that he saw any humor in our current situation. This was his forty-ninth mission.

The situation was on the verge of becoming impossible. We were down to almost 3,000 feet and the Italian coast was little more than a dark line on the horizon. I inched RPMs and manifold pressures upward. The cylinder-head temperatures crept slowly higher, then stabilized near the red line. The increased power lessened our rate of descent but didn't help our airspeed. We needed speed to help cool the engines, but the best we could do was mush along, nose high, a few miles per hour above stall speed. Jack was at the controls while I divided my attention among the altimeter, the temperature gauges, and the coast. I'd rather have been flying the ship. Staring at the gauges and their grim readings depressed me.

When we were close enough to see coastal detail, it was as we'd feared. High cliffs dropped sharply to the water. There was no beach on which to land, and the water was too deep for an assured ditching. We were bearing to the north of the promontory in order to bypass its 3,000-foot ridge.

The closer we came to the coast, the more tense and unsure I became. The cliffs looked to be as high as we were—they weren't, but the pressure of our circumstances affected our judgment. To be certain, I increased power on both engines and watched with apprehension as the temperature needles climbed above the red line.

Jack and I discussed jumping the crew at the coastline. We were well over 1,000 feet above the sea, but once we crossed the coast, we'd have much less clearance above the ground. To jump the crew, we needed sufficient time over shallow water to get them safely out of the ship. The only way to achieve that was by making a sharp turn so as to fly parallel to the coast. We were both of the opinion that we didn't have enough airspeed to hold our altitude during the turn. If we lost too much altitude, we'd probably have to ditch the ship in the water. The simple maneuver, a ninety-degree turn, was simply impossible.

We crossed the coastline with several hundred feet of altitude to spare. Before doing so, I called the crew on the interphone, explained the situation, and offered them the chance to jump. With the memory of Riley's experience fresh in everyone's mind, no one wanted to go into the water.

Proceeding inland, we skimmed along, several hundred feet above undulating hills, barely holding our own, hoping that the engines would keep running. We were much too low to bail out, but if we could keep going a little longer, it looked as though things might start to go our way. The end of the promontory ridge had passed to our left, and at 800 feet altitude we now had at least 400 feet clearance and the ground was shelving away. We were passing the last of the foothills.

Jack and I searched right and left, looking for Foggia Main airfield, which we knew to be in the area. Consequently, we were caught off guard when number-one blew.

Lynch yanked the throttle to *OFF* and punched the feathering button. We weren't certain of our exact location but we couldn't be more than a few minutes from the airfield. If we only had a radio, I thought, then regretted the useless yearning. Everything had gone overboard but hope, and that was rapidly running its course to despair.

When the engine blew, I jammed full RPM and throttle on number-three, and spun the supercharger to EMERGENCY. With only one engine remaining, we were going down. I called the crew on intercom and told them either to jump or take positions for a crash landing. We were five or six hundred feet above the ground, but without static lines to open their chutes as soon as they left the ship, jumping was risky. A crash landing in the forest was infinitely more dangerous; nevertheless they chose to stay.

When number-one blew, Jack pulled the nose a bit higher, to hold all the altitude he could. We'd both been craning our necks sideways to see past the nose of the ship, to see what lay directly ahead. It wasn't possible. We hadn't been able to see directly ahead since we'd shut down number-two.

Within a minute or so, number-three seized, and the prop chunked to an instant stop. The nose dropped sharply. As it fell below the horizon, the view to the front was like a picture flashed onto a screen. Immediately ahead, no more than a quarter of a mile, was the most beautiful runway in the world—Foggia Main! It wasn't as long as the runways at Manduria, but it was there; and we couldn't have been more perfectly lined up. Jack kept pushing the nose down to a steeper angle until it pointed directly at the near end.

"*Gear!*"

"*Flaps!*"

I hit the gear release button, slammed the lever down to lock, snatched the flap-control to the rear, and sat back to stare at the runway rushing up at us; and prayed for enough hydraulic pressure to set the gear locks. Other than wind noise, and creaking metal, the ship was unearthly quiet.

The gear had just clunked into lock when Jack hauled back on the control wheel, just in time. The wheels jarred onto the gravel surface, skipped, then rolled noisily as the ship's weight settled.

Unsure of our hydraulics, he braked early and hard to slow our speed. The aircraft decelerated rapidly, almost too rapidly. We came to a stop midway down the runway.

The last engine had quit, and we'd landed so quickly, I'd barely kept pace with what was happening. We'd probably been closer to death than at any time in the past. Only a miracle had put us at the exact point in space off the end of that unseen runway when number-three seized. Instead of gazing in awe at the quiet bomber sitting on the runway, we could just as well be lying in flaming wreckage in the surrounding woodland. I wondered if similar thoughts were coursing through my men's minds. They were drawn and quiet, just standing around, staring at each other, at our aircraft, or at British bombers parked nearby. I wondered if they really knew and had understood the extent of the danger we'd come through. There was no point in bringing up the subject now. We were on the ground. Nothing else mattered.

We'd gathered at the side of the runway and were wondering if the tower operator understood our plight, and had dispatched transportation for us and a tug for our aircraft. Several minutes had passed when we spotted a vehicle traveling at high speed toward us. Moments later, a large, red-faced British officer brought the "command car" to a skidding halt.

"What's the idea of stoppn' yr bloody engines?" he shouted. "Get thot bloody ahrcraft off my runway! Oi've got a flight of bloody Spits trying to land."

We stared at the fellow in amazement. The three feathered props were as obvious as his large nose bobbing in cadence with his angry words.

Our silence angered him even more. As his face grew to a purplish red, he screamed, "Get it off my bloody runway or I'll 'ave a dozer push it off!"

Jack had been standing silently, glaring at the officer. Instant anger clouded his face.

"You Limey bastard, I'll give you a thousand dollars for every engine you can start on "thot bloody ahrcraft!"

It was the next afternoon before we arrived at Manduria. Expecting a repeat of our previous problem with scavengers, I was primed and ready for battle. Fortunately everyone's belongings were intact. Just when I decided that I was being overly critical of the way the base was run, I learned that a clerk had not adhered to the seventy-two-hour rule for reporting lost crews. He'd sent a Missing in Action message.

When I finally calmed down enough to be rational I was assured

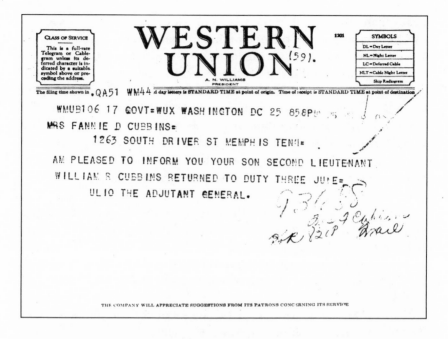

that a follow-up message canceling the MIA report would be sent. I was tempted to send another Red Cross telegram, but decided to let the matter ride. This turned out to be a good decision. Had I sent a telegram, my family would have become confused and disheartened beyond measure.

IX

The "wake-up" at four o'clock in the morning gave me a vacant feeling in my gut. A wake-up at that hour meant a long mission. Yesterday, July 2, the Group had bombed the Budapest marshaling yards. Since good weather was forecast to hold over the Balkans for at least several days, I figured we'd be heading in that direction.

The wake-up orderly informed me that Jack had the G.I.'s and couldn't make the mission. Lt. William Kapellar would be my copilot. I'd never met Kapellar but I knew him by sight; he was an original member of the Group, and was called Willie. I was pleased to have him for copilot and was delighted to be flying the left seat, but I felt sorry for Jack. With only six missions to go he was counting the days until his return to the States, and I knew that he'd be disappointed.[1]

During breakfast, I learned that Willie had already flown forty-eight missions. After today, he'd need only one more. Suddenly I remembered that Dave would finish his missions today. After we returned, we'd go to town and give him a farewell party he'd never forget.

Breakfast was the usual demoralizing affair: powdered eggs drenched in catsup; acid Spam that would sour a goat's stomach; and greasy toast lying limp in its own sweat. The coffee tasted and felt like raw metal. When we first arrived at Manduria I'd tried drinking the stuff black. That had been a bitter mistake. Two spoons of sugar and a generous lacing of condensed milk was my personal formula for rendering it impotent. But that created another problem. The aftertaste of condensed milk gave me an overwhelming desire to spend the rest of the morning scrubbing film from my teeth, but after briefing, our premission schedule didn't allow time for personal

---

1. When he missed this mission, it was determined that Jack, having completed forty-four missions, had done his part in the war, and he was returned to the United States.

problems other than a nervous pee at a nearby latrine, and another on the ramp before climbing into our bomber.

Walking through the black Italian morning, the aftertaste of two mugs of heavily creamed coffee thick in my mouth, it occurred to me that I should carry a toothbrush and a small tube of toothpaste in my flight suit. Why hadn't I thought of that before?

I missed Willie at breakfast but had no difficulty in locating him in the crowd milling about in the briefing room. Physically, Willie would stand out in any gathering of exuberant pilots. He was the quiet one, the one who looked as though he didn't belong.

Of medium height and slight stature, his very blond hair, blue eyes, and flawless pink skin made him appear to be no more than fifteen or sixteen years old. He reminded me of a young Messerschmitt pilot, a prisoner of war, that I'd met while attending B-17 school at Roswell, New Mexico.

Perhaps it was because we'd never met, but when we shook hands Willie was noticeably tense and quiet. We took seats so we could relax and chat for a few minutes before the briefing started. It didn't take long to determine the reason for his quiet tension. This would be his forty-ninth mission. One more after today and he could return home.

By the time the briefers arrived, the room was thick with smoke and the press of nervous bodies. The place was miserable, and about to become more so.

"Gentlemen," Tony barked as he jerked the curtain cord, "your target today is GIURGIU!"

I glanced at Willie. His face was impassive, devoid of reaction. I smiled thinly at my surprising thought, "I hope we're Tailend Charlie."

Giurgiu, a small Rumanian town on the Danube, was forty miles south of Bucharest. There were fighters in the area, but the worst problem would be the flak. The target, a tank-farm at the edge of the river, was defended by only three 88mm gun batteries: eighteen guns. The Wing's four groups had hit Giurgiu three weeks before. Over three hundred tons of bombs had been dropped with little success. Their notable lack of success had been caused by the remarkable accuracy of those eighteen guns. None of the shells in the initial barrages exploded too high or low, or off to one side, or too far ahead or behind the bombers. The first indication of flak had been instantaneous explosions, all of them in the lead box of the formation. None of our aircraft had gone down, but a number of them had been heavily damaged. Our three sister groups had each lost one aircraft. Many of the crews claimed that it was the most accurate flak they'd ever seen. Some wag had dubbed the batteries' gun director "Hermann the Fuse Cutter."

Join-up would be standard. We'd lead the Wing, pick up the 449th at 6,000 feet over Manduria, and the 376th and 98th over San Vito. Take a course over the Adriatic and cross the Yugoslav coast a few miles north of Albania. Our course would appear on German radar as though we were going to attack the marshaling yards at Belgrade. Well south of Belgrade we'd turn east in a feint toward Ploesti. Another deceptive course change would take us to our IP, where we'd turn southeast toward the target. The fighters at Bucharest would be airborne by this time and would probably attack us from the rear as we drew farther from that city. That was the problem with leading the Wing and the Fifteenth, as we so often did. The flak gunners would be fresh, and the fighters would have a clear shot at the lead formation. It is an honor to lead in battle, an honor that often falls to tough, capable groups like the Cottontails. Perhaps one day we'd look back on the experience and be proud of our record, and sacrifice—if we survived.

After the navigation and bombing briefings, the meteorologist informed us that the weather throughout the mission would be clear with visibility unlimited. Then came the hammer. Lt. Col. Bill Snaith was leading, and I was flying his left wing!

I'd never flown in the lead box. I'd wanted to, but had never been that lucky. But, flying that position to Giurgiu wasn't my idea of luck. I felt certain we'd been selected because of Ollie's skill with the bombsight. He'd recently rejected an offer to become squadron bombardier, I thought, because it meant leaving the crew. In declining the offer he may have given up a promotion to captain. I knew what the decision had cost him and was grateful.

My responsibilities in flying lead's left wing drove all thoughts of Hermann from my busy mind. The right wingman is deputy lead. In the event the leader or the deputy abort, or go down en route to the target, I become the deputy lead. If both are lost, I assume command of the mission and lead the Wing over the target. Willie knew this, and the thought of us leading the Wing probably gave him butterflies.

Mine were briskly fluttering in the residue of bitter brew churning in my stomach.

The position had only one redeeming feature. We'd be the third aircraft off of the runway, and wouldn't have to plow through blinding dust.

The personal equipment shack was in its usual bedlam. Everyone wanted his equipment at once so he could catch the first shuttle of waiting trucks. I thoroughly disliked the equipment routine. The PE sergeant had a shopworn ritual that was starting to get under my skin. Each time he slammed my chute onto the counter, he'd leeringly remark, "If'n hit don't work Lootinint, bring 'er back and I'll give yuh uh nother one!" He'd asked me on several occasions what I'd done with the chute I'd jumped at Vis. "I lost it on the way down," was my usual reply. He insisted that if I didn't return the parachute, I'd have to pay for it. I'd gone along with the joke for a while, but he'd played the record so often and abrasively that I was tired of hearing it. I'd plotted more than one ruse to get him into a B-24. Today would be a fine day for that unlikely eventuality.

"Hey Sarge, why don't you come with us? We got uh easy one today."

His silence was satisfying.

By the time we arrived at our aircraft, the gunners had completed their preflight checks and were huddled a short distance away, smoking and chatting quietly. They'd heard about the flak at Giurgiu. What they didn't know, and I was reluctant to tell them, was our position in the formation.

The ship was new. Freshly painted markings on the shiny metal indicated that it had not yet been on a mission. I walked to the rear and checked the serial number on the vertical stabilizer. The last three numbers were 159. It was an aircraft I'd recently ferried from the depot at Gioia. I ducked underneath the open bomb bay and stepped up on the catwalk. Lynch was standing there, holding onto a device that the crews had asked for but we'd not yet seen. It was a neatly coiled cable with a large snap hook spliced to the free end. The other end was fastened to the aircraft. There was another at the rear of the bomb bay, and yet another next to the camera hatch.

The cables could mean the difference between life and death for an unfortunate crew member. Heretofore, in order to get a wounded man out of the stricken aircraft, someone had to get a firm grasp on the injured man's parachute harness and the both of them would go out at the same time. Once outside, one would grasp the injured man's D-ring and push him away. It was a difficult and dangerous procedure. There was the obvious danger of being seriously injured exiting the aircraft through a small opening. Then there was the danger of the high velocity slipstream causing additional injuries to the two men. If the violence of the slipstream separated them before the injured man's D-ring could be pulled, he could fall miles to his death. If the assisting crew member didn't get out of the way as he pulled the other's D-ring, he could foul the man's chute, or himself be injured by the sudden deceleration of the other man. With this new static-line, however, all one had to do was uncoil the cable, snap the hook into the injured man's D-ring, and tumble him into the air. When the cable reached its full length, it would jerk the D-ring and open the parachute about twenty feet below the aircraft. It was a simple solution to a difficult problem.

Willie and I spent the next several minutes looking around, checking the engines, landing gear, and control surfaces. Finding everything in order, I walked a short distance away from the ship for a final cigarette and the traditional ramp-baptism ceremony.

My personal problems solved, it was time to climb on board. I placed my parachute in the pilot's seat and set the harness so I could put it on with ease. Next, I took off my overseas cap and dropped it and my flak vest onto the deck behind my seat. By the time I buckled in and was ready to start engines, Willie had completed the cockpit check and was standing by. Several minutes later, we eased out of our parking place to help lead the long line of bouncing behemoths to the runway.

As we flew northward, coastal mountains gave way to broad valleys overlaid with a patchwork of woods and farms. Although we were deep in enemy territory, we saw no flak or fighters. The pastoral panorama passing beneath us seemed detached from the terror of our mission, but its quilted surface was an unwitting ally. Natural features were markers that guided us unerringly toward our objective.

We were near the Rumanian border when my detachment with the scene below was shattered by deputy lead's voice in my headset. He'd developed engine trouble and was aborting the mission. Watching the ailing aircraft drop downward, I wondered if it would make it home. Speculation faded with the realization that I was now deputy lead and would have to think and act in that capacity until the formation returned to Manduria.

"Bombardier! Navigator! Did you catch deputy lead's transmission?"

"Roger," Ollie replied. "Understand."

"Roger. Pilot out."

Now that I was in a position of potential command, Green began feeding me navigation data. I was mentally rehashing mission details, trying to concentrate on the key points, things I'd have to do if I became the leader. Each passing mile brought increased tension. I was no longer thinking about flak or fighters; normal fears of being shot down had given way to new concerns. If lead was hit while we were between the IP and the target, there'd be no time to set up and engage the autopilot. I'd have to fly the ship manually, and I didn't want to miss the target.

Willie and I had been trading off at the controls. During the past ten minutes he'd been flying while I sporadically smoked a final cigarette and sucked on oxygen and a pretarget sourball. It was time for me to go to work.

I stubbed the cigarette and reached for a final swallow of water. The light weight of the canteen surprised me. I'd drunk more water than usual. The trip home was going to be dry. Refreshed by the icy drink, I fastened my mask, wiggled it to a comfortable seal on my sweating face, and buckled my steel-helmet strap.

"I've got it," I called to Willie on the intercom. We were nearing the IP and it was time to stick my wingtip into lead's waist window. By the time we cleared the IP, I was in position and holding steady. A few minutes later, Ollie called, "Bomb doors coming open! Systems ready!" and said he was synchronizing the bombsight on the aiming point. I'd have to hold the bomber very steady so as not to interfere with his tracking the target. The aircraft was tight against lead and handling smoothly with only minute power changes needed to hold position.

It seemed we'd been on the run an exceptionally long time when I saw lead's bombs dropping beneath his ship.

"Bombs away! Doors coming closed!"

Ollie's words had hardly died in the hiss of my earphones when the air about us erupted into an orange and black inferno that tossed us violently upward, and rained steel against the ship. The sound was instantaneous, then gone. But the sky continued to erupt like a field of volcanoes spewing unseen death, shredding the air about us.

The aircraft was mortally wounded. Number-three had lost power and was running erratically. I fought the controls to stabilize the swaying ship.

Number-three started to pick up power. As it was coming back, number-one started coughing. I was fighting erratic power, and pressure waves from exploding flak, trying desperately to stay with the formation. To maintain speed, I'd lowered the nose, then pulled to the left to clear the aircraft behind us. We'd entered the bomb run at 20,000 and had already lost almost 500 feet of altitude.

It was no use. We were going down.

The intercom was garbled with the shouts of gunners in the rear. I was so busy flying the ship and trying to get control of the engines, I couldn't divert my attention long enough to shout them into silence, to learn the cause of their panic. I thought that I'd heard the words "gas" and "fighters."

Then I smelled it, the deadly odor of 100-octane gas. At that moment, I felt the impact of several machine-gun bullets, or shrapnel, against the armor plate on the back of my seat. Instinctively, I ducked my head.

My eyes stung from the abrasive gas fumes. Leaning to the right, I looked aft in time to see Lynch drop from his turret and crawl toward the bomb bay. The entrance to the bomb bay was obscured by a heavy mist of gasoline. We were a flying bomb. I turned back to the cockpit and started flipping switches to their "off" positions.

As number-one picked up power, we lost power on the right side. Willie moved his hands rapidly on throttle and mixture controls in an attempt to stabilize the engines. I called him on the intercom and told him we had a broken fuel line. I again caught sight of Lynch heading for the bomb bay, carrying two rounds of .50-caliber ammunition in his right hand.

Having lost so much engine power, we'd dropped away from the formation. I searched the sky ahead, but the formation was nowhere in sight. We'd crossed the Danube and were over Bulgaria, still heading southeast on our bomb heading. That was no good, I wanted to be heading west. I banked the ship hard to the right to get back to the Rumanian side of the river. With engines alternately failing on either side, it was impossible to keep the ship in trim and relieve the strain on my legs. The wings were constantly dipping on one side as an engine died and the windmilling propellar braked us. Each time I decided to feather a prop, the engine would start running again.

I felt a hand on my shoulder and turned to look into the ashen face of Lynch. His mask dangling free so he could talk, he shouted, "We've got two fuel lines cut. I stuck .50-calibers in them but one blew loose. I'm going back to plug the other one."

Before I could tell him to get a walk-around bottle, he was gone.

The walk-around bottle was a portable oxygen tank. Though relatively small, it was large enough to be cumbersome and restrictive when working in close quarters. When full, the bottle contained a ten-minute supply of oxygen. We were at 17,000 feet and I figured that Lynch had been without oxygen for at least two minutes. During our brief conversation, I'd noticed that he appeared to be in critical need of oxygen. To make matters worse, he wasn't plugged into the intercom system and I couldn't monitor his physical condition or his progress in stopping the fuel leak.

Again on the Rumanian side of the Danube, I corrected our heading to fly parallel to the river. This brought us back to the withdrawal route the groups would be taking. We were not going back to Italy, but, if we followed the river, it would lead us to the Yugoslav border.

I wasn't certain of our position but I figured that it was at least one hundred miles to the border. Cross-checking our altitude and airspeed, I knew that we'd not be able to fly that far. Our only choice was to follow the river as far west as possible, bail out, and try to make it on foot to Yugoslavia. If we made contact with the Partisans, we would likely be all right. Our most immediate problem was stopping the flow of fuel before the ship exploded.

I was dividing my attention between the cockpit and the bomb bay. Lynch was not in sight. He either was in trouble or had bailed out. I discounted the latter; he wouldn't do that without telling me. I motioned Willie to take control of the ship and was unbuckling my seat belt when I heard someone shout. Ollie was standing at the rear edge of the flight deck. I pointed toward the bomb bay and motioned him to go there. He peered into the mist, turned and climbed onto the flight deck, snatched a round from one of Lynch's machine-gun belts, and disappeared into the bomb bay.

Turning my attention back to the cockpit, I saw that Willie was hard pressed to fly the aircraft and handle the engine controls by himself. He hadn't been able to keep the rudder trimmed and the strain was evidenced by his eyes and the perspiration showing around his mask.

Taking control once again, I waited impatiently for Ollie to return. After a minute or so, I knew that he, too, was in trouble. I didn't know where he was, or if both he and Lynch had succumbed to fuel fumes. I had to find out.

He hadn't jumped. I could see his chest pack lying on the flight deck.

"He could be dead," I reasoned. "What would I do with his body? I couldn't leave it in the aircraft. Something had to be done. Tracers from one fighter pass could send us the way of *Wells Cargo*, or worse."

The flak had ceased shortly after we were hit—probably because of our lower altitude. Within moments, the intercom had become strangely quiet. Shortly thereafter, I'd heard a single voice, either Matthews or Claverie, shout something that I hadn't understood. I'd heard transmissions from other aircraft calling fighter attacks, but nothing else. I'd tried several times to raise someone in the rear of the ship to come to Lynch's aid, but there'd been no answer. Because of fuel blowing about inside the bomb bay, I was reluctant to use the intercom for fear a spark would ignite the fuel. Having received no communication from the rear for several minutes, I decided that the rear gunners either had bailed out, were badly wounded, or were dead. Ollie's failure to return heightened my apprehension. I couldn't wait any longer. I had to find him.

As I motioned Willie to take control, the flak started again. I pulled my seat release, pushed my feet against the rudder pedals, and slid the seat back. The moment I took my feet off the pedals, an explosion thrust us upward. A large hole appeared in the side of the aircraft, just beyond my rudder pedals. Part of my instrument panel, and the side of my throttle quadrant, were in shambles. Willie's left hand and cheek were bleeding. He was staring straight ahead, ignoring his bleeding hand or fearing to look at it. The wounds appeared to be only scratches and had probably been caused by debris from the instrument panel.

I looked back to the hole in the side of the aircraft and drew an imaginary line to the instrument panel and throttle quadrant. Had I not moved my feet at that exact moment, I'd be looking at two bloody stumps. There was no time to think about could-have-beens, however. I slipped out of my harness, unhooked my mask from the regulator, and headed for the bomb bay.

My first full breath of 100-octane air was all I needed to understand Lynch's and King's ashen faces and the silence on the intercom. Initially I'd been angered when the rear gunners hadn't responded to my calls. Seeing the conditions in the bomb bay, and imagining what it must be like in the rear of the aircraft, I couldn't fault them for jumping. Their shouting, and the intercom call that I hadn't understood, had been their attempts to tell me that they were bailing out. Even in the cockpit I'd smelled the fuel fumes leaking into my imperfectly sealed mask and had endured burning and watery eyes, but I'd had no idea how bad the situation really was until I left my seat. Conditions in the bomb bay, and undoubtedly in the rear of the aircraft, were unbearable.

The bomb bay was filled with mist and flying droplets of fuel. Visibility was so poor I was on the catwalk before I saw Lynch. I didn't see Ollie, but Lynch was lying face-down, his body resting on the forward and rear doors. His face was jammed under the catwalk, with his feet pointed toward me. He was so close to the catwalk that I had to peer around the end of the bomb racks to get a good look at him. Were it not for the racks, it would have been a simple matter to hoist him up onto the catwalk and pull him out of the bomb bay; but the racks were a reality that would make getting to him very difficult.

I grabbed his left ankle and tried pulling him toward me. Reaching around the bomb racks was like reaching around the end of a fence. I couldn't get enough leverage to move him. Had I been able to stand on the bomb doors I could have moved him with ease. But if I stepped onto the doors our combined weight could break the doors loose, and neither of us was wearing a parachute. After making several attempts to move him, I concluded that it would take at least two people to do the job. Even then the task would be both difficult and dangerous. Someone smaller than I could work within the close confines of the bomb bay at much greater advantage. I was trying to concentrate, to think of who that might be, when I noticed that the light within the bomb bay was noticeably dimmer.

I headed for the cockpit. Dizziness and nausea swept over me. I was gasping for breath and finding it difficult to see. Feeling the edge of the flight deck beneath my palms, I lifted my right leg to place my foot on the ladder. I knew my leg was moving but couldn't figure how or why. I was trying to think about that when I noticed a brightness devolving into blue sky. Moments later, my vision cleared and I realized that I was sitting in my seat. I looked down at my oxygen regulator. My hose was connected, but my mask was dangling from my helmet. I snapped it in place, set my regulator to FULL RICH, and turned to see Willie staring at me. His face relaxed and he returned his attention to the aircraft. Though only semiconscious, I had climbed onto the flight deck, crawled to my seat, sat down, and connected my mask to the oxygen system. I had no recollection of anything after lifting my leg to step onto the ladder.

I thought that the engines had settled down, but they hadn't. Willie had reduced engine power to relieve the uneven thrust, and his action had cost us a lot of altitude. We were near 12,000 feet and dropping. He was following the river, but had no idea where we were.

I checked my watch. Almost ten minutes had passed since we'd been hit, and from the look of the terrain below us we were probably no more than twenty miles or so from Giurgiu. Our short flight into Bulgaria had cost us dearly. A glance at the altimeter and a quick calculation told me we'd still be many miles from Yugoslavia when we went down. I'd think about that later. For now, I had to find Ollie and get Lynch out of the bomb bay.

I couldn't imagine what had happened to him. Desperation was gnawing my mind when I sensed someone behind me. It was Joe Ukish. I'd forgotten he was still in the ship.

Unhooking my mask, I yelled, "Joe! Lynch is in the bomb bay. See if you can get him out."

Joe was much smaller than I, but looked to be strong for his size. Perhaps he could negotiate the crowded bomb bay and get Lynch out.

Moments later, he returned, breathing heavily, and looking very ill.

Catching my eye, he shouted. "I can't move him. I think he's dead."

"OK, Joe. Bail out!"

What happened next drove me to frenzied action.

His consciousness fading, Joe snapped his parachute onto his harness, bent down, and reached underneath the flight deck for what I knew would be the emergency handle that opens the bomb doors.

My mask tore loose from my helmet as I thrust myself out of

my seat and dove for him. Feeling his collar in my grasp, I heaved.

"Goddammit! Use the camera hatch!"

The look on his face told me that I'd shocked him into realizing that he'd almost dumped Lynch out of the aircraft. As he headed for the rear, I yelled, "Make sure everyone is out before you go!"

I headed for my seat and oxygen mask. There was less raw fuel filling the air, but I could feel the dizziness building.

I reconnected my mask, buckled into my parachute, and checked in with Willie. He was all right, but we'd lost a lot more altitude. We were below 8,000 feet and dropping. All four of the engines were running erratically.

Looking toward the bomb bay, I was trying to rationalize Ollie's disappearance when Green's head and shoulders popped up at the rear of the flight deck. He was wearing a walk-around bottle and appeared to be in good shape. He reached to unhook his mask as I unhooked mine and shouted. "Do you know where King is?"

"Yeah! He's here at my feet."

"Is he alive?"

Green disappeared momentarily, then reappeared.

"He's alive."

"Is there a walk-around bottle there?"

He disappeared again. Thirty seconds or so passed before he reappeared and shouted that Ollie was hooked to a bottle and breathing well.

"As soon as you can get him on his feet, you go ahead and bail out."

He nodded and disappeared again.

Apparently Ollie had plugged the fuel line, then passed out before he could get to the oxygen bottle beneath the flight deck. The reason I hadn't seen him during my trip to the bomb bay was that he was lying unconscious in the dark beneath the flight deck. Joe must have crawled over him but hadn't mentioned it to me. I puzzled about that for a moment, then realized that I hadn't asked if he'd seen Ollie.

I took control of the aircraft to give Willie a chance to check his harness in preparation for bailing out. The second flak barrage had stopped almost as soon as it had begun, and the fighters were attacking the retreating formations. We were in the clear with only one problem: getting out of the aircraft. Engines two and four were running normally again but one and three were erratic.

"Willie, as soon as we get Lynch out of the bomb bay we jump."

He listened to my words without showing any emotion. His bleeding had stopped, and I could see that he had nothing worse than a few scratches. Damage to my instrument panel was confined to the destruction of my flight instruments. They were no loss. I didn't need them to fly the aircraft on such a clear day.

We were over four hundred miles from home and running out of altitude. Our only consolation was that we'd be bailing out over level terrain. Our main problem would be that of avoiding capture after we landed. The land below was heavily farmed with few tracts of woodland to give us cover. Evading capture would be difficult, probably impossible.

A hand on my shoulder caused me to turn. Ollie, his face drained of color, was leaning forward, supporting himself on our pilots' seats.

"Ollie, can you and Willie get Frank out of the bomb bay? We have to get out as soon as possible."

"We'll get him."

I knew by the sound of his voice that he would.

"Use the static line at the front of the bomb bay," I shouted, as he and Willie dropped into the mist.

Turning my attention back to the aircraft, I increased engine power to slow our descent. The slight increase of power added measurably to the trim problem. At this low altitude it took considerable leg strength to hold the aircraft straight, both while retrimming and thereafter. The damaged fuel lines, I thought, were somehow interfering with the flow of fuel from the tanks to the engines. But the fuel lines in the bomb bay were used only to transfer fuel between tanks. The engines received their fuel directly from the tanks. If I could determine how the cut lines were causing the problem, perhaps we could fix it. But Lynch was the fuel system expert, and he was lying unconscious, or dead, in the bomb bay.

Regardless of how I rationalized his predicament, I knew that he was dead. I felt no sorrow. There was no time. That would have to come later. He'd died trying to save us and I couldn't bear the thought of leaving his body in the doomed aircraft.

A glance at the altimeter told me there was no time to fix anything. We had to get out of the ship.

Ollie and Willie had been struggling with Lynch for minutes that seemed much longer. A sudden squeal of the bomb doors and a rush of noise and air signaled they had succeeded. Looking aft I saw their backs as they bent over, obviously doing something to Lynch. Moments later a flash of white told me that he was out of the ship and his chute had opened.

Ollie and Willie wasted no time scrambling back to the flight deck. They'd seen our nearness to the ground through the open bomb bay.

"See that island in the river?" I shouted so that they could hear. A large island was visible about eight miles ahead.

"When you get on the ground, follow the river. I'll meet you opposite this end of the island at eight tonight."

It was a useless plan and I knew it. To travel through so much enemy territory in daylight and not be captured would be impossible. However, our need to get out of the aircraft was so urgent that there was no time to think the plan through.

They nodded agreement.

"*Go!*" I shouted, and motioned toward the bomb bay.

"Go, Willie!"

He'd never jumped before, and I'd been wondering if he'd balk, but he followed Ollie toward the bomb bay. I wasn't worried about Ollie. Although this was his first jump, my measure of his courage told me he'd go without hesitation. I watched Ollie take a position on the catwalk, then pause as Willie shouted something to him. He then stepped off of the catwalk and and disappeared from my view. Willie followed him immediately.[2]

I retrimmed the aircraft and pushed my seat back, got up, and stepped to the rear. A pile of flak jackets was jammed against the seat. I picked up the top jacket and threw it toward the open bomb bay. At that moment, the ship started into a right turn. I turned, grabbed the control wheel, and leveled the wings. After adjusting the throttles, I returned to the pile of jackets and started pitching them toward the bomb bay. I was reaching for the last jacket when the aircraft lurched to the left and pitched me against the opposite side of the ship. I struggled upright and I dove for the flight and engine controls.

The aircraft again stable and headed down the river, I grabbed the last jacket and flung it aside. My cap and four escape kits were lying

2. Forty years later, Ollie told me what had transpired during the few moments he and Willie paused on the catwalk. Thinking that Ollie had been with us when we jumped at Vis, Willie said, "You've done this before. You go first while I watch how you do it." Ollie, reluctant to undermine Willie's confidence by telling him the truth, tumbled forward.

where the jackets had been. In a flash I knew why I'd thrown the jackets away. I wasn't going to bail out without my hat. Hurriedly, I started stuffing escape kits inside the front of my flying jacket.

Again the ship fell off on one wing. While retrimming and balancing engine power, I was appalled to see how close I was to the ground. I could distinguish individual leaves on trees lining the river. "I couldn't be more than four or five hundred feet off the ground—if that," I thought. "I have to get out of here!"

I turned, grabbed the last escape kit and stuffed it into my jacket, grabbed my cap, and scrambled for the bomb bay. I'd already decided to pull my ripcord the moment I felt the slipstream. I stepped onto the catwalk, grasped the D-ring, stooped, closed my eyes, and tumbled forward.

I hadn't taken time to double up into a tight ball. A violent force whipped me uncontrollably and delayed my pull on the ripcord.

Within moments, I was aware of lessened wind and my tumble was slowing. I pulled the D-ring and opened my eyes to blue sky and neatly bunched suspension lines wrapped a full turn around my right leg. The lines were sliding upward toward the streaming canopy only a few feet beyond my boots. I'd tumbled through the lines of the deploying chute.

The sight of the lines sliding up my leg caused me to grin. I didn't know why, except that the lines sliding around my leg were funny. The white canopy flapping above me like a kite's tail was very pretty against the blue sky.

I was still grinning when the corded lines stopped sliding, the "kite-tail" flapped a couple of times, and the skirt of the canopy gulped air.

There were momentary impressions of an object brushing the left side of my face, a crushing impact, a confused spinning of earth and sky, then silence.

X

Silence became awareness, the quiet of a summer day. I was sitting on the ground with my legs spread apart. The familiar touch of earth beneath my hands helped focus growing perceptions. I was in a field that had been plowed and harrowed. My parachute had drifted to my right and collapsed near the edge of the field. A plastic packet, one of the escape kits I'd stuffed inside my jacket, lay near my left hand. That must have been what brushed my cheek a few moments ago, the thought flitted through my mind. Looking around me, I saw the other kits. All but one were within easy reach. I realized that I'd struck the ground with great force, but couldn't recall getting set to land. I searched my memory once more but could not recall the opening shock of my parachute.

A warning tingled in my mind. I placed my hands on my upper legs and rubbed them. They didn't appear to be broken, but something was wrong. The warning grew stronger. In an instant, I knew what it was. My hands were feeling my legs, but there was no responding feeling in my legs.

I've broken my back! I thought. I shouldn't be sitting up. No, my back wasn't broken. If it were, I wouldn't be able to sit; and I had no pain.

While I rubbed my thighs, my attention focused on the dark wetness on the right leg of my flight suit. The wet area was small, but it looked like blood. "Oh God, my leg is broken. The bone must be sticking out."

It didn't occur to me that, since my foot was still attached to my leg in a normal manner, my leg was probably OK. Fearing to look at the bloody white bone protruding through my skin, I let seconds pass before I screwed up my courage, leaned forward, and slowly worked the suit up my leg. As I pulled on the cloth I saw it dragging on a sharp point. I had to consciously force my hands to continue pulling the cloth.

Relief and disbelief came in equal measure. Instead of a bone protruding from the skin, a jagged piece of shrapnel, slightly smaller than the one that had pierced Lynch's helmet, was sticking out of my leg at a point about eight inches above my ankle. There'd been little bleeding. I learned why when I tried to remove the piece of shrapnel. It was wedged tightly between tough muscle and my shin bone. A second tug pulled it loose and freed the blood trapped inside my leg. The sight of the blood welling out frightened me, but within moments, the flow slowed to an ooze. I couldn't remember being wounded. In the heat of battle and the drama of following events, I hadn't felt the shrapnel strike me. It probably had happened when I had gone to look for Lynch. I had indeed come very near to losing part of one, or both, legs. The wound, though deep, was hardly more serious than a scratch. I removed the first aid packet from my parachute harness and tended the wound with sulfa powder and a compression bandage. I didn't need an infection: not here, hundreds of miles from home, and deep in enemy territory.

The thought came on a wave of deep loneliness. I'd been on the ground for several minutes without comprehending the import of having come down in enemy territory.

Where am I? I thought. Then I remembered. I was on the Rumanian side of the river.

The Danube was a hundred yards or so in front of me.

The distant rumble of engines caused me to look up. A formation of bombers was droning over, heading west, and growing smaller against the sky. It was either the 98th or the 376th—the last groups in our Wing. Whichever of the two it was, they'd taken a beating. Empty positions caused by missing aircraft had left the formation ragged.[1]

"They'll be home in a few hours," I thought. Regardless of the terror I'd endured in the past twenty minutes or so, I'd rather have been with them and taken my chances in combat than be here in the unknown. The thought became a burden, a crushing depression. I sat quietly, trying not to think about home, Manduria, waiting for the lonesomeness to wear itself thin, to let my faculties recover and regain control. Hopelessness overwhelmed me, leaving a cold vacancy in my mind and body.

---

1. Later I learned that it was the 376th. They'd borne the brunt of the fighter attacks and had lost five aircraft.

Instinct, then emerging thought, told me to start moving; do something, anything, to get my mind organized. Get out of the harness and hide the parachute!

It was an awkward task, trying to gather the canopy, wrap it with suspension lines and harness, and move it to the growth of pokeberry bushes at the edge of the field. After bundling the chute as best I could I pushed it ahead of me, crawling with my elbows toward the bushes. The blue-black berries were soft and wet. The slight pressure of pushing the bundle beneath the lower branches stained the white nylon with blotches of deep crimson. It was a silly thought, but I wondered if the stains would wash out.

The bundle snagged on something beneath the bush. I'd cleared the obstruction, but hadn't pushed the chute out of sight when I heard a shout from my rear. A man was walking rapidly toward me, shouting and waving his arm.

As he closed the distance between us what I'd thought to be a farm implement on his shoulder looked more and more like a shotgun. I reached for the .45 automatic in the shoulder holster.

"Damn!"

I looked down at the place where my automatic should be and discovered that I wasn't even wearing the holster. I'd never flown a mission without the weapon securely in place, where the hell was it? Then I remembered. When I'd climbed into the ship that morning, I was carrying the holstered weapon in my hand. I'd laid it on the floor next to the emergency bomb door valve while I passed the rest of my gear up to Lynch. Unthinking, I'd climbed to the flight deck and left my weapon lying on the floor of the ship.

I abandoned the chute and crawled frantically for the river. It was a futile effort. I'd moved no more than a few yards when my excited captor caught up with me. I rolled over and looked up into the smiling face of a man who seemed to regard me with the honest joy of someone who had found a treasured friend. He obviously had no fear of me nor intended any harm. He laid his shotgun on the ground and helped me sit up. His smile and demeanor were so infectious, I forgot that he was the enemy.

Anxiety gave way to relief. I'd not only had the good fortune to be captured without running the risk of being shot by a trigger-happy soldier, or axed by an excited mob of hate-crazed peasants, I'd been taken by a "friend" in a place where all were expected to be enemy.

I was puzzled. Why was the man so friendly, so outright joyful? I concluded that he'd seen me exit the ship at low altitude, had seen my chute streaming, and had thought that I'd been killed. Finding me alive had triggered within him the same sort of relief that his friendliness created within me. Whatever his reason, I was grateful for his concern.

Assured by his manner, I pointed to my legs and shook my head. Squatting at my side, the smile left his face as he clucked concern and reached to draw back my right suit-leg. I stopped his movement and waved my hand sideways to let him know my wound was of no consequence. I then rubbed both legs and made a half-hearted attempt to get to my feet. I noticed that my knees bent slightly and that feeling was returning to both legs, and with it, pain.

My effort to rise communicated my inability to stand. Clucking once again, he grasped me behind the knees and lifted them. With my legs jackknifed, he alternately rubbed them, and carefully bent and straightened each leg several times. I could feel life returning to my legs. Each stage of increased feeling brought an increase in pain. I motioned for him to stop, and tried getting to my feet. Placing an arm around my back, he straightened, lifting me with ease.

Although not tall, perhaps five-foot nine, his powerful shoulders and stocky frame spoke of strength from a life of physical labor. His leathered skin was that of a man who'd spent most of his fortyish years outdoors: a farmer. Bare feet protruding from rough trousers, the serviceable texture of his shirt, the look of open concern on his broad face mirrored a fine character, a simple and honest man. I was quite taken with him.

My first supported steps were accompanied by his smile and grunts of approval. After several minutes of walking in circles, with him lending a supporting arm, my legs were about as normal as they were likely to be for some time. All the while we were walking he was grinning and jabbering incessantly, and energetically waving his free arm. His arm motions, starting high and arcing downward, then pointing to my legs, testified to my belief that he'd witnessed my jump.

Suddenly he stopped and pointed to a group of a dozen or more peasants approaching us from across the field. In front of several men, many women, and a few children, were two soldiers carrying long rifles with very long bayonets attached. The crowd was talking noisily, with much arm waving. The soldiers appeared to be nothing more than peasants in uniforms, but their expressions were grim, their bayonets threatening.

My captor released my arm, placed his palms against my chest, and pushed gently. The quizzical look on his face asked if I could stand. I nodded "Yes." He retrieved his shotgun and took a staunch position between me and the approaching crowd. Holding the gun across his body with both hands, feet spread apart, his message was clear.

The argument with the soldiers started as they drew near. The soldiers, officious and bullying, appeared to demand that he turn me over to them. My captor was determined that I was his. The argument became critical about the time the crowd arrived. My captor, tired of arguing, shouted and pointed his shotgun menacingly. Had the situation not been serious, I would have laughed at the ensuing melee.

The soldiers and those in the front tried to retreat so rapidly that those behind bumped into and fell all over each other in noisy fright. After a few moments of shouting and arm waving, my captor quieted them. He then spoke at length in a normal voice. I could tell by the expressions on the soldiers' faces that they disagreed with what he was saying. It was like watching a foreign movie without the benefit of subtitles. However, words weren't necessary. Their tone of voice, expression, and pointing were all I needed to know what was going on.

When my captor finished speaking, one of the soldiers spoke strongly in defiance to what had been said. My captor spoke back in a voice of finality and waved the soldiers to the side. They complied by taking positions to the right, some thirty feet or so away. My benefactor then spoke and motioned the crowd to come closer. This they did, but with great timidity. Except for a man accompanied by a young girl, they seemed more interested in bunching together for mutual protection than in approaching me for a close-up inspection. Their antics and curious, half-frightened countenances, reminded me of a Punch and Judy show.

The man who'd been with the young girl walked past me, pulled my parachute from beneath the bush, and placed it on the ground in front of me. Except for hurried whispers, the peasants were attentive. Most of them seemed interested in the conversation taking place between the man and my captor.

It was an earnest conversation, with much pointing toward me, the parachute, and the girl. Several times my captor smiled at me and nodded approvingly. The man turned to the girl and motioned for her to approach us. She'd moved back into the crowd and had listened dejectedly. With head bowed, she walked toward us. As she came to a halt, the man, apparently her father, reached out and lifted her chin. I looked into the largest, darkest, most frightened eyes I'd ever seen. Smudges of dirt on her face were emphasized by very long and unkempt black hair. The yellow peasant blouse and red skirt would have been quite fetching had they been less soiled and presented under other circumstances. I could hardly tell her bare feet from the earth. I gauged her age at fourteen or fifteen.

I understood full well what was going on. My captor, enjoying the prospects, was encouraging me to accept the offer. In my circumstances, nothing could have been further from my mind. I looked directly at him and shook my head in a solemn "No." The man, looking as dejected as I felt, motioned the girl away, and rejoined the crowd. My captor picked up the chute and motioned me to move off in the direction from which he and the crowd had come. The soldiers fell in behind us, a few paces to our rear. The flock of peasants, jabbering like curious geese, followed at a respectful distance.

We'd moved only a short distance when I felt sharp pain in my right buttock. Shouting as I spun around to face my tormentor, I realized that one of the soldiers had pricked me with his bayonet. Seeing my pained reaction, my captor wheeled and brought his shotgun to bear upon the nearest soldier. So sudden was his movement, he caught the offending guard between the eyes with the muzzle of the shotgun. The droplet of blood forming above his nose told me that my captor had made an unarguable point. His screamed "Stei!" left no room for negotiation. He wanted the guards to back off and stay away from us. Turning to me he spoke "Hei!" and motioned me on. I followed at his side while exploring my backside to determine if I'd been injured.

The walk to the village, a half-mile or so distant, was accomplished without further interference. Nevertheless I repeatedly peeked over my shoulder to check the position of the guards.

The village was little more than a small collection of thatch-roofed wooden and masonry houses crowding a dusty road: a simple farming community, rude but charming in its tree-shaded existence. The appearance and mannerisms of the peasants matched the character of the village with movie-lot perfection. Everyone living there had gathered to ogle the American who'd interrupted their quiet, changeless lives.

The local jail was the only official-looking building in the village. Constructed of whitewashed masonry—probably baked mud—it too had a thatched roof. Its official look owed to the bars of a small window on the street-wall. We entered the building through the only door visible.

The spacious room seemed to occupy about one-half of the building. A single door led into the room with the barred window. Several chairs and rough benches were positioned along three walls. Seated behind an ancient desk at the far end of the room, a stocky sergeant was busily talking on the telephone. When we entered the room, he signaled to the party on the telephone that we'd arrived. There followed a period of protracted silence punctuated only by his series of "Da's," and affirmative head-bobbing. An officious man of forty-odd years, he was obviously receiving instructions from a superior. Throughout the conversation he sat at attention. Aside from the look of concentration on his dark face, the scene was quite comical.

Having said his final "Da's"—which I took to mean yes—he replaced the telephone receiver and sprang to his feet. His quick movement brought the guards to attention. Although I couldn't understand what was being said, I knew that I was to be taken into the adjoining room.

The room was bare except for a small table and two chairs in the center, and two boxlike beds against the rear wall. In addition to the window on the street side, a second barred window was centered on the side wall. Both were about two feet square, and glassless. One guard remained outside the connecting door while the other accompanied me into the room and motioned me to sit at the table or lie on the bed. I chose the bed but wondered about the advisability of lying on the blanket. It appeared to be made of woven wood-fiber.

The bed was an equally crude affair: a simple box frame of unpainted wood. The mattress was made of burlap stuffed with straw. There was no pillow. Not wanting to lie on the burlap, I covered it with the blanket and rolled my jacket into a pillow. I hadn't noticed my weariness until I stretched out on top of the blanket.

The trek to the village had been painful. My right knee was in bad shape, and the walk had caused my wound to throb with dull pain.

The tension of combat, my severe impact with the ground, and our bout with the guards had sapped my strength. As I lay on the bed listening to the murmur of voices in the adjoining room, a leaden shroud of loneliness and depression enveloped me once more. As I agonized over the fate of my crew, a kaleidoscope of battle images passed through my mind. I was confident that everyone had gotten out, but with enemy fighters over the target, I worried as to how they'd fared. The only casualty I knew of was Lynch. I hoped that the Rumanians would give him a decent burial. If the rear gunners had been attacked while in their chutes, there'd be more than one funeral. I considered the probabilities and decided that if there had been fighters near us, they'd have attacked our aircraft or attacked one of the groups following us. I didn't think it likely that they'd attack helpless men hanging in their parachutes when there were so many bombers in the area.

I thought about my mother, the terror and anguish she must have endured because of the telegrams she'd already received. The next one would worry her beyond measure. No one could possibly have seen me bail out, and I wondered if I'd be reported missing, or killed. In light of the problems we'd already had with the reporting system, "killed" was a distinct possibility. The thought depressed me even more.

I awakened to the realization that I'd been sleeping soundly. The room was barren and dim in the fading light. Within moments, memory and the darkened room brought back the loneliness that I'd escaped in sleep. I wondered where Ollie, Green, and Willie were. Having bailed out in rapid succession, they had undoubtedly been captured and were probably being held as a group, elsewhere.

Rising from the bed, I was dismayed by the stiffness that had seized me. The pressure of my feet on the wooden floor sent sharp pains tearing through my knees and legs. I knew from my experience with a volleyball injury that I'd suffered major damage to the lateral ligaments of both knees. Standing made me realize that my knees were not the only part of me that had been damaged. My insides, back, legs, every part of me was sore and stiff.

My first guard had been replaced by another soldier. There was just enough light for me to make out his blunt face and husky young body. He appeared to be about my age. My first stiffened step away from the bed brought a look of concern and hurried steps to assist me to one of the chairs. After lowering myself onto the chair I began to rub my legs. After several minutes of brisk and painful massage the stiffness eased, but remained in abeyance as if preparing for a new onslaught.

The guard, talking and motioning with his eyes and hands, gave the impression that he'd heard the story of my bailout and capture. At one point in his recitation, he demonstrated his knowledge by leaning down and lifting my right suit leg. When he looked at me and pointed to the bandage, I waved his concern aside.

The stained suit leg was attracting too much attention. If I had a chance to escape, it would be best to be rid of it. I pointed to the stain, made a pouring motion with my hand, then bent over and pretended I was washing it.

"Da," he murmured and left the room.

Following his departure with my eyes, I spotted my chute on the floor next to the door. It had been rebundled. The large folding machete I carried taped to the harness had been removed. Someone, probably the sergeant, had collected an interesting souvenir.

Following a brief exchange in the next room, my guard returned and said, "Da."

"Da," apparently, did mean "yes." I'd learned my first Rumanian word.

Minutes later another guard came into the room carrying a pitcher of water and a washbasin containing a bar of rough soap, a drinking glass, and a wine bottle artfully decorated with the drippings of many candles. After placing the items on the table, he inspected me while engaging the room guard in conversation. Satisfied with whatever it was he'd learned, he departed.

I removed my flying suit and spent several minutes scrubbing the leg. The soap produced little lather but it removed all but the slightest stain. I wrung out most of the water and dressed. Over twelve hours had passed since breakfast, but I wasn't hungry. Nothing is more effective than combat for killing one's appetite. But I was thirsty, damned thirsty. After I finished dressing, I filled the glass from the pitcher and drank.

Night had descended into the room, adding yet another layer of darkness to my cloak of gloom. The lighted candle helped contain my sense of doom, but it was the guard, his friendliness, his slow and deliberate attempts to talk to me that finally lifted my loneliness and guided my thoughts to the problem at hand—how to escape.

We were seated at the table with the candle between us. Intelligent, and possessing a nimble imagination, he'd been speaking slowly, one carefully enunciated word at a time, watching my reactions to see if I was getting his overall meaning. It was difficult, but I understood many of his gestures, and believed that I was following his thought.

He was trying to tell me that he knew about America and was determined to go there one day. It seemed that every fourth or fifth word was "America" emphasized by a broad smile. He was against the war and the Nazis. There was no question about his intense dislike for Germans. During our conversation, he noticed my look of understanding when he used the words Hitler and Deutschland, and tried using a few German words in the conversation. He didn't phrase any of his sentences in German. Rather, as a means of insuring meaning on a particular point, he'd resort to a German noun or verb. I couldn't speak German, but I knew enough words to catch the gist of his simple conversation.

His curiosity and respect for me were apparent from the outset. After lighting the candle, he'd leaned across the table and pointed a finger at the silver wings pinned to my flight suit.

"Peelot?"

"Da," I replied in my best Rumanian.

A rapturous smile spread over his face as he closed his eyes and tilted his face heavenward. His expression told me that he dreamed, as I once had, of flying. I uttered another "Da," as though I'd read his thoughts and confirmed his visions of flight.

We were interrupted by a commotion in the other room. At the sound of voices he smiled and made an eating motion as he stood to open the door.

My captor, bathed and shaved, still barefooted and wearing the same trousers, but now washed, had changed to a dingy white shirt buttoned at the collar and an old suit coat. Despite his barefoot, rumpled appearance, he looked quite elegant in his "Sunday best." Sensing that he honored me with his attire, I bowed stiffly and returned his smile.

He was gingerly carrying a large plate covered by a high metal cover. Beaming, he sat the plate in the center of the table and motioned for the guard at the doorway to bring the wine bottle and bowl that he was carrying.

The feast properly arrayed in flickering candlelight, my host produced a large spoon from his pocket and motioned for me to sit. No one can enjoy a candlelight dinner with two guards and even a friendly farmer looking on. I not only wasn't hungry, the villainous-looking stuff floating in the bowl looked as though it had already been eaten by someone with whom it hadn't agreed. Whatever it was, I prayed that it would taste better than it looked. My host's insistent urging finally won the battle with my squeamish stomach. I picked up the spoon and dipped it into the bowl. It took courage to put the spoon in my mouth.

Cold, greasy fish soup! It tasted as bad as it looked.

I glanced up to see my host shaking his head.

He raised the cover from the dish and revealed a large mound of steaming, cornmeal mush. I dug out a bite with the spoon and promptly blistered my mouth. The new guard's laughter, and my host's "Nui," helped me double my Rumanian vocabulary, but at a painful price.

He took the spoon, scooped out a chunk of mush and dipped it into the soup and handed me the spoon. The mush had heated the soup in the spoon and caused a remarkable change in its flavor and texture. Fish had never been one of my favored foods, but the concoction of hot mush and soup was quite tasty. I smiled my appreciation and ate. After swallowing several spoonsful, I decided to try the wine. I removed the twisted-paper stopper, put the mouth of it to my lips, and turned the bottle up.

Expecting wine, but getting a slimy, sour substance, the shock was almost more than I could handle. I nearly vomited. It took a moment for my taste buds to reorganize and send the proper signal to my brain. Clabber!

Having been reared on that gold-flecked product of the wooden churn, I consider myself a connoisseur of buttermilk. But clabber? I'd seen my cousin feed clabber to his hogs and and they'd slurped it with relish. But the idea of people drinking the stuff was revolting.

I tried churning it by placing my thumb over the mouth of the bottle and vigorously shaking it. I poured a bit of it into the waterglass to observe the effect of my churning. Slimy solids moved lazily through yellow whey and settled to the bottom. I smiled a polite "nui" to uproarious laughter.

I ate my fill of the soup and mush and drank another glass of water from the well-rinsed glass. My host and the guard were pleased, as was I, with my performance. I hadn't been offered lunch, and had taken my captors' lack of concern as an indication that they weren't going to make any special effort to provide for my comfort or well-being. There was no way of knowing when I'd be fed again. I was certain that I'd be leaving this place within a matter of hours, and if I were going to escape and remain free, having a full stomach might be a valuable asset during the first hours of freedom. This village was probably as close as I'd ever get to the Yugoslav border, and being guarded by a young man who appeared to be sympathetic gave me hope.

Shortly after I finished eating, the sound of voices passing on the street caused my host and the new guard to go into the other room. After many minutes of loud, almost violent arguing between the gravel-voiced sergeant and another man, the door opened. Backlit by glaring light from the other room, I couldn't distinguish their faces, but I knew it was the gypsy girl and her father.

Perhaps it was the magical quality of candlelight, but the girl was uncommonly beautiful, and at least a year older than I'd thought. She wasn't beautiful in the way of a mature woman. The glow of youth had not yet given way to experience and character that would in time sculpt her adult features. Standing next to the table with the candle-light adding form to her face, I couldn't recall having seen a face of such perfection. She and her clothing had been scrubbed from hair to foot. Were it not for the fear overshadowing her innocence I might have enjoyed the moment. What struck me most was my failure to have seen through the dirt and appreciate her rare beauty there in the field.

My host was not only pleased with her appearance, he seemed confident that I would now make the trade. My young guard, standing apart from us, listened attentively to the conversation and frowned his displeasure. I sensed that he knew the girl. Just as surely, he'd admired her for her manner and beauty. Many, I thought, would want to possess such a lovely creature. The longer I looked at those frightened eyes, the more ridiculous and incomprehensible the situation became. I didn't care what happened to my parachute, but I resented the man's offer of his daughter for a bundle of stained nylon. To hell with him!

The negotiations had hardly begun when I ended them. Glaring at the father, I took the bundled parachute from my host and thrust it at the girl. Her frightened reaction angered me even more. Impaling the father with another glare, I forced the chute into her arms and gave her a gentle push. Stealing a look of acquiescence from her father, she turned and walked toward the open door. The added weight of the parachute caused her bare feet to resound solidly on the plank floor. Seeing the small, frightened figure hurrying toward the door increased my anger.

I hadn't noticed the sergeant standing at the door, witnessing the transaction. I couldn't tell which of us he was glaring at, me or the father. The latter bowed his humble thanks to me, then to the sergeant. The bastard was almost bubbling because of my unexpected generosity. I thought that I'd have to get the guard to throw the man out of the room in order to get rid of him, but the sergeant solved the problem with harsh words that sent the man scurrying. Before the door closed behind him, the sergeant was giving the man a monumental tongue-lashing. From the sound of fury in the sergeant's voice, I wondered if he'd let the girl keep the parachute.

Finally alone, my young guard entered into a lengthy conversation with my host. I could tell from the frequent glances and nodding in my direction that he was telling him things that he'd learned about me. I am equally certain that my host was relating the tale of my capture and the problems we'd had with the two soldiers. Although I didn't understand a word, their gestures and facial expressions held clues as to what they were saying. They laughed without restraint at the "shotgun between the eyes" incident. My guard apparently knew and disliked the two soldiers, and was happy that my host had won the argument.

The quietness of the outer room told me that the father and his daughter had gone. My host, having shaken hands with me four or five times in a protracted good-bye, was gathering the remains of my dinner, when a shout and the sound of feet in the outer office hurried him along. The door slammed open to disclose the other guard frantically waving my host to get out, and for me to come into the other room. The guard retrieved his rifle from against the wall and escorted me to the door. My skin crawled with apprehension, a sense of brewing trouble.

XI

A single bulb suspended from the ceiling cast harsh shadows on the tense face of the sergeant standing at a stiff attention. He was listening attentively to the quiet speech of a tall, thin officer. The paucity of insignia on the officer's epaulets indicated to me that he was probably a lieutenant. Perhaps thirty, he was neatly dressed in tunic and trousers. A small holster, the type used with an automatic, was attached to his Sam Browne belt. Thin-faced, with a hawkish nose, his skin was unusually white: a stark contrast to the sergeant and the other Rumanians I'd seen. His sensitive face didn't belong with the uniform, and there was no hint of authority in his speech or manner. The woman standing next to him was quite the opposite.

She too was tall, but her pasty complexion and severe features had the look of arrogance. At the moment she was listening to the sergeant's reply to the lieutenant and looked as if she'd pounce on him as soon as he finished.

In midsentence she interrupted him with a harsh order, which he shouted to someone behind me. I was immediately seized and searched. Until then I hadn't noticed the two guards posted at the door.

While my belongings were being removed and placed on the desk, she sent my room guard scurrying for my flight jacket. It was promptly emptied of the extra escape kits. The woman recognized them and gave me a quizzical look, as if to ask why I had so many kits. Watching her examine my belongings, I wagered mentally that the forty-eight dollars in each of the kits would find their way into her purse. Consequently, I was surprised when she motioned the guard to return my Parker 51 fountain pen and one of the kits, but not before she removed the blood chit[1] and escape map. My cigarettes and lighter remained unoffered on the desk.

---

1. A blood chit is a piece of cloth the size of a large handkerchief with the American flag and a message written in several languages printed on it. In effect the chit is a promissory note against our treasury. The message states that the bearer is an American and that the U.S. Government will reward anyone who aids the bearer to escape.

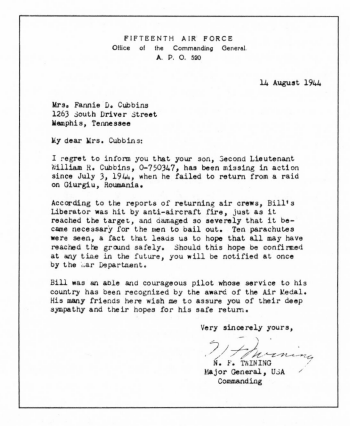

FIFTEENTH AIR FORCE
Office   of   the   Commanding   General.
A. P. O. 520

14 August 1944

Mrs. Fannie D. Cubbins
1263 South Driver Street
Memphis, Tennessee

My dear Mrs. Cubbins:

I regret to inform you that your son, Second Lieutenant
William R. Cubbins, O-750347, has been missing in action
since July 3, 1944, when he failed to return from a raid
on Giurgiu, Roumania.

According to the reports of returning air crews, Bill's
Liberator was hit by anti-aircraft fire, just as it
reached the target, and damaged so severely that it became necessary for the men to bail out. Ten parachutes
were seen, a fact that leads us to hope that all may have
reached the ground safely. Should this hope be confirmed
at any time in the future, you will be notified at once
by the War Department.

Bill was an able and courageous pilot whose service to his
country has been recognized by the award of the Air Medal.
His many friends here wish me to assure you of their deep
sympathy and their hopes for his safe return.

Very sincerely yours,

N. F. TWINING
Major General, USA
Commanding

Following the search, the woman berated the sergeant at length. While yelling at the frightened man, she repeatedly picked up items from the desk and slammed them back down to emphasize a point. The more she talked the more I wished to be elsewhere. Weasel-faced, and with eyes that emphasized an abrasive personality, she had an arrogance that bristled like barbed wire. Family resemblance between the two was so strong, she could have been the lieutenant's sister, but there was something about the rapport between them that made me think she was his wife.

During her lengthy tirade she darted hostile glances directly into my eyes. She had guts. I knew when she turned to face me that I had a problem, but I wasn't prepared for what happened.

We were standing a little more than arm's length apart. One moment she was in midsentence with the sergeant. The next moment she said, "What is your name?"

She'd spoken in perfectly enunciated English: British. Her words startled me so, that I didn't answer.

"Answer my question!" she screamed, and stopped short of stamping her foot. However, the movement brought her closer to me.

Angered by her outburst I looked at the lieutenant and wondered why he allowed her to carry on in such an abrasive manner. As far as I was concerned, she, a civilian, had no right to interrogate me.

"Look at me! My husband is not speaking to you. Answer my question! What is your name?"

Her eyes were filled with hate and fury.

"Second Lieutenant William R. Cubbins, AO 750347."

"Who is the pilot of your aircraft?"

I considered the question, then replied, "I am."

It was a mistake. Her rage mounted and spilled over into her next words.

"Do you take me for a fool?" she screamed. "The aircraft fell ten kilometers from here. It cannot fly itself!"

As she spoke her pasty face became livid.

"I am the pilot!" I responded sarcastically.

"You lie," she screamed. "You take me for a fool?"

I was caught off guard by her raving, and before I could move she delivered a vicious slap to my face.

I tried to stop my own blow but succeeded only in not hitting her with my full palm. I caught her with my fingers, but it was sufficient to stun her and move her backward.

As I recoiled and cocked my body for battle, the lieutenant stepped forward and grabbed her with both arms. Behind me, feet shuffled and a bolt clicked a round of ammunition into a rifle chamber. I froze.

Watching the lieutenant trying to calm his wife, I fought adrenalin and fury to keep from trembling. The trembling wasn't all from chemistry and fury. I expected to feel piercing pain from a bayonet, a rifle butt, or a bullet from behind. The next few moments were endless. I couldn't decide what to do next. I was so angry that I never thought about dying. I was ready to fight.

Had the lieutenant not taken so long to console his wife, the situation could have gone beyond repair. As it was, time replaced my rage with reason and fear. I straightened to a less aggressive stance, and peered over my shoulder at the source of the chambered round. The guard was standing with his rifle pointed at the floor, wondering what to do.

Out of the corner of my eye I could see my young guard, frightened and confused, standing at the door to the other room. His rifle, butt down, was resting on the floor.

As the shock of my slap wore off, the woman's speech got louder. I figured that she was demanding that I be punished on the spot. The lieutenant was saying "Nui," but it didn't sound convincing. Nevertheless, he was making progress.

I quietly thanked God for henpecked, understanding husbands, and simple-minded guards. The lieutenant's self-control was remarkable. Although he'd raised his voice a time or two, one would never guess that he'd just witnessed his wife being slapped. He'd never even glanced my way. The sergeant was standing against the wall, huffing and puffing with excitement. He didn't know what, if anything, to do. As far as I was concerned, nothing needed to be done. I realized the enormity of my action and regarded myself as a thoroughly subdued noncombatant.

Perhaps four or five minutes passed before all of us returned to a state of reasonable calm. The woman had not only calmed, she was acting more rationally than when I entered the room. Again I looked behind me for the guard with the loaded rifle. He was standing quietly with the butt of his rifle resting on the floor. I figured he didn't have the courage to shoot me without being told to, and the lieutenant wasn't the type to give that kind of order. I relaxed as best I could and waited.

The woman moved to the desk and picked up a large piece of torn map, apparently one of Green's, and addressed me in a firm but subdued tone.

"What was your target?"

"William R. Cubbins; Second Lieutenant; AO 750347."

"Why do you give me such a stupid answer?"

I thought that she was going to explode again, and I didn't want that to happen. I'd try reasoning with her. She'd already learned that I wasn't going to be abused.

"Look, lady, I'm a prisoner of war. All I have to tell you is my name, rank, and serial number."

"Why do you give me such a stupid answer? Why can't you answer a simple question?"

"I don't have to talk to you. You slapped me when I told you I'm the pilot. You tell your husband that I am a prisoner of war and that I'm not going to tell you anything except my name, rank, and serial number."

The hate of her stare made me wonder if I'd gone too far. I was now more than a little frightened at how rapidly the face-slapping had occurred and wondered if she would again lose her temper. Although the lieutenant hadn't reacted the first time, I couldn't rely on him to stay calm. I resolved that in future interrogations I'd remain silent. If pressed I'd try to be convincingly ignorant.

"Lady, will you please tell your husband what I just told you? I am the pilot. There was no one left in the aircraft. I'm not going to answer any more questions."

The tension in my voice was obvious. My words came out haltingly, like the speech of someone with stagefright.

She glared at me for a moment, then translated my speech. The left side of her face was red where my fingers had struck. Her countenance, drawn tight, emphasized her ferret-look and exposed her own tension. I doubted that she looked any more tense than I. When I slapped her I'd felt the blood drain from my face. Unless it had crept back without my noticing, I was probably still white-faced and looked as if I were ready to do battle.

The lieutenant watched me closely. It was as though he'd just this moment discovered my presence in the room. Until now he'd made a special effort to not look directly at me for longer than a moment's time. Now he was watching me constantly, but avoiding direct eye contact. The length of the translation indicated to me that she was embellishing what I'd said, or she was asking him about something that I couldn't decipher. When she finished, he looked at her thought-fully and spoke a quiet "Nui." After a few more words to her, he turned to my room guard and spoke briefly. Then, for the first time, we locked eyes. There was no way to tell his thoughts. His expression was without meaning. For all I knew, he could have been envying me for having slapped his shrew of a wife. There was certainly no hostility in his face as he nodded me toward the door of the other room. Halfway smiling my thanks, I turned to walk toward the door. Her quiet words stopped me.

"Tomorrow, you will be taken to Bucharesti and put in prison with the other American gangsters."

The words were spoken without expression, but her face mirrored hate. The click of the door behind me brought much-needed relief.

From the moment I'd watched the bomber groups heading for home, I'd been plagued off and on with a deep loneliness. For the first time in my life I'd felt the need for being in the company of peers. Like many people, I value occasional periods of isolation. In the daily routine of life, we are in contact with the lives of others —friends, family, or associates—in countless, familiar ways. During the past twelve hours, I had been forcibly isolated from all that was familiar to me. Everything about the day, the people, their dress, their language, their houses, their relationships with each other, every aspect of my circumstances was alien. The relative friendliness of my captor and the young guard had helped to some extent; nevertheless, my mood was such that I might as well have spent the day at the North Pole. Admitting to this hitherto unknown aspect of myself, my need to be with peers disturbed me and eroded my confidence. I wanted out of this place, out of this country. Despite the terrors of the day's events I preferred the rigors of combat to the circumstances and feelings I'd endured since landing in this world of terrible loneliness. I had no way of knowing it, but loneliness and the feeling of utter help-lessness would soon become the most formidable foes that I'd face.

Before sitting at the table, I poured a glass of water. God, I was thirsty. Something about the biology of danger, perhaps it was the flow of adrenalin, had left me with a momumental thirst. The candlelit expression on my guard's face told me that he too had been under severe stress. The woman had made things difficult for everyone. I'd been lucky beyond reason and I knew it.

It was after ten o'clock and weariness was a crushing weight. My knees ached and the rest of my body felt as though it had been battered by a thousand clubs. My wound was throbbing, but I passed that off to nerve sensitivity brought on by tension and my having stood so long in the office.

When I awakened from my nap, I became concerned about the soreness surrounding my rib cage. I didn't seem to have any broken ribs, but my sides were tender and painful. I'd struck the ground with such force that my body had been severely compressed. Internal and external pressures had probably damaged me in many ways. I was undoubtedly suffering from shock, and would be better off were I to lie down, but I didn't want to do that, not while there was a chance to escape. But time was against me. Each passing hour brought new and increased pain. I concluded that if I was going to escape I'd have to have help, and my young guard was the only immediate source.

While walking to the village, and again after the man and his daughter had left, I'd broached the subject of escape to my captor. I was reasonably certain that he hadn't understood me in the first instance, but he understood me perfectly at the time he, the guard, and I had been alone. He'd sympathized with my desire, but had declined to help. My only remaining possibility lay with the guard, and I had reservations about pressing the issue with him. With each passing hour piling symptom upon symptom of my deteriorating mobility, there was little value in getting the guard to help me escape, only to be caught. If that happened, he'd undoubtedly be executed. Nevertheless I had no choice but to ask. The decision would be his.

Following our return to the room he'd admonished me for slapping the woman. I'd agreed, and heaved a visible sigh of relief. I wanted to change the subject. He took my cue and began chatting and gesturing on the subject of America. It was a perfect opening for me to suggest that if he'd help me, I'd take him to America. Earlier he'd rejected my request by laughingly refusing; but this time, his refusal was a firm "Nui," to which he added, "Nein!" I wasn't certain, but I interpreted his lengthy remarks to mean that escape from Rumania was impossible.[2]

I attacked the problem from every conceivable angle. I explained my intended route; that all he had to do was help me get to the Yugoslav border; the Partisans would do the rest. If he hadn't known Tito's political affiliations, perhaps I would have succeeded. Each time I mentioned the Partisans, he'd frown and say, "Tito Communista!" Either I couldn't communicate to the point at which he clearly understood, or he simply didn't believe that I'd take him to America. To him—that is, to his sense of values and knowledge of the world —America may as well have been another planet. I longed for the blood chit the woman had taken from me.

Our discourse continued with quiet fervor for wearying hours. No matter what I tried, the answer was a polite "Nui." By two o'clock, we were exhausted. Signaling that I needed to lie down, I attempted to stand, but the long hours of sitting had left me painfully stiff. The guard rounded the table and helped me to the bunk. My failure to convince him to help me escape deepened my depression. Bidding him "guten nacht" I settled painfully onto the bed and was instantly asleep.

2. The best, perhaps only, chance for escape lay through Yugoslavia. Bulgaria was totally hostile to Americans. Being a non-European made the problem of escape infinitely more difficult. Americans look, stand, walk, do everything like Americans. We're walking billboards of our society.

XII

I awakened to bright sunlight and my guard shaking me out of a deep sleep. Weariness had aged his young face, but his voice rang with urgency. His frequent use of the word "Craiova" told me that I was leaving.

Craiova is a small city, about forty miles from where I believed this village to be. That puzzled me; it was in the opposite direction from Bucharest. Still, the idea of going there appealed to me. The city is only thirty miles or so from the Yugoslav border.

During my four-hour sleep, I'd stiffened. Noting my difficulty, the guard took my hand and pulled me to my feet. Knowing I'd never see him again, I offered him my flight jacket. He refused the gift and hurried me toward the door.

In front of the building an ancient bus was waiting, its small engine struggling to keep idling. Except for the driver it was empty. The lieutenant motioned for me to get on board. The sergeant, standing by the driver, waved me to the rear of the bus.

Hobbling along, using the backs of the seats to maintain my balance, I made it to the rear. The sergeant took a seat midway and sat with his feet blocking the aisle. The guard and the lieutenant took seats at the front.

The moment the bus pulled away from the jail I knew that I was in for an agonizing ride. We weren't moving more than fifteen miles per hour, but the jostling movements of the rickety bus were painful. I took advantage of my privacy and massaged my legs and sides, and did arm exercises to loosen my back and shoulder muscles. My arms were the only parts of me that seemed to have escaped serious damage.

The tree-lined road and farmland were peaceful, crude, untouched by the war, our clattering bus the only intruder in a living canvas of medieval art. It would be foolhardy for an American to try to travel through such countryside in daylight. Other than an occasional patch of woods there was no cover to hide one's movements. Were I to escape and try for Yugoslavia I'd have to travel at night, perhaps with no food or water.

After an hour or so we entered a village several times larger than any we'd passed. Ahead, a less dilapidated bus was parked at the side of the road. A crowd of civilians and soldiers was standing beside it, watching our approach. Our bus was braking to a stop when I caught sight of Ollie in the middle of the soldiers—and Willie!

I couldn't see Green. Was he injured in the jump? Had he avoided capture?

I pulled myself to my feet and made my way to the door. While waiting to step down, I searched the crowd. Yes, there was Green. Flickering hope died. Frank Lynch wasn't there.

I went immediately to Ollie and the others. Our reunion was marked more by relief than joy. Ollie stared at me for several moments of disbelief before he spoke.

"I thought you were dead. I watched the plane after my chute opened but I never saw your chute."

"I was pretty low when I got out. My damn chute almost didn't get open. I really hit hard."

Neither he nor Willie was injured, but Green, as before, had watched his chute come out of the chest pack. Four neat riser burns on his face—two on each cheek—had slicked and turned a yellowish-tan. He didn't mention them, but they had to be uncomfortable, even painful.

After an extended conversation between the lieutenant and the guards who had accompanied my officers, we got onto the waiting bus. The lieutenant, the sergeant, and the guard who'd come with us followed. I was grateful to be on the bus. Following our arrival the sergeant's crude shoes had hardly hit the ground when he'd launched into a heroic tale of my capture. The crowd, fascinated by his dissertation, had cast fearful glances in my direction. I'd been correct in my assessment of him. Given the wrong audience, the dumb bastard could get us into serious trouble.

After our initial greetings we seldom spoke. Each time we tried, a guard motioned us to be silent. When we boarded the bus the sergeant glared us into silence. The lieutenant, sitting in quiet contemplation, ignored us. It was just as well. There was no point in discussing escape plans in the presence of the enemy. The sergeant didn't concern me, but I had reservations about the lieutenant. His wife was so articulate it was hard for me to believe that he couldn't speak, or at least understand, our language. It was best to play it safe and leave each of us to his own thoughts.

Shortly after noon we entered Craiova. The marshaling yards had been bombed a month ago, but there hadn't been any damage along our route. Nevertheless, the raid had left its destructive imprint on more than twisted railway tracks and the shells and rubble of bombed-out buildings. War had struck terror and sorrow in the hearts and minds of Craiova's people, and had left a bitterness that would endanger us.

Near what I judged to be the center of the city, the bus entered a military compound. The garrison was situated at the intersection of a cobblestoned boulevard and a lesser street. It was an attractive place, an old military post surrounded by a masonry wall. The corner of the wall at the street intersection had been left off to provide for a wide, angular entrance set with iron gates. Inside, trees shaded the garrison in a pleasant manner. Judging from the size and appearance of the post, it was a major headquarters.

We dismounted and were ushered into a large building where we were left under guard in an empty room. Within a half-hour, an air raid siren set up its terrifying wail. What a hell of a way to celebrate the Fourth of July, I thought. Guards hurried into the room and moved us outside to a slit-trench that had been dug into green lawn. I hadn't noticed them when we arrived, but trenches were scattered throughout the lawn. Most were crowded with soldiers. Ours was occupied by several officers, who looked us over then ignored our presence.

Suddenly antiaircraft guns boomed thunderously. No shells passed overhead, but the blasts from the nearby guns were extremely noisy. I wondered if we'd be able to hear the bombs coming down. At one point, between barrages, I heard the faint sound of engines but couldn't see the aircraft because of the canopy of trees. I figured that the guns were firing at bombers on the way home from a target located elsewhere, or at a reconnaissance plane photographing the marshaling yard. Whatever the cause, the alert didn't last long. The "all clear" sounded and our guards collected us for the return trip to the room.

Along the way, we were stopped by our escort lieutenant in the company of an elderly officer whose ornate epaulets suggested that he might be a general. Other officers, all of whom wore impressive insignia, kept a respectful distance while the lieutenant and the general chatted. As they talked, the general examined us with care. It was as though he were inspecting new personnel, or equipment, for his own army. Something about his manner told me that he approved.

Back in our room, all of us were nervous and quiet. The raid had emphasized our helplessness in a new way. Not only were we at the mercy of the enemy, but our own forces could become a major source of danger. The only solution was escape, but there was little point in my entertaining that idea at the moment. My physical condition was hopeless, and since the others hadn't broached the subject, I was willing, even thankful, to bide my time and see what happened next. Weary from the lack of sleep, I stretched out on the concrete floor and dozed off.

I was awakened by a voice speaking Rumanian. A guard had come to escort us to a small mess hall. The food was simple and tasteless: watery cabbage soup, several small boiled potatoes, and a piece of dark bread. I wasn't hungry, but I could feel a vacancy in my stomach. Pain and the soreness in my body masked any pangs of hunger that I might have felt.

Later that evening Ollie and I were taken to a nearby room. Two Luftwaffe pilots—a lieutenant sitting behind a wooden table, and a sergeant standing near its end—were waiting to interrogate us. The lieutenant was thin, his face pallid beneath meticulously combed black hair. Alert eyes that darted from one of us to the other indicated a nimble mind. His black tunic with Sam Browne belt, riding breeches, and polished boots, were typical of the dress I'd seen of Nazi officers in news clips. It was his cold, impassive look of arrogance that bothered me most.

The sergeant, tall and muscular, appeared relaxed, almost friendly, in his gray uniform with long trousers. There was something about his blond, boyish good looks that puzzled me. It took a moment but I found the answer. He had the mannerisms of an American.

When we left our room we had no forewarning of where we were going or for what purpose. Consequently my first sight of the Germans was accompanied by a feeling of apprehension. I knew that we were about to be interrogated, but the lieutenant's casual "Come in, gentlemen" disarmed me.

His accent wasn't British. It was more like American or Canadian English with only a trace of German. I was puzzling over where he'd been educated when the harsh sound of his revolver slamming down on the table startled me.

"Where is Tito?"

I looked at the map spread on the table. It was the same piece of map that had survived the crash of our ship.

Thoughts blazed through my mind. Each flash jolted me with a new fear. He knew that I'd been in Yugoslavia! I'd be tried as a spy and executed!

Before he asked the question, his eyes had darted from my face to Ollie's, then back to mine, and so on. The moment he asked the question, however, he read my reaction and turned his full attention to me.

"Where is Tito?" he demanded, as his hand slapped the table top.

I looked at Ollie's frozen face then back to his.

"I don't know," I replied without conviction. All the while the sergeant had been casually watching me but had said nothing.

"What is your name?" he now asked.

"William R. Cubbins, Second Lieutenant, AO 750347."

"And yours?"

Ollie responded with the stock answer.

He not only looked like an American, he sounded like one. There was no trace of German in his speech. His brogue was almost as Southern as my own.

The lieutenant had picked up his revolver and was handling it in a careless manner.

Was he going to shoot us, or, the odd thought struck me, play Russian roulette with us as he continued to ask questions?

Instead of asking another question, he calmly introduced himself and the sergeant. The next several minutes of chatty conversation did much to relieve my tension. The sergeant had lived in Wheeling, West Virginia, as a child. His family had returned to Germany in the late thirties. Although the lieutenant didn't volunteer any personal information about himself, he was very good in his attempts to draw us into friendly conversation.

I noticed that neither of them had made a note of our names or serial numbers. The only thing on the table upon which they could have written was the map. I was running such thoughts through my mind when the lieutenant suddenly asked, "What is the number of your squadron?"

"William R. Cubbins, Second Lieutenant, AO 750347," I replied.

He gave me a faint smile and said, "Lieutenant, you can answer my question; there isn't anything that I do not know about your organization."

I thought, Bullshit! He doesn't know anything about us. But he did, and his next remark shocked me almost as much as had his question about Tito.

"Your Captain MacQueen certainly knows a lot about the Norden bombsight."

The son of a bitch had us nailed! He knew that we were from the 723rd Squadron. Alarming thoughts raced through my mind. Had it been a lucky guess? The odds against that were too great. Had the stabilizer markings of our aircraft been forwarded to a place where they'd been identified and that information sent to these interrogators? Perhaps the ship's Form 1 had survived the crash. It might carry the squadron number on it. That was what the Rumanian lieutenant was carrying in his briefcase: the map fragment and God only knew what else.

I glanced again at the piece of map lying on the table. He wasn't as smart as I'd thought. He didn't know a damned thing about our bailing out over Vis. If he did, he would have already threatened me with that knowledge. I was trying hard to convince myself of that, but his remark about MacQueen worried me.

Before we arrived at Manduria, Henry MacQueen had been the operations officer of our squadron. Jack had been a close friend and had often spoken of him. The MacQueens had a new baby and Henry had the habit of carrying a pair of infant shoes on missions for luck. I recalled that he was not known to be alive. At that point, something lurking in the recesses of my memory popped into my mind. He'd said that Henry knew a lot about the Norden bombsight. That wasn't likely. Henry was a pilot, and pilots don't know very much about bombsights. Another thing, B-24s have Sperry sights. There's no reason they can't be equipped with the Norden and some probably were, but the Norden was common only to the B-17s. A chilling thought hit me. If he knew I was from the 723rd, perhaps he also knew that I was a B-17 pilot and I didn't want to be interrogated about the Norden sight, which we still regarded as being Top Secret. Hell, he hadn't pursued his question about Tito. Maybe he didn't know as much about us as my imagination was crediting to him. I had to break my trend of thought. I was worrying myself as much as he.

"Is Captain MacQueen alive?"

I knew that in asking the question, I was confirming my squadron, but I didn't care. Its only importance was in the shock value of disclosing such knowledge to us and we'd survived that. He'd frightened me, but I was determined that I wasn't going let him get the advantage of me again.

"Yes," he smiled. "He is in the prisoner of war camp in Bucharest."

"How many guns are there on the P-51?"

"I don't know," I replied. "I think twelve."

I didn't know, and I thought it was time to play dumb. "Do you know, Ollie?"

I could have bitten my tongue. That was a helluva thing to have said. I'd put Ollie on the spot. But Ollie, so far unmolested by their questions, replied with a stony-faced "I don't know."

Hell, I thought, they know how many guns there are on a P-51. They've shot down enough of them to know everything there is to know about the aircraft. The same thing applies to bombsights. They probably have enough salvaged Nordens to equip a good-sized bomber force.

Our answers to the P-51 question seemed to satisfy their requirement to interrogate us. Other than the question about Tito, they weren't interested in anything that we were likely to know. The invasion of France, and the Russian army driving toward Rumania and Germany, meant that it was only a matter of time before they lost the war, and they knew it.[1]

When we stepped into the hallway, Ollie turned to me.

"Are you all right?"

"Yeah, I'm OK."

I wasn't, but I didn't want him to know it. I was upset with myself for having let the lieutenant frighten me with his question about Tito. I'd felt the blood drain from my face and was ashamed.

"You don't look so good," he persisted.

"I'm OK."

I felt like hell, and I didn't want to talk to him or anyone else. I turned and hobbled away.

The next day seemed endless. There was nothing to do but lie around and mope over our misfortune. I'd told the others that we'd

1. I didn't know it until weeks later, but the question about Tito had been legitimate. German forces had mounted a campaign to capture him. Unknown to the Germans, his staff had recently escaped from Yugoslavia and set up headquarters in Italy.

be taken to Bucharest. That surprised them, as it had me. Before being shot down, no one had ever talked about prisoner of war camps, not even the briefers. Now that we were prisoners the locations and nature of the camps were of vital concern. Since the Rumanians and the Germans hadn't disclosed any information other than what I had learned from the lieutenant's wife, the only thing we could do was wait and see. Her parting remark about "gangsters" had confused and unsettled me. I couldn't imagine what she'd been referring to.

It had been two days since we jumped. My stride had shortened to about twenty inches and my insides felt as though they'd torn loose from their moorings. Being with my three officers helped my spirits, but my physical ailments were beyond solution other than that provided by time.

Late in the afternoon the Rumanian lieutenant and the sergeant came into the room and motioned for us to follow them. Holding onto the stair rail and twisting my body, I let myself down a step at a time. By the time we reached ground level I was in need of a rest. I wasn't tired. My torn leg muscles were burning from the exertion.

My first indication that we were leaving the compound came when we headed down the road toward the gate. At least that was how it started. The mob had other ideas.

The scene at the gate was one that I'd seen before—in a Frankenstein movie. In the midst of thirty or more peasants armed with rocks, clubs, pitchforks, axes—there was even a scythe—a dozen soldiers were pushing and shoving, trying to clear the area in front of the gate, and around a large black carriage waiting a few yards beyond.

It was a magnificent vehicle, with its lacquered body, crimson velvet upholstery, and two handsome black horses prancing nervously in the screaming mob. For whatever the reason we were going for a carriage ride. That is, if we survived; and that was currently in doubt.

It was a fearful sight. A mob of crazed peasants pressing the guards, shouting and brandishing their weapons. Three of their shouted words were in clear but accented English: "Gangster! Murderer! Criminal!" Their anger and the resolute manner in which they fought with the guards were unmistakable. They intended to kill us.

Our arrival at the gate had the effect of a signal to both groups. Until now the guards had merely been trying to contain and calm the crowd; but now that it was time for us to leave the guards were no longer just pushing people, they were jabbing and striking men and women alike with their rifles. Several blows I witnessed were intended to cause grievous injury.

I couldn't imagine how word had gotten out that we were in the compound, nor could I understand why the mob was so angry at us. No bombs had been dropped during the air alert yesterday. Another curious thing was that everyone was dark-skinned and in peasant dress, yet we were in the heart of a city of 70,000 people. Speculation was pointless. The only things that mattered were that the guards were pressed just to defend themselves and that we had to go outside the protecting gate.

As the gates were flung open, I was pushed forward by one of the guards. He kept pushing and jostling me against soldiers who were engaging the crowd. Instead of moving directly to the carriage, we circled its rear to the far side. Along the way, I caught a glimpse of an old woman, her withered face disappearing from the blow of a rifle butt. I ducked my head to protect it from clubs and flying rocks. Had the crowd not pressed so tightly, they would have had more freedom to deliver their blows and missiles. As it was, I reached the carriage untouched. Before I could get my foot on the high step, someone put a shoulder to my rear end and all but deposited me onto the seat. I felt pain, but paid it no mind. The desire to escape the crowd was paramount.

The driver was on the driving perch. The lieutenant was beside him. The sergeant had taken a seat next to Green and was facing the rest of us. Our own guard had mounted the footman's perch and was yelling and waving his rifle at the driver. The moment my fanny hit the seat, I heard the driver whistle and caught the hurried slap of rein leather against straining rumps. I couldn't see at this point. I'd bent down and covered my head with my arms, but I could hear well enough to visualize what happened next.

The carriage lurched forward amid the frightened cries of people being knocked to the cobblestones by charging horses. I wasn't certain, but I thought I felt two bumps as steel-tired wheels rolled over parts of some hapless victims. As the carriage broke free of the crowd, several rocks struck the sides and rear. A few moments later I straightened up and looked around. Miraculously, none of us had been injured, and we were speeding down the cobblestoned boulevard at a clip that would outdistance foot-pursuit.

We traveled about a mile, then the carriage slowed. I peered around the driver's perch and saw an open area ahead. It was the marshaling yard. A small wooden shack sitting between tracks, a few yards from the boulevard crossing, appeared to be our destination. As the driver turned toward the shack, I searched behind us for sight of the mob. An intervening rise of the boulevard blocked my view. I was worried that we hadn't gone far enough from the mob. The lieutenant, the extra guard, and the sergeant were our only protection and they'd be as straws if the mob caught up with us.

Huddled in front of the shack, jabbering and pointing at us, were the strangest-looking men I'd ever seen. All of them were tall, or so they appeared in their high, sheepskin hats. The hats were cones with their points bobbed off. Long, unkempt hair hanging from underneath hadn't seen the service of scissors for years. Each was dressed in a rough shirt and black pantaloons held up by a length of rope, or cloth, anything that would serve for a belt. Their most curious items of dress were the pieces of sheet rubber sewn to stay on their feet. The makeshift shoes flopped comically as they duck-footed out of our way.

Each had a bundle rolled in cloth tied at the ends with a rope that also served as a carrying strap. The arrangement was worn like a bandolier, with the rope passing over a shoulder and under the opposite armpit so as to allow the bundle to rest against one's back. Their dark skin and filthy condition betrayed them to be nomads, probably gypsies. Despite their constant jabber and comical manner, they were a pitiful lot. Victims of tradition, or war, their poverty and circumstance were saddening to see.

The lieutenant motioned us toward the shack. When we stood to climb down the gypsies sprang away like frightened chickens. We and the lieutenant went inside, leaving the sergeant and the guard to take posts outside.

The shack was built of rough-sawn lumber and was barren except for wooden benches along the walls. The lieutenant issued instructions to the sergeant, then came inside and closed and latched the door. The latch, a simple turn-type, was a short piece of wood attached to the door by a nail. It would be useless if the mob found us.

There were two windows: one each in the front and rear walls. Outside I could hear the sergeant telling the gypsies his version of our capture. I stood and looked through the front window. He was well into the tale, and from what I could see he'd just arrived on the battle scene in a tank, had captured us singlehandedly, and was marching us to jail.

No, my imagination had gotten ahead of the brave fellow. He was pointing his rifle skyward jerking his arm as he downed our mighty bomber singlehanded. I had to give him credit, he really knew how to stretch a simple story.

His audience had grown considerably. It now included several townspeople who peered in through my window and were immediately waved away by the lieutenant.

The tale ended with the sergeant standing and inviting his admirers to take a peek at his captives. Instead of coming to my window, they crowded toward the door. I looked at the door and saw several knotholes, and a large gap between two boards. Watching the comical scene through the window, I was the only one in the room who was prepared for what was about to happen.

At least a half-dozen of them were trying to see through the crack and holes at the same time. The press of curious bodies was too much for the latch. The door burst open and spilled several gypsies and a townsman onto the floor. Thoroughly frightened, the gypsies yelled and scrambled to get to their feet and out of the shack before we ate them or did them some other grievous harm. My gang, caught by surprise, was momentarily bewildered and frightened. The lieutenant showed a side of himself that I had decided he didn't have. Coming as close to anger as I'd ever see him, he followed the last of the gypsies through the door and ordered them away. Then came the sergeant's turn. The lieutenant's tongue-lashing, coming in front of his former admirers, must have been painful to him. Thoroughly deflated, he sat quietly on an outside bench and smoked a well-used pipe.

Late evening settled through the windows, softening shadows in the bare interior of our refuge. Early morning and dusk had always been my favorite times of day. Each of us in the makeshift railroad station was quiet in his private thoughts, disturbed only by the murmur of voices some distance away. For some reason—perhaps it was the golden quality of twilight bathing the interior, or hunger and memory of that supper in the village when my thoughts had turned to the delights of country buttermilk and cornbread—whatever the reason, my mind strayed to that peaceful summer of 1935 when my grandmother and I spent several weeks with our cousins who lived near Como, Mississippi.

Cousin Oester was a dirt farmer whose chief crop was the few bales of cotton the family harvested from sunbaked earth. Plowing and harrowing behind a mule, chopping weeds between rows with worn hoes, then picking the capricious crop by hand—that is, what the boll weevils left—were endless, back-breaking labors that had to be done. Cotton was their only cash crop. President Roosevelt's edict to destroy surplus hogs and cattle had robbed small farmers of that traditional source of income. "What we can't eat or sell don't get raised," my cousin had explained. Most farmers were dirt-poor, but poverty of the pocket, though troublesome and demoralizing, had made only temporary inroads in most folks' spirits. Day after day they held on, clinging with a tenuous grasp on hope, on faith in the better times that seemed always to be just over the hill, or around the next bend of a dusty road.

I'd spent many evenings such as this sitting on the edge of worn porch planks, listening to crickets chirping their weather forecast, the squeak of treasured rocking chairs, an occasional "splat" of tobacco juice making a splashy spot in the deep dust of the yard. I'd learned right off to stay out of Cousin Oester's line of fire during those black country nights. Sitting here in this foreign land, trying for the moment to forget my hunger and the danger of our circumstance, I thought how alike were Cousin Oester's house and this distant shack.

Squatting some thirty or forty feet from the dirt road, his house was two rooms separated by a spacious breezeway that connected full-length porches across the front and back of the structure. The building was tied together by a tin roof that sang soothingly to the cadence of rain pelting its blistering surface. My cousins delighted in chiding their city kin by insisting that the center breezeway let twisters—tornadoes—pass harmlessly through.

The large room on the left was Cousin Oester's bedroom. Guests, such as my grandmother, shared that room. The large room on the other side of the breezeway served as both kitchen and living room. The only thing dividing the two areas was the narrow strip of flooring showing between a threadbare rug and well-worn linoleum. The living room part doubled as a bedroom for my two young cousins and myself. Saturday baths were taken in a galvanized laundry tub set in the middle of the kitchen floor. The house, like life on the small farm, was simple but sufficient.

Kerosene lamps were the only lighting, and were used sparingly, normally to light one's way to bed, or to visit the outhouse. At ten cents a gallon for coal oil, one didn't waste fuel. After a day of drudgery in the fields, or with the endless other tasks of life, one usually followed the sun to bed.

It was the quiet between supper and deep night that I enjoyed most. After the dishes were done, the family gathered on the front porch and chatted lazily about "that upstart, Hoyt Wooten, who'd left Como and Senatobia in a huff and gone off to Memphis to build his radio station and that big house on Highway 51 so's folks back home would have to pass it on their way to the city."

If there was a revival at the small church down the road, Cousin Oester would worry about the lack of hard money to put in the plate. "We'll have the preacher come to Sunday dinner, and maybe one time for supper," he'd pronounce to settle the issue. Most often, the talk was about the work of the day and the tasks that had to be done tomorrow. I had listened quietly and enjoyed their verbal footnotes to life. Except for nationality, and customs born of heritage, Cousin Oester and his family were not very different from the Rumanian peasants. Even the lieutenant sitting quietly in the far corner was little different from me. Yet, because of the trappings of politics and other aberrations of the mind, we were enemies. I was grateful for his understanding and forbearance, which seemed at odds with the politics of his country. I bore him no ill will, nor he me.

My thoughts were interrupted by an increase in the volume of chatter outside. Shortly I heard the familiar sound of a train puffing slowly toward us. The sergeant's voice coming through the closed door to alert us wasn't necessary. The engine was hissing to a squealing stop.

XIII

The wooden cars and steam engine were vintage European. Small and quaint by American standards, they seemed appropriate to the nineteenth-century pace of this strange land. Gypsies were scurrying about, jockeying for favorable perches on the sides and roofs of the half-dozen passenger cars. Those on the roofs shifted about, or stayed put to protect their places as still more of them scrambled up coach ladders to squeeze precious inches of space from those already on top. Each ladder had its own occupants, who would hang sideways to allow those climbing to pass them by. If a hanger became dislodged, the climber often stopped and claimed the space. Arguments were spirited, but went no further than verbal exchanges. The poor wretches reminded me of a flock of magpies scrapping over a morsel of food.

We waited with the lieutenant while the sergeant and the guard boarded a car to clear space for us. From our vantage on the ground, we could see and hear all that transpired. For the first time I sympathized with the sergeant. The car, looking as if it were ready to burst from the press of humanity within, was being packed even tighter by the two men who were being loudly resisted by passengers being dispossessed of their seats and standing room. After a short wait, the lieutenant shouted through the glassless window and ended the arguments.

Squirming our way through the confused mass, we took seats near a front corner of the car. The sergeant and the guard pushed and shouted to clear more space in the aisle so they could stand guard with room to maneuver their rifles. I'm certain that the sergeant made remarks that embellished himself vis à vis his dangerous charges. The people nearby made room as they stared at us in frightened wonder. Encouraged by their attention, our Rumanian Don Quixote launched into his familiar tale. The lieutenant ended the dissertation with a few words that left our hero subdued.

Inspecting what I could see of the car, I noticed a number of large bullet holes in the ceiling and end wall. Charring around the holes had been caused by incendiary ammunition. The car had been strafed by fighters, either ours or Russians'. The terror caused by the attack was easy to visualize, and I wondered if the train had been packed as now. Perhaps I was trying to justify my own part in the war, but, I thought that when we dropped our bombs, those in the target area at least had the benefit of the warning siren to send them scurrying for shelter. The people in this car never had a chance. Reddish-brown stains of brutal reality darkening my seat, and the wall only a few feet from where I sat, were mute testimony of that.

God, what had it been like for the poor wretches riding on the roof? For reasons that I had not yet discovered, my own capture, the possibility that I might be killed, were acceptable outcomes of war, but what happened here wasn't war. I hoped that the fighter jocks had been aiming at the engine, that the death clinging to these scrubbed stains on the seat and wall was caused by accident, a mishap of war.

The train lurched forward and almost upended the guard and the sergeant. After the initial movement, they balanced themselves by standing spraddle-legged and leaning on their rifles. It would be a long ride for them. Bucharest was at least a hundred miles to the east. Considering the speed of the slow-moving train, I judged that we wouldn't arrive until daylight. I didn't look forward to an overnight ride on wooden seats, but the grim message of the battle-damaged car made me thankful to be traveling at night. I had an earnest desire to be in Bucharest and away from this train by 10:00 A.M. at the latest. Satisfied that nearby passengers meant me no harm, I settled my aching body into the least uncomfortable position and closed my eyes.

Discomfort, and frequent stops, made unbroken sleep impossible. Shortly after midnight I awakened long enough to notice that the guard was still standing, but the weary sergeant had displaced a civilian from his seat at the end of the car. He wasn't alert, but every few minutes he'd shift his aging frame from one uncomfortable position to another.

Shortly after 1:00 A.M. the train slowed, then stopped. The night was moonless black. Within moments a man walked past the car, shouting a message that sent weary passengers scrambling for the door.

Their sudden movement startled me. Sensing danger, I'd started to rise, when the lieutenant motioned us to remain seated. He knew what was going on and wasn't concerned. Reassured, I settled back onto the seat until the crowd thinned and he signaled us to follow.

Climbing down from the train was painful, especially when I dropped stiff-legged to the ground. In front of the train, people, brightly lit by the engine's headlight, moved rapidly alongside the track, then disappeared as though the land had opened and swallowed them.

"A bridge must be out," I thought. "We'll have to cross a stream and catch a train on the other side." I looked into the lighted darkness to see if a train was waiting, but our headlight didn't disclose anything ahead.

We followed the crowd, taking advantage of the headlamp to light our way. The further we drew ahead of our engine, the blacker the night became beyond the cone of diffusing light. We'd moved off of the track bed and were walking at the edge of the gravel. People were still well lit but the ground now merged with the night. Unable to see the ground, I found it difficult to walk on legs that didn't respond well to the uneven surface. Each stumble brought a new wave of pain. I sensed that we were near the edge of a creek bank but the glare of the light interfered with my night vision. One moment my feet were on firm earth, the next moment I stepped into thin air and slid down the steep bank.

The pain of contact was severe but short-lived. After being in the beam of light overhead, the creek bed was more black than black. A perfect opportunity to escape, the thought flitted through my mind. But the unexpected change of trains had caught us off guard, and there was no time to formulate an escape plan. For whatever it was worth, we'd been handed an opportunity and hadn't taken advantage of it. Since we didn't know our location, our inaction was probably for the best. There would be no value in an unsuccessful escape. The attempt could cause the enemy to take measures against us and make any future attempt more difficult.

Leaning on Ollie's shoulder, I managed to wade the stream without further ado. I couldn't tell if the water was muddy or clear, but the bottom beneath my feet was gravel, perhaps a ford.

I was concerned about keeping the bandage on my leg dry. I could hear water splashing beneath my feet, but it seemed no deeper than an inch or two. I'd examined my leg while at the garrison and it had looked fine. A scab had formed and closed the puncture. Nevertheless, I had sprinkled the last of my sulfa powder on it, discarded the soiled gauze, and rewrapped the injury with the bandage wrapper. My sulfa exhausted, and my bandage in its final stage, I couldn't afford to let the wound become contaminated by muddy water.

On level ground again, I saw the dark image of the train, lights out, waiting just ahead. Securing seats was a repeat of the routine at the other train, with one overriding difference. I was so desperately tired that I no longer cared what the people gawking at us were thinking. I fell into sound sleep.

Sunlight and the noisy train brought me back to reality. The countryside was more crowded. We were nearing Bucharest. I looked at my watch; it was after eight. I'd slept for at least six hours and was surprisingly refreshed. I was stiff and sore but I felt better and more alert than at any time during the past three days. Loneliness had been replaced by curiosity. In no immediate danger, I'd come out of my shroud of depression and reentered the real world, one ravaged by hunger.

It took considerable time for the engineer to work the train through bomb-damaged tracks and switches to its final stopping place near a street. After the passengers departed the lieutenant signaled us to get up and walk to a small bus parked nearby.

Bucharest, the little we saw of it, was a picture of Old World charm. Its cleanliness, its varied architecture and broad boulevards with tree-lined esplanades bespoke the beauty and grace of a city traditionally at peace with itself. The streets we traveled were mostly avenues of commerce. However, curtained windows in the upper floors of most buildings showed that they were also residences. Overall, the city reflected the grace and vitality of people who in other times had enjoyed life's more gentle pleasures.

Much too soon, the bus turned into an entrance in a high masonry wall. Was this the prisoner of war camp? It was a military compound but, except for the guards at the entrance gate, the few soldiers I saw inside were unarmed and seemed to be going about their duties in the fashion of headquarters types. Searching the compound as best I could, I noted that two sides of its rectangular shape were formed by two-story stone buildings. The other sides were thick, masonry walls.

At the far end of the compound, a long, single-story building sat a few feet from the wall. A second low building occupied the center of the cobblestoned yard.

The bus stopped in front of the building next to the entrance gate. Motioning us to remain seated, the lieutenant stepped off the bus and disappeared into the building. He'd been gone for at least ten minutes when two guards hurried out of the building, boarded the bus, and shouted an order. The sergeant and our guard reacted with equal gruffness in motioning us to leave. Outside the bus, the guards pointed us toward the single-story building at the far end of the compound. A guard was standing beside the open door, and American faces stared at us through barbed wire lacing glassless windows. This couldn't be the main camp; I was certain of that. It was far too small to hold the hundreds of prisoners the Rumanians surely had collected by now. Perhaps those inside would enlighten us. Like good Indians, we walked single file toward the building.

Inside, some "fallen eagles" lay dispirited on double-decked bunks, while others waited hopefully for our arrival. I looked around the room for my gunners and other familiar faces but saw none. For a group of strangers, it was quite a reunion.

"What outfit are you from? When did you go down? What got you: flak or fighters? Do you know so and so?" On and on it went, the usual fly-boy talk.

The feeling was strange, but being cast with others of similar misfortune is an elixir to one's own spirits. Misery does indeed enjoy company. All were officers, and as far as I could determine, had been shot down on the same day we had. Some were from the 49th Wing and had been shot down over Bucharest. Most were from our Wing and had suffered the same fate as we at Giurgiu.

According to our new comrades, the garrison was only a collection point and interrogation center. We would move to the permanent camp as soon as all the prisoners from the July third and fourth raids were assembled and interrogated. While being interrogated by a Rumanian, they had been told that the officers and sergeants were in separate camps, which were located in different parts of the city. According to the interrogator, the prisoners were well-treated. The "well-treated" smacked of propaganda. However, I had to admit that other than the lack of food, and having been slapped by a shrew of a woman, I hadn't been abused—but neither had I been well-treated.

I figured that we'd find out soon enough what they meant by "well-treated." At the moment I was damned hungry and wondering when we'd be fed. According to those already here, I'd remain hungry, because the food left practically everything to be desired.

After an impoverished dinner of cabbage soup and dark peasant bread, we were taken away, one at a time, for interrogation. None was gone for more than fifteen minutes. I was the second to go.

The guard led me through the dark compound to a building nearby. Along the way, I made up my mind that I wasn't going to tell the bastards anything but my name, rank, and serial number. Upon reaching the proper door, the guard knocked and waited for a response from within. A male voice apparently bade the guard to send me in alone.

The room was bare except for a worn library table with a chair in front and behind it. A somber Rumanian officer was standing behind the table, waiting for me to enter. His American voice surprised me.

"I am Capitan Cristi. Please sit. What is your name?"

"William R. Cubbins, Second Lieutenant, AO 750347."

"I didn't ask for your rank or serial number," he snapped.

His show of anger surprised me. The guy looked as if he couldn't whip a marshmallow, and as far as I could tell he wasn't armed. I decided he had a chronic case of irritation. I could understand that. He'd spoken only twice and had already irritated me. He reminded me of a fat wet mouse.

"Lieutenant, pick up the pencil and fill out the form."

I grasped the paper lying on the table and read it. The first few lines were similar to dozens of military forms I'd filled out as a cadet. There were spaces for my unit number, type and number of aircraft, the location of my base, etc. Without bothering to read the entire form, I picked up the pencil and filled in the name, rank, and serial number boxes, and shoved the form toward him. He knew what I'd written on the paper, but he glanced at it anyway.

"If you do not complete the form, we will not notify the Swiss authorities that you are a prisoner of war."

As he pushed the form back to me he continued with his poorly disguised propaganda.

"If we do not notify the Swiss, your unit and your family will never know what happened to you. When the war is over you will stay in Rumania."

He'd made that last remark through a sickly smile. It was all pure bullshit. He knew that I recognized it as such and was suddenly genuinely angry.

"If you do not write down your home address, you cannot send letters to your family."

I didn't like the sound of his shouting *that* with such conviction. I figured that his words were more than an idle threat but I was determined that I wasn't going to give in to anything he said. I ignored him.

"Have you ever been to East Chicago, Indiana?"[1]

"No," I replied.

"I lived there for many years."

I could believe it. He sounded like a damnyankee. There was only a trace of accent in his speech. After about five minutes of his monologue, I figured there wasn't a whole lot that I did not know about Rumanian Captain Cristi. I felt that he was trying to disarm me and I wasn't falling for the ruse. I now knew quite a bit about him, but all he knew about me was my name, rank, and serial number. He had to be the most incompetent interrogator in the Rumanian army.

Following his lengthy autobiography, he tried several questions about my home and religion. I repeated my stock reply of name, rank, and serial number.

"Lieutenant, you are going to be our prisoner for many years. Before you go home, you will answer my questions."

I almost said "bullshit!"

Fully irritated, he yelled, "Go back to your building!"

That suited me perfectly. During the course of his monologue, he'd disclosed that we would be taken to a school that served as the prison for officers, and that we'd leave in two days. On my way back to the barrack, I decided why I'd taken an instant dislike of the man. He was so American, I considered him more a traitor than an enemy officer. I didn't care for the ordeal of being questioned, even by him, but I was delighted that the "dreaded interrogator" had turned out to be a "wet noodle."

---

1. Cristi, I later learned, was wont to tell a prisoner that he was from Detroit, or West Virginia, or whatever place popped into his mind at the moment.

After a breakfast of bread and weak tea, I headed for the latrine. The next few minutes would provide me with one of the most memorable experiences of my life.

The latrine, a one-room building, stood alone in the courtyard, a sort of centerpiece to the compound. Along the length of the wall opposite the entrance door was a line of built-in floor scallops with raised foot pads. A small drain hole was set in the bottom of each scallop, near the wall. A guard, an older man, stood facing the wall, taking aim at the hole in the floor so as not to splatter his shoes and leggings. I'd no sooner taken a similar stance when the room dimmed perceptibly. I glanced over my shoulder to see what was blocking the light.

Standing in the doorway, filling the doorway, was a man, a human pear set on long legs. His bald, too-small, bullet head sloped toward narrow shoulders and a vast midsection much too large for the Sam Browne belt encircling him well above his waist. To complete the comical shape, huge riding breeches draped from underneath his tight tunic and disappeared into cavalry boots that emphasized knock-kneed legs. Every detail of his appearance, from his ponderous size to the tiny pistol holster on his belt, made him seem a caricature of a man. The feature that captured my attention were the cruel, piglike eyes staring hatefully at the guard's back.

The poor guard never had a chance. Before he could look around and see the danger, the fat apparition squealed like a frightened pig and charged with all of his three-hundred-plus ponderous pounds of unleashed fury. Before the soldier could respond to the squeal, the "human pear" closed half the distance between them. That's when the poor fellow made a tragic error. He tried to spin, stop urinating, come to attention, salute, and run, all in a totally simultaneous and uncoordinated movement. He didn't complete a single one of his erstwhile objectives. His tangled feet slipped on wet tiles and caused him to fall forward on his hands and knees, facing the door. That would have been fine had he been able to get his feet beneath himself and bolt for the opening, but luck had deserted him. Still trying to salute from his all-fours, then two-knees and one-hand stance, he put himself in a trap. Taking full advantage of the inviting target, the "pear" aimed a kick at the soldier's vulnerable rear end. The kick was delivered with such vengence the man moved forward several feet before he landed flat on his face on the hard tile. Squealing all the while, the infuriated "pear" began trying with all his might to stomp the poor man through the floor. The guard was trying with equal fervor to avoid the murderous boots. He did manage to escape from most of the stomping, but made it no further than all fours before another mule kick caught him in the seat of his pants and propelled him half-standing toward the door. In midstride, he lost his balance and again sprawled face down on the floor. Seeing that his tormentor was not in pursuit, damned if he didn't again try to stand, salute, turn, and run, all at the same time, and with the expected disastrous results. But this time he fell on his belly in the gravel outside the door. In a wild scramble energized by pure terror, he got to his feet and bolted out of sight.

During our short stay in the garrison I made friends with the senior officer of our small group. I'd never met a more brash, devilish, or daring rascal than Capt. Arthur John Stavely. Perceptive beyond his thirty years, Art didn't know the meaning of "captured." "Prisoner of war" translated inside his fertile mind as "war by other means"—his war, his means.

Intelligent, educated, articulate, and a native New Yorker, he'd learned to fly as a youngster, and imparted aviation lore in the manner of Jimmy Doolittle. Indeed, the two had much in common beyond their physical resemblance. Art had an unrelenting drive to be doing something, anything, and if for no other reason than for the plain hell of it, as now.

"We gotta bust outta dis joint!"

The affectation was vintage Dead End Kids, but the devilish glint in his eye carried a different message. I had the distinct impression that he would never attempt to escape. If he ever had a desire to escape our prison walls, it would be in order to acquire the larger population beyond as victims. Barbed wire was only an inconvenience to him. It didn't keep him in, it protected those on the other side of the wire from him. I soon recognized the risks of throwing in with such a fellow, but I decided that come what may we'd find our way through the prisoner of war ordeal together.

Amused by my Southern brogue and rebel willingness to engage the enemy, he brainstormed me for ideas we could use to harass our jailers. Before we could bring any of our thoughts to fruition, however, our numbers swelled to the point that it was time to move us to the schoolhouse.

Outside our barrack door, a dozen guards had formed two columns. An officer entered the room and motioned us to follow. The twenty or so of us formed a column of POWs, two abreast, between the lines of flanking guards, and moved off toward the gate. The formation was quite military, and for good reason. These guards weren't farmers in uniform, or parade soldiers whose only business is to look good. Armed with automatic weapons, grenades, and bandoliers of ammunition slung across their shoulders, they were tough, admirably disciplined combat troops. They weren't abusive, but if one of us straggled or engaged another in conversation, a warning look and words were followed by the guard moving closer to ensure that we responded to his indication to "close it up," or whatever.

Our parade ended on a nearby thoroughfare set with streetcar tracks. The street was bordered on one side by a continuous row of two-story buildings, and on the other by a board fence. We gathered in a group against the fence, while the guards surrounded us with a half-circle that extended into the street.

Within minutes a half-dozen townspeople gathered only a few feet away. Almost immediately, one of their number launched into a lengthy speech. The speaker, a man whom I judged to be in his twenties, was cleanly dressed in a rumpled shirt, trousers, and white tennis shoes. His thin frame gave him a look of chronic hunger and emphasized his anger. The more he talked, the more angry he became. Done with whatever it was that he was saying to the crowd, he turned and started berating us. The officer and the guards watched, but did nothing to stop him.

Encountering no interference from our escort, he took a position between the crowd and us and began a tirade which he directed in equal measure to both groups. His most frequent words were pantaloona, gangsters, and criminals; the latter he spoke in clear English.

Each time he said pantaloona, he grasped a trouser leg and shook it, then pointed to various parts of his body. The fellow was upset about something relating to his clothing.

Suddenly, Art was in the fore of our group and making his own speech, in German, echoing the words "gangster" and "criminal" back to the Rumanian.

Hearing Art speak German, the man switched to that language. Art, now understanding what the man was saying, became very red-faced. Within moments, they were yelling at each other. Art would speak. The man would translate for the crowd, then lambast Art with his gangster-criminal diatribe. The argument grew more heated until Art yelled something that brought the man up short. The man turned and literally hissed his translation to the crowd. The crowd gasped. The guards became alert.

The officer ordered the crowd to move away and motioned several guards to enforce his order. After moving a short distance, the civilians fell to arguing among themselves. When things settled down, I asked Art what had happened.

"The poor guy said his wife and children had been killed in an air raid. The only things he had left were his pants. He'd borrowed the tennis shoes and shirt from friends. Then he started giving me a lot of crap about me being a gangster and a criminal. He finally made me mad."

"What did you say that made him so mad?"

"I told him that we didn't start the war; he and his Nazi partners started it."

Without knowing the man's problem, the anguish etching his thin face had been so deep I'd felt sorrow for him. When Art started speaking in German the man's anguish had turned to anger, then hatred.

Art's version of what had transpired couldn't possibly account for the crowd's and the guards' reaction. He had said something that shocked them, something that he didn't want to discuss with us. Now that the incident was over, he'd regained his composure and acted as though nothing had happened. The approach of a streetcar ended the matter.

The trolley, a tandem of decrepit cars, was much smaller than its American counterparts. While the officer entered the lead car to speak to the motorman, guards entered the trailing car and ordered the half-dozen passengers to leave. They hurriedly complied and entered the lead car, with hardly a glance in our direction. When the seats of our car became filled, the remaining guards boarded the lead car and the trolley moved forward.

The moment the cars started in motion, the rear of the lead car became jammed with angry people thrusting their arms through barred windows and shaking their fists at us. It seemed that everyone in the lead car was trying to get to the windows to berate the criminals and gangsters in the car following. I was reminded of a small child who had run into its house before summoning the courage to shout taunts at the neighborhood bully. The officer let them blow off steam for several blocks, then ordered them to be quiet. I almost enjoyed their comical display of vengeance. Nevertheless, I was relieved when they finally quieted. The remainder of the ride was uneventful.

XIV

A side from the parting jeers of streetcar passengers, we marched the distance to the schoolhouse without incident. Shortly before we turned onto a side street, a guard tower rising from inside the corner of a wooden fence told us we were nearing our destination.

The schoolhouse, a two-and-a-half story stone structure, crowded the narrow side street a sidewalk's-width from the curb. The school's window glass had been replaced with barbed wire. Despite threats from the guard in the corner tower and another posted in the street, prisoners crowded the windows to check out the new arrivals.

The appearance of some—their unkempt hair and clothing, some in no clothing except their underwear—reflected the rigors of captivity and reminded me of some Italian prisoners of war we'd pitied at Marrakesh.

A few wore beards and proud moustaches, and were well barbered. I searched the windows for a familiar face but found none. They in turn surveyed our group with a like purpose. The faces of some who searched in vain let loneliness reclaim them and pulled away from the windows. Others, despite the dehumorizing stresses of captivity, taunted us with the old cadet admonition, "You'll be sorry!" Art and I responded with clenched fists and equally earnest shouts of "Gangsters! Criminals!" The tower guard and our escort became threatening in their efforts to clear the windows and put an end to the spirited repartee between us and those inside, who seemed uncommonly happy about our arrival.

Entrance to the camp was by way of the rear yard, through a gate in a wooden fence. The fence, capped with several strands of barbed wire, continued along the street to a guard tower, then led away from the street to form the rear wall of the compound. Inside the yard, the entrance to the school was by a broad set of steps rising a half-story to a landing. There were no prisoners in the yard—only the gate guards and several others, spaced to ensure that we entered the building.

Standing on the landing were two armed guards and the maniacal "pear" that I'd encountered in the garrison latrine. The "pear" stared at us for a few moments, then turned and walked through the open doorway. Oh God, I thought, is that brutal bastard in charge of our camp? The officer who had accompanied us from the garrison motioned for us to follow.

We moved down a wide hall to a large room on the side of the building away from the street. It was the school's gymnasium. Except for rows of wooden bed frames, the room was empty. Three large, glassless windows strung with barbed wire were set in each of the side walls. Black shutters were mounted on the insides of the walls so they could be operated from within the room.

Art and I selected neighboring bunks near the center of the room and perched on the sideboards to await the next development. After ten or fifteen minutes guards came in and went to a locked door at the far end of the room. I hadn't thought of it until then, but there was another room, probably the gymn's equipment room, between the end of our room and the outside wall. If we could pick the lock, I thought, the room might provide an escape route. I maneuvered for a peek at the space beyond the partially closed door, but the guards were already returning with their arms loaded with mattresses and blankets.

While we were arranging our bedding, old prisoners came in to get the latest war news. They already knew of the invasion of Normandy and were disappointed that we couldn't add any meaningful details. For the first time I realized how little I knew about the ground war outside of Italy. Caught up in the demands of our own combat, I had never asked Intelligence how the war was going elsewhere, and I had rarely ever glanced at the *Stars and Stripes*—our newspaper. Cut off from the outside world, I would soon come to crave the nutrition of information as I would that of food.

Old inmates filled us in on camp routines, and inquired about our units and about friends who were still flying or had been shot down. Upon learning that I was a Cottontail, my inquisitor would laugh and ask, "When are they gonna send you guys your aircraft so you can start flying missions?" I accepted their good-natured ribbing and assumed that the camp held a large contingent of Cottontails.[1]

1. With twenty American bomb and six fighter groups in action over Rumania, an equal distribution of prisoners would come to less than 5 percent of the total per bomb group. As it was, of the 1,127 Americans returned from Rumania, 133 of them (12 percent) were

During our getting-acquainted session with the "old heads" (men shot down in April and May), we were officially welcomed by the Senior American Officer (SAO) of the camp, a major. The son of a bitch marched into our room and proceeded to inform us that *he* was in command; that while it was our duty to escape, we *would not*; and that we *would not* do anything that could upset the routine of the camp. "Your gunners," he continued, "are in a camp located in a military hospital near the marshaling yards. The commander of both camps is Lieutenant Colonel Victor Ioanid. You will respect him but will come to me on all matters."

His clipped manner of speech, and "Gentlemen this" and "Gentlemen that" bespoke a warped perspective as to who and where we were. Indeed, had we not been where we were I would have thought his manner comical. Instead, apprehension squeezed my gut. The prospect of being commanded by a man with deep-rooted psychological problems was grim. I was about to speak out when his abrupt "Carry on, gentlemen!" probably saved me from a court-martial. Watching him march away I thought, "Piss on you, Buster!"

The mutinous thoughts coursing through my mind were unsettling. "What the hell could you do with a guy like that, ignore him?" I asked Art. My growing discomfort ended with a shout from the hallway: "Chow call!" We scrambled for the door.

The mess hall, a room the same size as ours, was located in the basement directly beneath us. We had only to walk out our door, onto the stairwell, and down to the mess hall at the foot of the stairs. We'd been told that the best air raid shelter in the building was a small space beneath the stairs at the basement floor. On the way down I noted the concrete and steel construction of the staircase and mentally agreed that the point was well taken. Getting to the shelter first would pose a problem, but our vantage on the stairwell gave us a good shot at it.

Cottontails. The next largest contingents were from two more groups of the 47th Wing: the 449th, with ninety-seven prisoners, the 376th with eighty-four. The third largest contingent, eighty-five, was from the 463rd, a B-17 group. The reader is cautioned that the prisoner figures do not accurately reflect aircraft losses. For example, of the ninety 47th Wing aircraft lost over Rumania, twenty-eight were from the 450th and twenty-seven from the 449th. The 98th and 376th shared the remaining thirty-five losses. The only valid statistical conclusion that one can draw, in view of the large population of 450th men, is that Cottontail crews had been more fortunate in bailing out of their aircraft.

Rectangular tables with flanking wooden benches were arranged in rows throughout the dining room. Each table seated ten prisoners, five to a side. One of the old heads, Capt. Theodore Stanley, was waiting for us. Ted led us to a table midway into the room, abutting the wall. After we took our seats, Ted briefed us on the mess routine.

We would sit at the same table each day, and in a specified order. The order of seating was determined as we were now sitting. It was necessary to establish a "pecking order" and routine to insure that each received his fair share of those items of food that would be placed on the end of the table to be passed along. We would keep our seating order throughout the day, then shift each morning. This allowed the wall-men from the previous day to have first access to the strawberry jam served at breakfast. It was a matter of conscience that the two men at the head of the table would spread a bare amount of the jam on their bread. As the bowls progressed down each side of the table, the amount one dared take became progressively less. By the time the bowls reached the far end of the tables, the amount of jam left was often little more than a smear in the bowl. Had it not been for the rotation system, the portioning of the jam would have caused serious problems. Even at that, the daily disappearing act often brought strong remarks from the men seated next to the wall.

The food was brought to the tables by strange-sounding fellows who turned out to be Russian prisoners. Although friendly, their sanitation practices were not compatible with our more delicate constitutions. Had it not been for the efforts of Ted and Lt. Anthony Namiotka, our health would have suffered even more.

The kitchen was run by a Rumanian captain whom Ted considered a reasonable man. The captain purchased our food from nearby markets. Originally the diet had been a routine of wormy soups, hard salami, and hard bread containing foreign substances of which the most notable found so far were a fence staple and glass, and the combination guaranteed diarrhea. While they were given only limited access to the kitchen, on several occasions Ted and Tony accompanied the captain to market. However, the increasing hostility of civilians ended the practice. Despite such barriers, our mess officers were able to improve the quality of the fare.

Communication with the captain and cooks involved four languages. Ted and Tony would discuss some situation in English. Then Ted would speak French to the captain. Tony, who was fluent in Polish, could make himself understood to the Russians and could understand enough of their language to translate in English to Ted. Ted would complete the cycle in French to the captain.

The food left much to be desired. We were each given a small bowl of soup, another small bowl of chopped salad, a thin slice of dark bread, and a mug of dark liquid that looked like coffee—if you drank it straight away. I didn't. Its aroma, a scent that I couldn't identify, worried me until I decided the stuff changing color in the mug was potable. After the first swallow, it wasn't too bad. More important, it was hot. After a few weeks, I came to like it.

The salad, what there was of it, was lettuce garnished with bits of watercress, onion, cucumber, and sometimes radish, but with no dressing. Except for a random bit of bitter cucumber, the salad's only flavor was "green." Eating it was much akin to playing Russian roulette. One never knew when a bite would savage one's taste buds with the bitterness of gall. I tried keeping track of each bite, an inventory as it were, in an effort to identify which bite was likely to be bitter. I never won.

The soup was the centerpiece of the meal. It contained the minimum number of strands of cabbage to qualify for the name. There was little else to distinguish it except bits of matter that looked suspiciously like bug particles. We were lucky at that. The old heads delighted in regaling us with tales of their early fare. On several occasions they'd been treated to a delicacy: sheep's-head soup. It had been a challenge to get through a bowl of the stuff in the hope that one wouldn't encounter a large eyeball staring up from the spoon or rotten teeth rattling in the bowl.

Some claimed the bread to be the centerpiece. Indeed, the caloric content and strong flavor of the bread were strong points in support of that contention. It was a peasant rye, so hard and stale that I was baffled as to how it had been sliced. I tried to cut it with the short hacksaw blade from my escape kit, but the teeth gummed up and wouldn't faze the tough slice. With some effort it could be broken with one's fingers. I tried soaking it in the barley brew, but that was too time-consuming. Prying it between clenched teeth worked best. I could break off a small piece and chew it with reasonable results, but one never did that before banging it against the tabletop. Striking the table was intended to divest the bread of its tenants: weevils. As often as not, the tiny creatures would literally rain out of a slice. It was easy to tell the rye seed from the weevils; seed doesn't squirm in protest at being evicted from room and board. Although I never knew how the bread was sliced, I did learn how it was brought from the bakery. It arrived in a horse-drawn cart that was also used to haul cow manure for the guards' garden. Nothing was too good for gangsters and criminals.

If one's mind was not allowed to dwell on the weevils, the saliva-moistened bread was tasty. The bug-particled soup was more difficult to negotiate, but the slivers of cabbage won the flavor contest. I ate them: every particle.

Eating this food was not without its humorous side. After a week or so I concocted a spiel to use on new prisoners. I'd explain in detail about the weevils and the fresh protein inhabiting the soup. "Don't worry about it," I'd tell them, "No one can eat the food at first. After you've been here a week, you'll be so hungry you'll shake out the weevils, dip out the roaches, and savor the rest. Toward the end of the second week, you'll be so hungry you'll eat the food, bugs and all. By the end of the third week, if anything tries to get away, you'll catch it and put it back in the bowl."

After lunch, Art and I drifted about, chatting with old inmates and looking for past acquaintances. I found one: a copilot whom I'd known at Colorado Springs. The only officer of his crew to survive, he had been shot down on his first mission. He didn't know how his NCOs had fared, but believed that they'd gotten out of the aircraft. It was a subject that had been on my own mind and I didn't know what to do about it. At the moment I could only hope that they were together at the other camp. However, what the SAO and others had said about the place being near the marshaling yards gave me second thoughts as to their safety.

Their camp had already experienced several near-misses by American bombs intended for the marshaling yards. In one extraordinary instance a bomb had hit a hospital building next to the prison compound. Although the building was not part of the camp, it was the building in which our wounded were kept. The bomb hit the far end of it, did extensive damage, and killed a number of Rumanian soldiers. Americans at the opposite end of the building were unhurt. The incident left Rumanians with a superstitious belief about the accuracy of our bombsights. Some were convinced that the bomb had been intentionally dropped on the Rumanian end of the building. The story was the kind from which legends are born. Legend aside, the story deepened my concern for my gunners' safety.

Art and I spent most of the afternoon inspecting the the schoolhouse and the floor plan as well as where the guards were stationed, their alertness, and what the guards in the towers would do if we stuck our heads out the windows. The inside guards were older men of peasant stock who either ignored us or became fearful when we tried to talk to them. Our guess was that they were illiterate and poorly trained. Although the tower guard at the street intersection looked to be the same type, he wasn't. Each time we poked our heads out of a window he'd yell at us and wave us back inside. If we didn't withdraw our heads immediately, he'd raise his rifle and aim it at us. Easily the most aggressive guard we saw, he'd bear watching as a potential source of trouble. I wondered—fleetingly—if he would shoot. His actions convinced me that I didn't want to risk finding out.

The floor plan of the building was E-shaped, with the gym wing forming the center arm of the E. The center hall, about ten feet in width, ran the length of the building and connected with entrances at each end. The main entrance was at the front of the building, at the sidewalk. Its doors were kept locked and a dense barbed wire barrier on the entrance steps sealed the doors from the hallway. We had entered the building at the south end. The doors at the north end were locked. However, by looking out a window of a room at the north end we could see a small yard and the buildings on the far side of the wide street we'd marched on as we approached the school. We couldn't see the street or its streetcar tracks directly in front of the school because of the board fence. However, looking across the northeast corner of the fence where the tower guard who'd threatened us was posted, we had a good view of the street for a short distance before it disappeared beyond a wooden building, a tavern, sitting on the corner opposite the guard tower. To our left an interior board fence connected the front of the school to a brick building which seemed to form the west boundary of the prison com-pound. This interior fence also created an inaccessible yard next to the gym that projected westward from the main body of the school. In effect, the interior yard was a no-man's-land between the wall of the gym and the front yard of the school. But to be an effective barrier to escape, the interior yard would have to be manned during the night. I made a mental note to check that as soon as night fell.

Inside the building, classrooms—sleeping areas for the prisoners —lined both sides of the main hall and the wings. The second floor was identical to the first except that the room above the gym was the school auditorium, and there were windows in place of doors at the ends of the main hallway.

The main stairwell sat in the center of the building, on the west side of the hall. It ran from the basement to the attic. The stairs leading from the second floor to the attic were blocked by a dense entanglement of barbed wire which the Rumanians thought impenetrable. It wasn't. The old heads had worked an indiscernible passage through the wire so they could hide during head counts. By varying the number of men in hiding, it was possible to make the Rumanians think that prisoners had escaped when there had been no escape. It was a useful device, one designed to keep Colonel Ioanid confused and off balance. The ruse was effective.

The poorly lit basement had the same central hall and room configuration as the upper floors. It wasn't off-limits to us, but for various reasons most of its numerous rooms were kept locked. Opposite the dining hall, next to the stairwell, there was a tiny canteen where we could buy soap, cigarettes, toothbrushes—but no toothpaste—and toilet paper. Next to the canteen was a locked room filled with weapons, ammunition, bombsights, radios, clothing, etc., items that had been salvaged from our wrecked aircraft. I thought it strange that such salvage would be kept in the building with the POWs, especially the machine guns and ammunition. At the end of the hall was the boiler room, which was also our shower room. Just north of the stairwell, on the opposite side of the hall, was a small room that was kept sealed by a gate fashioned of iron bars. It looked like a jail cell, and on occasion was used as such. The standing-height tunnel led to a manhole in the street. Mentally I bet that the manhole cover was welded shut. Col. Ioanid—called "Fat Stuff" by the old heads—had an office and sleeping quarters in two rooms just inside the basement entrance. A Rumanian lieutenant, known as Cockeyed Pete, lived in another of the basement rooms.

Art and I agreed that getting outside of the building wouldn't be too difficult. One way would be to lower oneself out a window overlooking the side street, then cross the street to the tree area surrounding an Eastern Orthodox church which sat only sixty or seventy feet away. Getting through the window would be child's play. The barbed wire was very loose. If necessary, we could easily cut it with our hacksaw blades. We couldn't see a guard on the street, but old heads assured us that at least one was posted there during the night hours. It would be easy enough to check his position and activities when the time came.

Many of the prisoners who had been in the camp for weeks and months tended to be lethargic and noncommunicative, particularly on the subject of escape. Several were openly suspicious. Others tended to look down their noses at us. We were the new kids on the block. We were untested, and hadn't paid our dues in sharing their common misery. No one came right out and said as much, but many appeared to harbor feelings of tenure-seniority. I understood the basis of their attitude—the air raids they had endured without the benefit of shelters and the terror that gripped them when they'd suffered a diphtheria epidemic in May. I didn't challenge their superior position of experience in suffering the ravages of being a prisoner; but to me, being senior meant sharing their experience in a helpful way with the new prisoners. As it was, if we didn't know the right question to ask many of them would tell us nothing. Fortunately, several were quite helpful, especially on giving the background of the guards.

Most of the guards were older men. The old heads believed them to be mostly illiterate farmers who spent six month tours in the army between harvesting and planting new crops. Younger, more physically fit men were sent to combat. During the course of our inquiry, we picked up a good bit of history on the various POW camps, and the town's "gangster" prejudice about Americans.

April 4 had dawned clear over Rumania. Improved flying weather and the Fifteenth Air Force's strike the day before against the marshaling yards at Budapest, Hungary, and Brod, Yugoslavia, meant the time was drawing near when the new American armada of heavy bombers in Italy would unleash its fury on Rumanian oil refineries and other targets vital to the Axis Powers' war efforts.

At 10:00 A.M., air raid sirens started their wail and sent Bucharest's citizens scurrying to neighborhood slit trenches and to shelters in the basements of substantial buildings. It was their first practice air raid alert. Many grumbled over the Germans having disrupted their lives with the unwanted drill. Consequently, when the alarms sounded again, later that afternoon, many ignored the warning and passed it off as another German harassment. That was most unfortunate.

The Fifteenth hit the Bucharest marshaling yards and an airfield with 313 B-17s and B-24s. Pressed by heavy fighter attacks and intense antiaircraft fire, eight bombers (seven were from the 449th) went down. On the ground, the lack of civilian reaction, and stray bombs resulting from the fierce air battle, caused the deaths of at least five thousand people. Rumor placed the death toll as high as fifteen thousand. The low-level raid against the Ploesti oil refineries the previous year had killed only one civilian, and that was due to a striken bomber crashing into a prison building. Whereas the low-level raiders were respected, the large number of civilian deaths caused by the Bucharest raid created so much anger within the populace that the high-level crews came to be viewed as gangsters and criminals.

The following day, April 5, the Fifteenth had returned in force to strike oil refineries at Ploesti—the opening round of what would become one of the war's greatest and most bitterly fought air campaigns. The resulting battle saw thirteen more heavy bombers (five from the 450th) go down. In two days the number of American prisoners of war in Rumania virtually doubled.

The low-level raiders were being held in a boardinghouse at Timisul, a small village in the Transylvanian Alps some twenty miles south of Brasov. Since the facility was already crowded and there would undoubtedly be many hundreds more prisoners taken before the war ended, another camp was needed to hold the new prisoners. Initially they were incarcerated in a military compound, the Royal Garrison, one of seven old forts that had ringed medieval Bucharest. Life for the new captives was uncertain at best.

Officers were locked up in a small one-story building set in the compound yard. NCOs were consigned to rooms in a multistory barrack that formed one end of the compound. The building also served as a barrack for German and Rumanian soldiers.

The prisoners were kept closely confined and were given little food. Indeed, their captors appeared to be at a loss as to what should be done with them. Medical care for those who became ill was practically nonexistent. Interestingly, their Rumanian guards were highly fearful of them.

After a few weeks of starvation and severe crowding, the prisoners threatened to escape if they weren't given more food and allowed to go outside. The Rumanians relented and let them have access to the cobblestone courtyard, but not before they set up a machine-gun post to cover the area. One machine-gunner, a dark-skinned peasant who posessed a bad temper, rankled the prisoners with his harsh attitude and threatening manner. One day, when a prisoner called him tigan—a gypsy—he sprayed the yard with machine-gun fire. Fortunately, no one was injured.

There had been several escapes from the garrison but none were ultimately successful. Lt. Joseph Athenas and two of his gunners escaped and were gone for three days. The Rumanians knew almost at once that the NCOs were missing but they didn't find out about Joe until he was recaptured. The officers in Joe's room had stuffed his fleece-lined helmet to simulate his head. Rolled blankets and a pair of borrowed shoes protruding from beneath a covering blanket made it appear that he was fast asleep. During the day the ruse was disassembled. The first night that he was gone the bed-check guard was frightened away by a prisoner giving a classic performance of a dog barking.

Bed checks and daylight head counts were often amusing. Prisoners would move about and thereby prevent an accurate count. The guard, thinking someone had escaped, would summon a corporal or sergeant, who would then be subjected to the same treatment. The second or third counter would then summon an officer, who would count the prisoners correctly and berate his own men for their stupidity.

The most life-threatening aspect of life in the garrison came from air raids. On the night of May 3, an RAF bomber crashed nearby. During the final moments of its death dive, it sounded as if it would crash inside the compound. Then on the night of May 6, a bomb exploded only fifteen yards from the officers' building. The following night the RAF returned and a bomb exploded in the roadway separating the prisoners' buildings. The officers' building suffered major damage, but no one was seriously injured. Again on the verge of mutiny, on May 8 the prisoners were marched to their new home at the schoolhouse, Scoala Normala Caterina, or Central Seminary, formerly a teachers' school for women. Within another month the influx of new prisoners had swelled the population of the school and the garrison to the point where they had both become overburdened. Consequently the officers still at the garrison were brought to the schoolhouse, and the NCOs at both locations were moved to a permanent camp set up for them in the westernmost building of the Regina Elizabeth Military Hospital.[2]

While wandering about the school, I noticed an aspect of captivity that was forboding to me. It was the tendency of some men to lie on their bunks, lost in loneliness. They seemed to be afflicted with the same terrible malaise of hopelessness I'd endured during my first days of captivity. I wondered if after a while I would again succumb to that immobilizing trauma. The more fortunate prisoners, those with the ability to accommodate themselves to their circumstances, were busily chatting, reading, or playing bridge with cards that had been carefully cut in half to form two decks. Bridge tournaments went on around the clock.

There were night people other than the inveterate card players. They were those who unhappily found themselves to be delectable to lice and the bedbug's palate. By staying awake at night and sleeping during the day, they were bitten less frequently. It seems that bedbugs were less ferocious in daylight. One fellow we saw was in pitiful shape. On one leg alone he had several scabs that were easily larger than my hand. Worse, I saw no indication of medication on his sores. Medical care, as evidenced by those being literally eaten alive, was almost nonexistent. Several diphtheria victims could only make whooshing noises when they tried to speak.

What disturbed me most was the prisoners' seeming lack of cohesiveness, that unifying force that organizes men's desires and energy. I couldn't tell if the problem was caused by cliquism that fragmented them into small groups, or poor leadership, or if the pressures of their circumstances had demoralized them to the point where their whole thought turned inward. I came to believe that part of the problem was a lack of leadership and organization.

By the time the evening chow call sounded, Art and I were uneasy

2. By the time I arrived at the camp, Fifteenth Air Force had bombed Rumanian targets on twenty of the preceeding ninety-five days. During this time the British lost 30 Halifax and Wellington bombers over Rumania, and we lost 113 four-engine bombers over Ploesti alone, not including the aircraft lost on the August 1, 1943, raid. Those 113 bombers carried 1,130 men, of whom approximately 40 percent survived to become prisoners. By the time the last mission against Ploesti was flown, on August 19, 1944, that target complex had cost us 223 B-24 and B-17 aircraft: approximately 2,230 men. Add to those figures 45 British bombers and the American fighters that were lost, and even a 40 percent survival rate pressed the Rumanians in their efforts to keep up with the influx of prisoners.

and unsure as to how we'd approach captivity. Neither of us was willing to bide his time lying on his bunk or playing cards. We both needed something to concentrate on, something to occupy our minds, preferably something that would keep us busy mentally and physically. Our efforts to uncover organized escape activities had drawn a gamut of reactions ranging from blank stares to near open hostility. All in all we had been summarily rejected by many of the senior inmates, and we were angry. Art and I agreed; we'd form our own clique.

Dinner was almost identical to lunch. There was the weevily bread, ersatz coffee, and the inevitable cabbage soup. But the salad was different, and there was a bit more of it. Resting on the top of the lettuce were several marble-sized boiled potatoes, and a small chunk of white cheese shot with black particles that looked suspiciously like mouse manure. The cheese was made from goats' milk and contained so much acid it bit back. It was only a small piece, perhaps a half-inch square by an inch or so long. In view of the way it stung the inside of my mouth, I was thankful it was not larger. To my delight, the cooks had left the bitter out of the salad. There was just enough of the food to whet my appetite and leave an angry gnawing inside me. I wondered if in time my stomach would eventually shrink enough to spare me the chronic feeling of hunger.

Under other circumstances, the golden glow flowing in through the gymnasium windows would have created a moment to treasure. As it was, the waning light bathing the barren walls filled the room with a warmth shredded by loneliness. What conversation there was was hardly more than a murmur. The changing of the guard in the hallway had been noisy, but now a vacant peace came with the dusk and ended the long and tiresome day. I was on the verge of dozing off when someone flicked on the room lights, thereby signaling more conversation. I was sitting on my bunk, chatting with Art, when we were interrupted by guards—on the ground, outside our windows —shouting something that we couldn't understand. After a few calls that grew angrier with each repetition, I made out, "Nix Illumina!" (Actually, "niche illumina.")

"Nix Illumina!" "Nix Illumina!" "Nix Illumina!"

"What the hell's that all about?" someone asked.

I could tell from Art's quizzical expression that he might know the meaning of the words, but he wasn't certain.

It wasn't full night, but the dark filling the open windows was black in contrast to the lighted walls. We were sitting on our bunks casting inquiring glances at each other, when the voice on the north side of us became frantic.

"Nix Illumina! Nix Illumina!" The guard screamed, panic shrilling his voice.

Bang! Whiiinng! The ricocheting bullet tore a shower of plaster from the ceiling.

Bang! Bang! Bang!

Whinggg! Whinggg! Whinggg!

Guards standing on the ground on both sides of our wing of the building were firing their rifles upward through the open windows. We dived for the floor.

Guards in the hallway took up the call, "Nix Illumina," and the sound of running feet and excited voices approached the gym from the hall. The place was in bedlam!

Within moments, the room filled with Fat Stuff and guards. Sounding like a hog in a slaughterhouse, Fat Stuff ordered the guards to close the shutters.

The inside guards shouted at the outside guards to stop shooting so they could close them.

When the firing finally stopped, Fat Stuff, at the point of attacking the inside guards, relaxed and stepped into the room. A simple flick of the light switch beside the entrance door would have solved the whole problem. Fat Stuff had been within easy reach of the switch as he stood outside the door screaming at the guards. I concluded that our chief jailor didn't function well under pressure, and that could be bad.

At this point the SAO and an American lieutenant arrived on the scene in full huff. The SAO demanded to know what had happened. Art explained our side; the lieutenant, a Jewish lad, explained in Yiddish to Fat Stuff. Fat Stuff thought for a moment, then spoke in German to "Yiddish," who then translated to English.

"When night falls, you have to close the shutters or turn off the lights!" he admonished. "The Rumanians don't want British bombers to use the schoolhouse for their aiming point! 'Nix Illumina' means no lights."

I was astounded that the fat colonel wasn't raving mad at us. After seeing him try to mutilate one of his own the day before, I thought that the shooting would have caused him to lose all control of his temper when dealing with us. He was indeed a strange fellow. He was angry, but his anger was at the guards and the SAO, because we had not been told the blackout rules. Satisfied that we understood, Fat Stuff and his entourage departed, leaving us to our own thoughts.

The ricocheting bullets had left no doubt of the danger that had struck suddenly and violently. One doesn't treat the situation of bullets flying angrily about as anything other than a deadly affair that could recur at a moment's notice, for whatever reason. Such was the problem of being a prisoner of war: being at constant risk, at the mercy of one's captors. But there was something about the incident that made my initial fright give way to anger. It was the Yankee cursing coming from the older prisoners in the hallway. I resented their taking sides with the enemy by cursing us for the incident. In our ignorance, we were innocent. That knowledge only made the other prisoners' attitude toward us seem more despicable. But that wasn't what was nagging in the recesses of my mind. I didn't know what it was, but I wasn't going to let the feeling rest until I figured it out. The night being warm, we turned out the lights and opened the shutters.

Sitting in the darkened room, we reconstructed the sequence of events, from the sound of the first "Nix Illumina" to Fat Stuff's surprising behavior and the way he had rationalized the incident. It was as though he were trying to excuse our behavior; or else he was trying to pretend that nothing serious had occurred. No one doubted that he had considerable authority, but he apparently didn't have free rein with us. He had much more freedom to brutalize his own men. In view of the disdain in which the older prisoners held him, Fat Stuff was a man who could be swayed for our own benefit. He certainly had his amusing side.

Art sounded as though he'd enjoyed the excitement. To my way of thinking, ricocheting bullets were totally without humor. However, as we talked, I became caught up in the prankish aspects of the incident and was intrigued by the possibilities for taking advantage of the blackout rules to harass our captors. Art seemed to be of a similar frame of mind, as was Flight Lieutenant L. F. Tichbourne.

We'd met Tich, a Royal Australian Air Force pilot, at the Garrison. He and Ollie had struck up a friendship at the outset. A tall, rawboned specimen whose quiet toughness was born of experience, Tich never left any doubt where he stood on an issue. He knew himself, his capabilities, and had a decisiveness that bespoke an unshakable self-confidence.

Tich had the heart and soul of an adventurer. Before the war he'd been a gold miner, a "hard rock" man in western Australia. He and his two partners had run a profitable operation, but not one that would make them wealthy. They'd wrested just enough of the precious metal from the land to justify their labors. I felt that Tich hadn't suffered the privations of that existence for mere wealth. The yellow metal was likely his excuse for being there. But now, he had no reason for being cooped up in this schoolhouse. Being a prisoner of war offended him. His only thought was to get out of this place. Lying on the rough bedding in the black room, I wondered if he'd join Art and me in our efforts, whatever they turned out to be. As a result of the shooting incident, he'd become a willing conspirator, but like the rest of us he hadn't formed any ideas as to what our next move should be.

It had been a long and eventful day. Stretched out on the mattress, wondering if my navel was in fact resting on my spine, I suddenly realized that most of my pain and body stiffness had disappeared during the day. I tried lifting my legs and bending my knees. My legs worked, though not well and not without pain. Nevertheless, I was making progress toward full recovery. I pressed on my bandage. My leg was sore at the point of the wound, but it too was improving. In the morning, I would remove the bandage and let the air harden the scab. I was thinking about that, the wound and tomorrow, when . . .

XV

" . . . damn bedbugs!"

Frantic slapping and Green's angry voice penetrated my sleep-hazed mind. The slapping sound was the flat of his hand striking his flying suit. Willie was laughing at the comical figure, his knobby legs protruding from shorts as he danced about, attacking his clothing to dislodge repulsive tenants. I sat up to watch his exhibition of shadowboxing with the limp flying suit.

All were awake and checking their clothing. I looked down at my shorts and saw one of the ugly vermin creeping slowly along my right leg.

After flicking the unwanted visitor onto the floor and smacking it with a boot heel, I removed my shorts and checked them for additional members of the family. My shorts were clear.

Removing my undershirt, I found two more, which I turned into spots on the floor. Uninhibited cursing accompanied the sound of drumming bootheels. Everyone had a collection of the hateful creatures. Art, lying on his bunk with an amused look on his face, suppressed one comment after another. I wasn't certain of what was on his mind, but if it had to do with breakfast I didn't want to hear it.

"Cub, save those things and give them to the guards."

Given a different target, it was an intriguing idea. A handful of bedbugs in Fat Stuff's room might encourage him to fumigate the building. If we had had a container, I'd have saved the eleven bugs that I had picked off my flying suit and smashed on the floor. I was puzzled as to why they were so taken with my suit. I turned it inside out several times to make sure I'd removed all of them. Reluctant to put the suit back on, I joined the others by stripping the blanket off the mattress and carefully checking both items. No bugs. I took the mattress off the frame and checked all the boards. Still no bugs. It was hard to believe that all of them had crawled out of the mattress and onto my clothing, but finding no more I felt much better.

No one had been bitten. I wondered if I would enjoy the same immunity from bedbugs as I have from other insects. I don't know why—perhaps the reason has something to do with my chemistry —but mosquitoes, ticks, chiggers, and a host of nameless nemises that torment others ignore me.

The call to breakfast ended Operation Deadbug and sent us scurrying for the mess hall. The meal was as we'd been told. A cup of ersatz coffee, a thin slice of weevil-ridden bread, and strawberry jam. This being our first experience with the jam, there was none left for the men at the wall end of the table. Considering the sharp edge of hunger, the amount of grumbling from the end-men was slight. It would take us a while to adjust to the inequities and injustices of captivity. The condition of many of those who'd been here for three or four months indicated that an extended stay could hold serious consequences for our physical and mental well-being. In the long run we would suffer the ravages of starvation equally, but if we could maintain a sense of humor we would survive.

Following breakfast and throughout the day, Art and I circulated among the prisoners to learn as much as we could about the camp and the feasibility of escape. There had been several escapes from the schoolhouse but in each instance the escapees had been captured and returned to the camp within a matter of hours. The greater difficulty was not in getting out of the schoolhouse, but in remaining free. One escapee had been inveigled by a young woman, possibly a prostitute, who took him to her room, then excused herself to go and purchase a bottle of wine. She returned with two policemen. The three who had escaped from the garrison had done well while traveling at night. Misled by the ease with which they'd walked for two nights, they tried traveling during the day, only to be recaptured. Nevertheless, several of those with whom we spoke appeared determined to escape.

Our inquiries had still not turned up any evidence of an escape organization. Considering the necessity for secrecy, this was understandable. On the other hand, too much secrecy was not in the best interests of morale or the amount of aid that would be required from other prisoners to help the few who chose to escape carry out their plans.[1] For whatever their reasons, those intending to escape preferred

1. Many years later, I learned that there was an escape committee, and that a tunnel entrance was under construction beneath the steps of the stairwell at the left side of the stage. The stairs terminated in the basement, behind a locked door in the kitchen. The

to plan and work alone, or in groups of two or three at the most. On balance it appeared that the decision to escape, although it was our duty to do so, was a highly personal decision that had been exercised only by a few. Some persons of exceptional daring had made that choice. On the other hand, considering our lack of training and preparation for the difficult art, I could not fault those who hadn't attempted to do so. At the moment, escape for me was little more than a shadow of an idea tucked away in the recesses of my mind.

My disappointment at not finding an escape organization in operation was a small matter compared to my resentment over being greeted with suspicion each time we broached the subject. Being treated thus by fellow prisoners depressed and angered me. I felt as though I were an "outsider," and was indecisive as to what I should do. Without tangible objectives I would soon have no momentum or direction and would become as dispirited as many of those I'd met.

Following a skimpy dinner of cabbage soup, bitter salad, bread, and ersatz tea, we gathered in the gym to consider how we'd handle the "Nix Illumina" problem. Discussion was fruitless. No one relished ricocheting bullets, yet we did not want to give in to our captors. Twilight was accompanied by the weariness of useless talk. No decision had been made, and it appeared that the enemy had won by default.

I was sitting quietly on my bed watching the dark deepen to black beyond the open windows when our dilemma resolved itself in a most natural manner. I don't know which of us made the first move. Our response was spontaneous and universal. Before the first "Nix Illumina" faded into the night, everyone in the room dived for the floor. Immediately, an outside guard fired his rifle into the air, thereby setting up a chorus of "Nix Illuminas" accompanied by guards on both sides of the building firing through the open windows. About the time the guards emptied their rifles, a commanding voice quieted them.

Most of us were on our feet and wondering what would happen next, when an irate squeal announced the arrival of Fat Stuff and his

---

prisoners had learned to pick the lock of the stage door and would work at night using crude tools they'd fashioned or had smuggled into the camp. The tunnel was an ambitious undertaking requiring their chipping and scraping through at least two feet of concrete. Once through the concrete it would have taken many feet of earthen tunnel to pass under the west fence of the compound. While the secrecy of such a project is paramount, those responsible carried their security to the point where many prisoners were denied an element of hope that could have made their incarceration much less painful.

entourage. He wasn't just angry, he was nearly apoplectic. The Rumanian captain accompanying him, a stranger to us, was angry enough to be dangerous. The captain barked an order at a sergeant; the sergeant shouted at several guards, who went scurrying to close the shutters. At that moment, the SAO and his Yiddish-speaking interpreter arrived in their usual huff.

Fat Stuff screamed at the interpreter as though he were responsible for our refusal to cooperate. Instead of explaining what Fat Stuff had said, the lieutenant berated us for not complying with the blackout order. We gathered around the entourage and listened attentively. The expressions on most of the faces in our group registered resentment at the lieutenant's words. My own thought was, "Who the hell does this guy think he is?"

Red-faced and glowering at the lieutenant, Art addressed Fat Stuff directly.

"This is your prison camp, and you have many men. If you want the windows closed, have your men close them."

As the lieutenant intrepreted Art's speech in Yiddish, the expression on Fat Stuff's face was as though he'd discovered the wheel. I gained the impression that Fat Stuff found Art's suggestion to have merit. But the Rumanian captain's reaction was a picture of exploding fury. Whatever he was saying, it included the words "criminals" and "gangsters" and was spoken with much fury and indignation.

Considering their difference in rank, one would think that the colonel wouldn't tolerate his captain's refusal to obey an order, but not so. As the captain railed on, Fat Stuff appeared to agree with his logic and nodded agreement as he fixed his gaze on the Rumanian sergeant. The sergeant came to a stiff attention and looked as though he were being sentenced to fight on the Russian front.

The issue settled, Fat Stuff spoke briefly to the American lieutenant, then listened as though pleased with himself as the lieutenant interpreted. The lieutenant's look of amazement was fitting company for his words.

"The sergeant will close your shutters from now on."

Our SAO, who'd not uttered a word during the entire affair, stood dumbstruck for a moment, then turned and marched angrily from the room.

We had won a small victory by getting the concession from Fat Stuff and by frustrating the SAO, but we weren't satisfied. We didn't *want* a solution to the problem. Intuitively we wanted the conflict to continue. I felt angry, but I wasn't certain why. Perhaps it was an extension of the anger I felt toward the SAO and those prisoners who were hostile toward us because we had caused the first shooting incident. It could have been a reaction to the frustration I felt because of my misfortune in having been shot down and captured; it could have been the feeling of helplessness that had plagued me from the moment I'd looked up from that lonely field and watched the formations of bombers returning home. There was also an element of fear, and the desire to strike back in hope of eliminating the cause of my fear. In trying to rationalize my anger, none of my thoughts, singly or in any combination, offered a logical basis for my feelings. Uneasiness kept me awake for what seemed to be endless hours before weariness and sleep released my troubled mind.

I awakened late to hurried sounds of people scurrying for breakfast. I had slept soundly for a few hours, and felt refreshed and full of unbridled hunger. It was a curious aspect of my physiology. My mental alertness and vitality seem to peak with hunger. The lean 1930s back home had conditioned me to function despite the cavern in my belly.

Following a breakfast that only teased my hunger to new heights, I drifted about the corridor and rooms, trying to meet others and pick up information about the camp. For the first time, I met three more subjects of His Majesty's Empire. Two of them, Captain Bird and Flying Officer Egles, were delightful fellows. The third was a tiny weasel of a man who would have been alone in any crowd.

Snotty, as he introduced himself, was a living Joe Blftsk. His intent stare gave me the impression that he saw rather than heard words. Obviously uncomfortable in his filthy, woolen uniform, he exuded a sense of remoteness as distant as his homeland, New Zealand. He was a warrant officer, but the Rumanians didn't understand his rank and had shifted him from the officers' camp to the NCO camp, then back to the schoolhouse. Snotty was not only betwixt and between in rank, but he seemed lost within the strata of ordinary humanity. During the ensuing weeks, I noticed that hardly anyone ever spoke to him. All in all, his appearance and manner were as unsavory as his name.

"How do you spell your name?"

"It's Snotty—S-N-O-T-T-Y," he spelled laboriously in his native brogue.

"Is that your real name?"

"No. It comes from my uniform."

I'd been wondering about his uniform. I'd never seen one quite like it except in movies about the British army on this or that far-flung frontier. It resembled a "dress" uniform except it was built of rough, gray wool and utilized typical British trousers with a baggy seat. But it was his jacket that caught my eye.

The jacket was tight-fitting, came only to the waist, and was ornately adorned with brass buttons. Two rows of buttons ran from the waist to the tight stand-up collar. Each sleeve had a row of at least a dozen small buttons extending from the cuff almost to the elbow, but on the outer face rather than the rear edge of the sleeve, as is the modern custom in tailoring.

"Warrant officers wear the uniform of naival midshipmen," he continued in his nasal accent. "H'it comes from the auld daiys of sailing b'fore the mast. Midshipmen were young blokes with runny noses which thiey wiped on their sleeves. So the naivy sewed buttons on their sleeves to keep them from wiping their snot," he said as he dragged the row of buttons on his right sleeve across his more than ample nose.

Engaging the little fellow in friendly conversation had been a mistake. For the next several days he dogged me like a dirty shadow, saying little, just peering intently at my words with his weasel eyes.

Captain Bird, a South African pilot of a night-flying B-24, was a clean-cut, quiet man, perhaps thirty or so, who always looked as though he were "on post" in his neat summer uniform replete with tunic and ribbons. I enjoyed his colorful tales about life in South Africa, how the natives made a strong drink of betel nuts chewed and spat by the women and left to ferment in hollow logs. One version of the potent brew, "Scorpio," was so named because of the live scorpions added to the concoction to give it "kick." The scorpions added so much kick that it was unlawful to brew the deadly drink.

In time, because of his quiet courage and sedate attitude toward our circumstances, Bird would become an emotional anchor for me. During low moments, I'd seek him out and elicit a fine tale of the Empire's early battles with the fierce Zulu, whose resistance to the white settlers was not unlike that of our own American Indians.

Fine fellow though Bird was, my favorite was Flying Officer Dudley C. (Pop) Egles. Pop was a big, garrulous man who'd probably never had a down day in his twenty-two years. Embattled from the outset of the war, Pop had been shot down twice during the North African campaign. He'd survived a night ditching in the Bay of Sollum, been rescued, then crashed in his Wellington in the desert some three hundred miles behind the German lines. The long walk had relieved him of the soles of his feet.

On the night of May 7, his Halifax had been shot to ribbons over Bucharest by a rocket-firing Messerschmitt 110. He had bailed out, been captured, and was impatient for our release so he could "Give the ruddy bastards another go." I'd soon discover that no matter how close the bombs thundered around our camp, the Mad Englishman, rather than huddle in fear or safety in the basement, would sit in an upstairs window or pace about while shouting, "Press on, Chaps! Give 'em a bloody good pasting. Come back tomorrow!" We who huddled found Pop's spirit damnably indomitable.

Following a supper of our usual fare and half-humorous speculation about the bits of brown in the cabbage soup, Art and I wandered hungrily about pausing to watch several bridge tournaments and to listen to a heated argument about when the war would be over. Neither debater advanced convincing, even rational, points upon which I could foresee the end of our captivity. News of the invasion of Normandy had given the prisoners renewed hope, but that was short-lived. The thrust of most arguments was related to the impact of the invasion upon Germany's will to fight. For my money, Normandy was a remote place where too many men were dying for too little territory gained. My own opinion was that it would take more than an invasion to bring the enemy to heel. Nevertheless, these friendly dissidents held views upon which they were willing to risk large sums of money that they didn't have to prove their point.

It was getting dark outside. Tiring of bridge and banter, Art and I made our way to the gymnasium. Most of the fellows were already stretched out on their crude beds, or searching mattresses and blankets for bedbugs. I was weary from lack of sleep and the pressure of boredom, and had found a reasonably comfortable position on my bunk, when all hell broke loose.

I raised up just as Art threw the Rumanian sergeant back through the doorway. In an instant everyone was up and rushing for the door to assist Art, whom we thought was being attacked by the sergeant.

By the time I reached the doorway, Art had the old sergeant bent over the stairwell railing and appeared to be trying to heave him into space. The guard standing opposite the stairwell had jacked a round into the chamber of his rifle and was yelling at the top of his lungs as he gestured menacingly with his bayonetted rifle.

Before any of us could crowd through the doorway, other prisoners from our floor and the floor above arrived on the scene and added considerably to the noise and confusion.

Within moments, the combatants were separated and held apart, though still struggling in their fury. By the time the SAO arrived, Fat Stuff, the Rumanian captain, and several guards were screaming and kicking their way through the press of prisoners. Art, spotting Fat Stuff's approach, launched into an impassioned speech—in German.

No longer angry, and obviously enjoying his own words, Art was eloquently inviting a confused and angry Fat Stuff to step into the gym to discuss the matter "as gentlemen."

Fat Stuff ordered the growing army of guards to disperse the prisoners to their rooms, then followed Art into our quarters. I had so much trouble convincing an officious guard that I belonged in the gymnasium that our conversation moved rapidly toward a return to the former state of violence. Embarrassed by his error and a sharp rebuke from the captain, the guard gave me his blackest look as he lowered his rifle and let me pass.

"Was ist los, Hauptman Staveley?" Fat Stuff asked in German.

Art replied through the interpreter: "Your sergeant came into our quarters."

"Hauptman Staveley, I told him to," Fat Stuff replied through the interpreter. "He came to close your shutters."

Art was grim as he spoke. "Herr Colonel, your sergeant is an enlisted man. These are officers' quarters. We do not allow enlisted men in our quarters."

The SAO, aghast at Art's effrontery, was about to speak, when he too was struck with the expression forming on Fat Stuff's face. As the interpreter translated Art's reply, Fat Stuff nodded an almost imperceptible agreement that lent understanding to the amazed expression seizing his red face.

The bastard had been hoisted on his own petard. His constant attitude toward his own soldiers was one of hateful fury; yet he had ordered an enlisted man to enter officer quarters. It didn't matter that we were the enemy. The inviolable separation of officers and troops that existed in his own mind, ridiculous as it was to us, was a sacred relationship to him. The captain, apparently the commander of our guards, held a different view. Having heard Art's reply, he was black with rage. His immediate solution to the problem was to shoot Art; and he was more than willing to personally do that with his own pistol, which he fondled in its belt holster.

Fat Stuff listened attentively, then argued with him for the better part of a minute. Fearing that he was losing the argument, or for whatever reason, the giant gnome snapped to red-faced attention and squealed the captain and guards out of the room. The last of our unwanted visitors had hardly cleared the door when we looked at each other in amazement, then howled with laughter over the totally preposterous outcome of a dangerous situation.

The incident had developed on the spur of the moment. Art had been to the latrine and was returning when the sergeant followed him into the room. In a flash Art thought of the "officers' quarters" reason to refuse him entry and had intended only to start an argument. He'd stopped and turned so quickly the sergeant collided with him. Thinking he was being attacked by a dangerous enemy, the sergeant fought back. At that point Art had no choice but to run or defend himself. Lying in the darkened room, I wondered what the nimble-minded Staveley would think of next.

XVI

By morning, the story of Art's scuffle with the sergeant had spread throughout the camp. Many of the prisoners found humor in the incident, while others gave us hostile looks. Several confronted us with scathing comments and charges that "You're going to get somebody killed!"

They had a point. The incident could have easily gone in another and more ominous direction. Nevertheless I resented their attitude, which I considered too docile. There was a great imbalance of fear in our circumstances that needed to be either modified or compensated for. Fresh from combat, my instinct was to join forces and continue the war by other means. We weren't just captives, we were under the uninhibited control of an enemy, and our wits marshaled in common purpose were our only defense. My impression of life in the camp, except for rare moments of humor, was that it had become a litany of helplessness and fear. I couldn't see myself submitting to quiet captivity, vegetating until the war was over, hoping and praying that I would survive. Neither did I want to die or be responsible for the death or suffering of others. It was a dilemma for which I had no solution. The more I thought about it, the more I became lost in its complexities and emotional aspects. My own emotions, particularly my anger over having been rejected by so many of the older prisoners, worried me as much as did their rejection. I read my emotions as a danger sign and knew that I would somehow have to rise above them. Talking to the Britishers helped. Unlike the Americans, Pop Egles and Captain Bird seemed to be enjoying the scenario unfolding in the gymnasium.

Following breakfast, Fat Stuff, suspecting the incident with the sergeant may have been a cover for an escape, held a surprise roll call. With no forewarning, we were rounded up and herded into the northern part of the first floor hall. Fat Stuff sat at a small table positioned at the south end of the hall and checked each prisoner's dogtags against a roster as we moved past him. After being checked, each prisoner was shunted to the rear yard until the count could be completed.

The old heads were jubilant. The procedure not only gave us an opportunity to confuse Fat Stuff, but we would get a chance to go outside in the sunlight. They had been campaigning for weeks to get the SAO to insist that they be allowed to go outside each day to relax or exercise in the open air. Fat Stuff, fearing someone would escape from the crowded yard, would not hear their pleas, and the SAO was too ineffective to force the issue.

The count proceeded with what I figured must be the usual delays. Several of the old heads couldn't produce their dog tags, claiming they'd left them in their room, and the guards wouldn't let the prisoners return for them. Fat Stuff was furious. He had never been able to count the prisoners with the assurance that he had the right number. Unknown to him, on previous counts several prisoners had made their way through the maze of barbed wire on the upper stairs and had hidden in the attic. On other occasions, after having been counted, they found ways to pass their dog tags to those who had not been counted. When Fat Stuff came to a name the second time, he would assume he'd made an error. He couldn't let his own men know this. Believing that he was responsible for the error must have been painful to him. His irascible behavior during each count indicated that he dreaded the duty.

When I stepped to his table he snapped, "Dog tag!"

I removed my tag chain from around my neck and dropped it clinking onto the table.

He stared at the tags for a few moments, searched the lists for my name, then glared hatefully as he spoke.

"Zecon Lootinit Coobins?"

"Da!" I snapped back at him.

"Not you tag!" he squealed.

"Da! My tag," I clipped, staring over his head at the blank wall behind him. I wanted to laugh at the silly bastard, but didn't dare. From the way his bald head was glistening, I figured he'd already screwed up the count and was in no mood for further harassment.

He slammed the tags onto the table and pointed angrily toward the exit door.

"Aus!"

I went.

I wasn't outside for longer than ten glorious minutes when he abandoned the count and ordered everyone back inside. He was upset with us but was venting his wrath on the guards who were dodging his blows and panicking in their fervor to herd us inside as quickly as possible.

The head count wasn't the only surprise that Fat Stuff had in store for the upstarts living in the gym. When we returned to our room, we were greeted with the sound of voices and busy activity outside the north face of our wing. Soldiers were busily building something beneath the center window. We were puzzled by the long timbers and the pile of boards lying on the ground. Determining what they were doing was made more difficult by the guards' threats whenever one of us attempted to peer outside to monitor the construction. By midafternoon, however, their purpose was clear. They were building a guard tower close against the outside wall. By dark, our fate was sealed. The tower was manned by a guard with a "grease gun" which he could poke through the open window to spray the inside of our room with lethal messengers.

For three days, the battle had been joined. On this fourth night we capitulated. At the sound of the first "Nix Illumina," someone thoughtfully flicked the light switch. Resentful in our defeat, the roomful of men was quiet long before the last eyelid closed in fitful sleep.

I awakened early with an uncomfortable feeling in my gut and headed for the latrine. Yesterday, Sunday, had been the day that held the one variation in our weekly diet. At breakfast, in place of the ersatz tea, our mugs had been filled with sour milk. The Rumanians claimed the milk had been soured by our bombing, a ridiculous claim at best. Whatever the cause, sour milk was a Sunday staple, and the older prisoners drank it without comment. I was reluctant to for fear of becoming ill or worse. But hunger and the instinctive need for sustenance caused me to drink the fouled stuff. True to my expectation, today I had diarrhea.

The latrine was a replica of those we'd seen in Algiers, except there were no commodes. A row of recessed scallops lined the wall opposite the entrance. I dreaded the stench of the place, the feces smeared on the wall by guards who had no paper, but there was no alternative.

After relieving my discomfort, I walked down the hallway toward the rear entrance. Morning sunlight backlighting the guard at the doorway was inviting. As I approached the open doorway, the sound of a commanding voice coming from the rear yard drew me on. The guard waved me closer and pointed through the doorway. Cockeyed Pete, a lieutenant whose right eye—or left—was doomed to focus outward to infinity, had his three truck and one ox-cart drivers standing at attention while he inspected them and gave them their orders for the day. The occasion was a daily ritual.

Pete was standing in front of the soldier nearest to the building. While his tone of voice was conversational, the guard was frightened. Without warning, Pete reached foward, patted the man's cheek several times then slapped him. It wasn't a vicious blow, but the sound of the slap told me that it must have stung. Pete smiled as he continued to speak, and pinched the man's cheek as though in a playful manner.

Slap! He hit him again.

Suddenly, Pete waved his arms and shouted, his face only a few inches from that of the quaking soldier. Just as suddenly, he smiled and spoke softly. Another pinch, a loud slap, then a barked command.

The soldier stiffened, did an awkward about-face and bent forward at the waist. Pete immediately delivered a moderate kick with his booted foot to the man's exposed backside and sent him stumbling away. Smiling with evil pleasure, he stepped sideways and placed himself in front of the next driver, and started the ritual anew.

One by one, in equal measure, the hapless men were subjected to his cruel sense of humor. Having booted the last man to a frantic dash for the compound gate, the bastard laughed at the retreating driver and walked nonchalantly into the basement of the schoolhouse.

Pete was far from being a pitiable character. Rather than accepting empathy because of his handicapped vision and wild appearance, he minimized his physical defect by acting in a barbarous manner toward those who were defenseless. The caste system of the Rumanian army was the real culprit. Pete and Fat Stuff took every opportunity to enforce the system for no purpose other than their own sadistic pleasure. As far as I could tell, Pete's duties did not bring him into direct contact with the prisoners. Nevertheless, he would have to be considered a threat to our well-being.

Following the incident, I beat a hasty retreat to the gym for my cache of toilet paper. It was crude paper, purchased with part of my allowance at the canteen. Despite its rough texture, it was a blessing.

My bout with the contaminated milk wasn't the only physical problem confronting me. A soreness in my jaw left me troubled about a foreseeable problem that I dreaded.

While at Colorado Srings, my lower, right wisdom tooth had made its growing presence known in an excruciating manner. When the tooth punched through the gum, a flap of highly sensitive flesh lay on top of the tooth. Each day had brought a marked increase in pain as the tooth thrust upward against inflamed flesh. After several days the pain was constant. I couldn't close my mouth to eat. A friend had needled me by suggesting that I go to the dentist and let him slice the flap free with a scalpel. I'd found his advice terrifying and refused to go until I couldn't stand the pain. After a few moments in the dentist's chair, I was embarrassed by my stupidity and lack of courage. One quick glance in my mouth and he dipped a swab stick in a tiny vial of carbolic acid and touched the tip of the swab to the offending flap. In an instant the pain was gone.

Here in a prisoner of war camp, I knew I'd not be so fortunate. Under no circumstance would I ask for medical attention from an enemy doctor. The tales I'd heard from the old heads convinced me that asking for medical help entailed too many risks.

Crunching stale bread with my teeth greatly accelerated the rate at which the flap became sensitive. By Thursday it was so painful I couldn't close my mouth. By Friday I knew that I had to do something to solve the problem. I'd been sucking on my bread for two days, and even that had become too painful to endure. There was only one solution: I had to bite the flap free.

Time and again I tried clamping my teeth together, all to no avail. The moment my jaws started to close, I'd gasp in pain and discover that I was involuntarily opening my mouth even wider. Attempts to snap my jaws shut had irritated the flap to the point that the pain brought tears.

Desperate to end my suffering, I placed my left hand under my chin and grasped the top of my head with my right hand and tried to force my jaws closed. The pain almost made me cry out. Resting for a few moments to let the pain subside while I contemplated my next action, I was confident that I knew how to rid myself of the offending flap.

Sitting on the edge of my bed, I switched hands so that my right elbow was resting on my right knee, with the heel of my hand under my chin, and my left palm was pressing firmly down on the top of my head. "One, two, three, push." I bent forward, bit, and pushed with both hands.

Pain exploded in my mouth and squeezed tears through clamped eyelids. I heard, or felt, the offending flesh burst and crush between my teeth. The effort left me gasping from pain, with the taste of blood in my mouth. Wiping tears on the sleeve of my flying suit, I walked to a window and spit blood and bits of flesh into the yard. If the raw gum didn't become infected, it would soon shrink and heal.

The next day I was hardly aware of my former misery. My immediate concern was, What is Art up to now?

He'd been in fine spirits at breakfast and had disappeared immediately thereafter. I didn't see him again until lunch. We bummed about the place for a couple of hours before he excused himself and promptly disappeared for the rest of the afternoon. I didn't find him again until a few minutes before dinner. He was sitting on the side of his bunk with a silly grin on his face, staring at nothing. One look at his eyes and I knew. He wasn't just tipsy, the guy was at least "three sheets to the wind." It took considerable urging, but I finally got him to go down to the mess hall and eat.

After dinner we returned to the gym, whereupon he thrust his hand underneath the head of his mattress and pulled out a liter bottle of clear liquid. He uncorked the bottle, took a healthy swig, and passed the bottle to me. Tears rolling down his cheeks caused me to sniff the open bottle before upending it. It smelled potent and had an aroma similar to the rahkia I'd sampled in Yugoslavia.

I tried a mouthful. It was almost pure alcohol. The stuff torched my raw gum and was impossible to swallow in one gulp. I finally got it down and joined Art in a wet-eyed salute to its potency. The bottle made its tearful round of those present and returned to me. The first mouthful still burning in my gullet and stomach, I declined a second draught of the liquid fire.

He'd given his watch to a guard to be sold in the city. Part of the proceeds were used to buy lighter fluid and the booze, which he called tuica—pronounced, *swee*-ka.

Tuica is distilled from plum brandy. Repeated distillation increases the alcoholic content. Normally it is distilled once or twice. I figured that Art's had been distilled at least three times. He would have been better off drinking the lighter fluid and burning the tuica in his lighter.

Shortly before dark Art decided to take Cockeyed Pete to task because of his harsh treatment of the drivers. I didn't know where in the basement Pete lived, but Art, during one of his forays, had spotted the villain's lair. He led me waveringly but unerringly to a door in the dimly lit hall and started pounding on it with both fists. I should have thrown him over my shoulder and beat a retreat, but it was too late. Before I could act, the sound of angry cursing from inside the room was punctuated by the door being flung violently open. A thoroughly disturbed Cockeyed Pete glared hatefully at us with one eye, then the other, or so it seemed. We had interrupted his dinner, but upon identifying us he relaxed and waved us enter.

A single, low-wattage bulb cast a yellow glow over the table but left the rest of the room in shadowed darkness. Despite the shadows, I could see well enough to tell that Pete lived like a pack rat.

"Was ist los, Hauptman?" he asked Art as he settled back in his chair and continued his meal. What was left of the ham butt was greasy but inviting. He'd already eaten some sort of green vegetable and potatoes and was finishing the meal with slivers of greasy ham and peasant bread. A dark, labelless bottle still contained some of the red wine he was swigging from a cup. The man ate like a pig, leaning low over the table, slicing off pieces of ham and popping them into his mouth, then licking his greasy fingers. Sly glances with one eye or the other—I couldn't tell which—signaled that he was enjoying eating in our presence.

"Was ist los?" he growled.

"You're a lousy soldier," Art slurred.

"Was?"

"Du bist eine schlecht soldat!" Art repeated his statement in German.

Pete sprang from his chair, leaned over the table, struck his breast audibly with a clenched fist, and screamed something unintelligible —to me—in German.

I was taken aback by his violent reaction, but not Art. He was unfazed by Pete's explosive response.

I watched Pete's face and eyes for a telltale sign as to the depth or sincerity of his anger, but the guy's skewed eye had me buffaloed. I couldn't tell for sure which one of us he was glaring at, or whether he was glaring at either of us. I hadn't understood his German, but I concluded that he was arguing the point with Art. Then came the greatest surprise.

"I best soldier!"

The Cockeyed One could speak some English! The bastard was a lot smarter than I'd credited him to be.

Art, also leaning forward with his face merely inches from Pete's satanic leer, shouted, "You're a lousy coward!"

"I'm a brave soldat!" Art shouted as he sat back down at a stiff posture of attention.

"I'm ready to die for my country!" he continued.

"You ready die?" Pete said as he sat back in his chair, a slow grin, then an evil leer taking hold of his crooked-eyed countenance.

"I'm ready to die for my country," Art insisted as though inviting the leering Pete to draw his pistol and shoot him on the spot.

Worry grew to near-panic as I sat frozen and watched Pete's right hand creep across the table and his fingers close on the handle of a dirty meat cleaver lying next to the ham.

Art, seeing Pete's arm raise up and back, his hand with a firm grasp on the cleaver, stiffened his erect posture and shouted, "Split me in two!"

That did it. The cleaver had reached full height and Pete seemed to be gathering strength in his arm for one mighty blow. I sprang to my feet, grabbed Art in a bear hug and wrestled him out of the chair and toward the door.

As I glanced back at Pete, the overhead light cast dark shadows on his leering face. He had the look of a cockeyed Satan until his countenance crumbled into uncontrolled laughter. I found little humor in the situation. In my view Pete was too cool a character. His cockeyed appearance masked creditable intelligence, and his sadistic concept of humor could be deadly. I was thankful that his duties did not require us to deal with him.

It wasn't easy getting the half-limp Art up the stairs and onto his bunk. Persuading him to lie down was out of the question. He had only one thought: he had to sacrifice his life for his country.

Sitting on his bunk in the dark and fondling the small bottle of lighter fluid, his thoughts took a turn to the bizarre. In his tuica-laden mind, the lighter fluid was nitroglycerine. Not satisfied to sacrifice his own life, he challenged all of us to martyrdom.

If we would give our lives for our country, he'd take the nitroglycerine down to the boiler room and blow up the schoolhouse. That there was no fire in the furnace never occurred to him. It was our duty to die for our country.

We were humoring him with the issue still in doubt when his unique genius for devilry came up with an alternative we all found appealing. He'd blow up the guard in the tower outside our room.

Had it not been so dark we could have seen his movements and stopped him.

Before anyone realized what he was doing, he'd ripped a leg strap off his flying suit, and stuffed it into the neck of the bottle. In daylight, cold sober, and with an arsenal of a hundred bottles, Art probably couldn't have duplicated what happened next. Our first indication of what he was about was the sudden flicker of his cigarette lighter. The lighted wick and bottle moved rearward, then hurtled through the darkened room. There was a small sound of glass breaking against masonry, then a dull whoosh as the fluid caught fire in a soft explosion of blue flame out through the open window. The whoosh was accompanied by a yell, followed moments later by the meaty thud of the guard's body hitting the ground.

The bedlam of shouting guards outside the building sent us scampering in the dark for our bunks. Within minutes, the squealing voice of Fat Stuff could be heard through the black window spaces as he berated his men in an attempt to discover what had happened. There was no question that he figured we had something to do with it, but no one came to the gym. I felt sorry for the guard. We had no idea as to the extent of his injuries. For all we knew, the man could be lying on the ground, dead from a broken neck. What had been born as a prank, more on Art than on the guard, had become a dangerous, perhaps deadly situation for all. There was no telling what measure of revenge Fat Stuff would take against his prisoners.

XVII

The roar of Messerschmitt engines overhead brought an involuntary tightening of muscles and nerves. Conventional wisdom claimed, "When German fighters assemble on Bucharest airfields, an American raid will soon follow." Considering the dozens of fighters that flew in during the next hour, I figured the Fifteenth was mounting a maximum effort.

There had not been a raid for six days. The last had been on July 9, against Ploesti. The 450th hadn't taken any losses, but we'd gotten new prisoners from the 98th and 449th. I'd wondered why we didn't debrief the incoming prisoners for war news and post it on our bulletin board. Most of the information we received was gotten through bull sessions, and was so contaminated with speculation one couldn't be certain how the war was going. Unfortunately air crews knew little about the ground situations on the various fronts.

If personal conviction could be taken as expertise, many were expert in forecasting which target would be hit today. Many more were convinced that the Luftwaffe had a direct channel of communications to an agent in Italy who supplied information about our raids before the bomber crews were even briefed. Indeed, Captain Cristi and Sergeant Dali—the latter a ne'er-do-well scion of a wealthy Rumaninan family who seemed to have little to do except ride around on his black BMW motorcycle and try to collect information from us for the Gestapo—had both alluded to "prior knowledge" of our raids. In view of my own experiences with enemy fighters that seemed to be on hand regardless of the country in which our target was located, I tended to agree. I hadn't noticed fighters assembling prior to the July ninth raid, but if the Fifteenth showed up today I'd be convinced.

The upcoming raid wasn't my only worry. At any moment I expected the hammer to fall because of last night's incident with the tower guard. During breakfast the SAO seared our table with frequent scathing looks. We later learned that Fat Stuff had awakened him during the night and given him holy hell. Fat Stuff hadn't been able to get anything intelligible out of the injured guard. All the man knew was that he'd been standing on the far side of the tower with his back toward the window. A sudden blue light and intense heat had caused him to lose his balance and fall. He had regained consciousness lying on the ground. Luckily, a sprained ankle and a large bump on his head—the latter received when he stumbled backward against a tower leg—were his only injuries. Fat Stuff knew that we had something to do with the matter, but was at a loss as to what. He issued a severe warning to the SAO regarding our conduct, but pressed the matter no further.

The old heads, although very angry at us, were of the opinion that the Fat One was already in so much trouble with his superiors because of escapes that he was probably reluctant to make an issue of the incident and draw more unfavorable attention to his inept administration of the camp.

Shortly after nine o'clock, the air raid siren sang out. The noise not only was loud and irritating, but also acted as a Pavlovian trigger that could galvanize us into immediate action, day or night, awake or fast asleep. In less than a second I was off my bunk and streaking for the door. I was fast, but not fast enough; the niche beneath the basement stairwell was already overflowing with huddled bodies. I was looking around for an alternate place to squat when it occurred to me that nothing was happening yet other than the wail of the siren. Embarrassed because of my nervousness and uncalled-for speed in scrambling to the basement, I sauntered off looking for Ollie or Art.

At least thirty minutes passed before flak guns roared their hateful sound. A battery of 88mm guns nearby hurled its awesome missiles almost directly over our building. The high-velocity shells made a fearful rushing noise as they split the air overhead. There was no "whine" as is heard on movie soundtracks. Because of their extreme velocity, eighty-eight-millimeter shells have a distinct sound: like gods of death rushing madly about the heavens in search of souls.

With my back to the basement wall, my elbows resting on my knees and my hands clasped behind my head in a crash-landing position, my mind visualized the worst sort of things—mainly, that the direction of antiaircraft gunfire was a sure indication that one or more groups was on a bomb run directly at us. I was waiting for the impact of the first two hundred bombs to come at any minute and wondering

American POWs buying melons following release from captivity, Bucharest.

Opera House, Bucharest, showing bomb damage by Luftwaffe. The POW officers' camp was located approximately one mile away.

Sherwood Mark

NCOs talking with former guards searching through ruins of the POW camp for their belongings after the Germans destroyed the building.

courtesy Lt. Col. Gunn

This is the ME-109 that Prince Constantin Cantacuzene flew from Popesti Air-drome to Italy, with Lt. Col. James Gunn aboard, to arrange for the rescue of the American POWs.

Cantacuzene and Gunn, right, toast their successful flight to Italy.

American ex-POWs and Rumanians gather around a B-17 prior to takeoff from Popesti Airdrome.

Homecoming, Bari: not all the ex-POWs were in good shape after their ordeal.

Sherwood Mark

American ex-POWs inspecting engine of a Rumanian ME-109 at Popesti Air-drome.

Army Air Force official photo

Author receiving the Purple Heart Medal at ceremonies at Manduria after return from POW camp. Col. R. R. Gideon, the new commander of the Cottontails, is affixing the ribbon. Lt. Col. William G. Snaith is at far left of picture.

Sherwood Mark

B-17s lined up at Popesti to fly American POWs to safety.

Author at Popesti Airdrome, on morning of rescue mission, with Rumanian air force personnel in background.

Sherwood Mark

Scene at Popesti Airdrome. Col. Kraiger, the OSS team commander for the rescue mission, is wearing cap. Lt. Col. Bill Snaith is holding camera.

Happy ex-POWs arriving at Bari, Italy.

Ex-POWs being deloused, Bari.

courtesy Lt. Col. Gunn

Maj. Gen. Nathan Twining, commander of the Fifteenth Air Force, and Brig. Gen. Charles Born (wearing sunglasses) greeting the first group of ex-POWs to arrive at Bari.

Army Air Force official photo

Crew of the *Swashbuckler* following release from the POW camp. Left to right, standing, C. Dittman, J. J. Ukish, F. M. Davis, Jr., L. Claverie, J. D. Matthews; kneeling, W. R. Cubbins, W. J. Kappelar, O. H. King, B. S. Green, F. W. Lynch

how we could possibly live through such massive explosive power. But no bombs exploded, and the firing stopped as suddenly as it had begun. I looked up and saw several old heads making their way up the stairs. Embarrassed over my fearful reaction, I followed them on legs weakened almost to the point of trembling. When I arrived at the first floor landing, a group of prisoners were crowding the open doors at the end of the hall. The guard was nowhere in sight. Wondering what was going on, I walked down the hall and joined them.

They weren't doing anything in particular, except peering at the sky and speculating as to the reason the flak guns had started firing, and hoping to catch a glimpse of the air action. One remarked that the best thing to do during a raid was to watch outside for the action in order to see if the bombs would hit near us. It seemed a reasonable thing to do. Anything would be better than huddling fearfully in the basement, expecting to be blown to shreds at any moment. I thought about stepping onto the outside landing for a better view, but falling shrapnel could cause one grievous injury. We couldn't tell whether the guns had been firing at fighters that had wandered into range during a dogfight, or whether a bomber had inadvertently drawn too close while fending off fighters, or reconnaissance aircraft had made a run over a nearby target. Since the guns remained quiet, we assumed that Ploesti was the target and we had nothing to fear.

But I *was* afraid, and ashamed. It was no longer a fear of bombs, but of a mind-corroding fear of fear itself. I had never known such fear during combat. The heat of the action kept mind and muscles busy and limited the time one had to contemplate the imminence of death. Here in the prison where we were helpless to act, and without air raid shelters, the mind was free to conjure up infinite ways in which one could die a violent death. What with poor diet and being at constant threat of the whim of our captors, none of us had the physical and psychological strength that we'd enjoyed before that last mission. Being shot down almost always causes a trauma that sooner or later takes one in its debilitating—often crushing—grasp. Having experienced such a high level of fear when the antiaircraft gunfire started firing, I was puzzled and worried over my reaction. I recognized that I would have to reach deep inside me, to heretofore unknown depths in order to summon the courage to fight this new unreasoned fear. I wondered if I'd find that courage.

Several days later it was midmorning and I was lying on my bunk resting. The effect of poor diet on my energy was making itself apparent. I'd weighed about 190 pounds at the time I was shot down. I could only guess at my weight now, but it was significantly less than it had been two weeks before. My flying suit seemed to fit more loosely with each passing day. I was feeling relaxed, when a hurried movement and a shout announced the arrival of a new group of "criminals."

They were a sorry-looking lot, sauntering along between two lines of armed escort. It was a large group, in triple column, perhaps forty of them, led by a mummy. Despite the new bandages wrapping both hands and his face and head, there was something familiar about the mummy's frame and gait. I leaned through the loose barbed wire and sang out the familiar "You'll be sorry!" The mummy looked up, peered at me through black eye holes, and answered.

"No sorrier than you, Cubbins."

His voice told me his identity. It was Bill Snaith.

There'd been several occasions during the two weeks since I'd been shot off his wing when I'd wondered if he'd made it. It wasn't an unkind thought. When we returned from Vis, we'd been greeted by then new–Lieutenant Colonel Snaith. His arrival at the school-house signaled the end of the incumbent SAO's authority. Bill was an aggressive fellow who would be effective in dealing with Fat Stuff.

Several days later, he related the details of his being shot down. He had led the strike on Ploesti on July fifteenth. Seconds after releasing his bombs, his aircraft had received a direct flak hit in the bomb bay. The shell had turned the ship into an inferno. Unable to get out of the cockpit, which was filled with searing flames, he'd sat back in his seat, covered his face with his hands, and waited for the release of death. At almost that same instant, the ship exploded, killing his crew.

His first conscious thought had been the discovery that he was falling on his back, about two hundred feet below the flaming wreckage of his aircraft, and faced with a terrible dilemma.

"If I pull my rip cord, will the wreckage fall on me? If I don't . . . ?"

He'd taken the only option available. He grasped the D-ring and pulled. His body was instantly decelerated by the deploying parachute, and the wreckage passed harmlessly overhead before falling through his altitude. But that had not been the end of his ordeal. Being the mission leader, and landing near the target, he'd had to endure the thundering destruction of the bombs of the groups that followed: the rest of the Fifteenth's hundreds of bombers on an all-out attack.

The Rumanian soldiers who captured him turned him over to the German defenders of Ploesti. That was fortunate. German doctors treated his burns before passing him back to the Rumanians.

During the next several days I wandered about the schoolhouse looking for friends among the new prisoners, and seeking information on the progress of the war. I found no one that I knew, and learned little about the ground action in France and Italy. The air war was another matter.

Over Germany, Austria, and Rumania the Luftwaffe was out in force. Improved fighter escort was producing record kills, but the bombers were still suffering heavy losses. Ploesti remained unconquered. Whether from the favorable atmospherics of summer weather, improved air raid warnings, or experience, the smoke screen was making the refineries even more difficult to find. The crews felt that Ploesti, already bombed twice during July, had become Fifteenth's highest priority target and would draw more raids during the month.

Among the new prisoners was an American who was not a new prisoner at all. He was only new to the camp. Lt. Ralph W. Hisey, Jr., was tall for a fighter pilot. His easy stance was that of an athlete. His manner of dress—an RAF flight jacket and trousers tucked into RAF flight boots—was unusual attire for an American pilot. When I first saw him he was standing alone in the hallway, with his head bent forward as a hawk in search of prey. Curious as to how he'd acquired his British garb, I introduced myself.

Ralph was a P-38 pilot from the First Fighter Group. He'd been shot down on the tenth of June but hadn't arrived at the schoolhouse until early July. He'd been badly mistreated during extensive interrogation by the Gestapo, and the more he thought about it the angrier he had become. Ralph Hisey was "madder'n hell."

The reason for German Intelligence's interest in Ralph was that this was the first time that a refinery had been dive-bombed. During escort missions P-38s often dropped down to the deck and shot up everything in sight, but dive-bombing the refinery was a new tactic.

The daring operation was, therefore, of vital interest to both the Germans and the Rumanians.[1]

Following the construction of the new guard tower, life in the gym threatened to settle into unbearable dullness. Our poor and meager diet sapped our energy and desires. A few of the prisoners' spirits and energy levels were so low that we had to drag them from their bunks, force them to stand and move about, and to go downstairs for meals.[2]

Fortunately only a few prisoners had deteriorated to such an advanced state of demoralization. The problem did not seem to be related to the length of time a man had been in the camp. One fellow who arrived with our group was already in such a state; his spirit was dying inside an otherwise healthy body. We tried calisthenics as a means of developing energy. That seemed to help a bit, but exercising inside the building was difficult, and drew too much attention from the guards and made them nervous. Our psychological situation improved markedly when Snaith finally convinced Fat Stuff to allow us to go outside. At first we could use only the rear yard. If very many of us went out at the same time, the yard became quite crowded. Fat Stuff eventually relented and allowed us to use both the front and rear yards.

1. Fifteenth Air Force, frustrated by the high-level bombers' difficulties in finding their aiming points underneath the smoke screen, devised a plan to catch the enemy by surprise.

Two groups of P-38s—one group carrying bombs, the other providing them escort—would take off from Italy, stay at treetop level to their Initial Point, then climb rapidly to 8,000 feet. The bombers would dive on the Romano Americano refinery before the smoke screen could cover the target. In essence the raid was similar to the low-level raid by B-24s on August 1, 1943. Major differences between the two plans—shorter mission distance, the P-38's higher speed en route, easier navigation, and fighter escort—gave the bomb-carrying fighters a better chance for success than the bombers had enjoyed. Each pilot would individually aim his bomb, and be able to get to and away from the target at a much higher rate of speed than could the B-24s. The plan looked good—on paper.

At daybreak forty-six P-38s of the Eighty-second Fighter Group, each carrying a 1,000-pound bomb, took off from their base at Vincenzo, skipped over the Adriatic and worked their way across Yugoslavia flying at ground level, then followed the Danube to a point southeast of Bucharest. The plan was to stay to the east of Bucharest, fly northward, and attack the target from an easterly direction, through the back door. Except for the loss of seven aircraft that aborted the mission for various reasons, and one that the pilot abandoned near Nis, Yugoslavia, all went well until the course turn at Bucharest.

As the force swung around Bucharest, it encountered a fleet of German bombers, transports, and biplanes that had scrambled off their airdromes to avoid being attacked on the ground. The element of surprise lost, a number of escorting P-38s of the First Fighter Group, and two of those carrying bombs, engaged the low-flying enemy aircraft for a veritable "turkey shoot." Hisey joined in the melee. After shooting down one—perhaps two—Dornier bombers, he became heavily engaged with four German fighters.

One morning I awakened, sat up, stood, saw the world go gray, then black, and fell backward onto the bunk. I lay quietly for a while and watched the ceiling take form and clear. I again tried getting up. This time, I remained seated on the edge of my bed until my vision cleared, then stood and waited for it to clear again before attempting to walk. During the balance of the day I had no further problems. From that morning on, I had to get out of bed in stages, going slow and easy and pausing at each stage until I was on my feet. Once standing, I could move about without any further difficulty.

Our physical limitations did little to impair our occasional harassment of the inside guards. This was particularly so if there was a guard we didn't like. Most of them were so dull and so poorly trained that Fat Stuff didn't trust them to carry a rifle with a shell in its chamber. Some would have been more dangerous to themselves than to us. However, their rifles always had a fully loaded magazine beneath the bolt. They were allowed to load a shell into the chamber only when they were threatened or if it became necessary to fire the weapon. When threatened, their usual procedure was to lower the muzzle of the rifle and noisily operate the bolt so we could see the shell slip into firing position in the rifle's chamber. We appreciated

---

With one of his two engines shot out and his wingman missing, Hisey maneuvered wildly at treetop level in an attempt to elude his pursuers. Within moments, his remaining engine was in flames. Thinking that he would die at any moment, he punched his "mike" button and calmly announced, "This is it; I guess I've had it." None of the surviving P-38 pilots saw him go in, but they reported his radio call to their base. After making the call, he spotted a field and successfully bellied the burning aircraft to a safe landing.

The thirty-six remaining bomb-carrying fighters of the Eighty-second Group pressed on despite head-on attacks from German fighters and withering antiaircraft fire, climbed to 6,000 to 8,000 feet, and dove at their smoke-covered targets.

The Romano Americano, the fourth largest of Ploesti's eleven refineries and heretofore only moderately damaged by the high-level bombers, lost one cracking plant and a large storage tank, and had three other refinery units damaged. Not satisfied with the damage to the refinery, the P-38s turned their attention to the Ploesti marshaling yards and the airfield.

Maneuvering wildly, often only feet above the ground, the attackers expended their ammunition against targets of opportunity. Their final score included two troop trains and ten other trains strafed, ten locomotives destroyed, three tank trucks fired, three heavy gun batteries silenced, three enemy aircraft destroyed in the air, and three others on the ground. Such destruction was not achieved without its price. The Eighty-second lost eight of its thirty-six dive-bombing aircraft.

The First was also heavily engaged. Its Seventy-first Squadron, having engaged and shot down at least eight twin-engine bombers and six other aircraft, was hit with waves of Focke-Wulf 190s and ME-109s. During the fierce engagement Lt. Herbert B. Hatch shot down five of the FW-190s, probably destroyed a sixth, and damaged a seventh. He was the only member of the Seventy-first Squadron who made it back to their base. While the First

that, of course. It was important to know if a guard's rifle was ready to be fired. It also played into our hands.

Someone would approach a guard we didn't like, make him angry enough to load a shell, then turn and walk away. As often as not, in anger or confusion, the guard would forget that his rifle was ready to fire. If so, sometime later, after he'd calmed down and his rifle butt was resting on the floor, a group of us would again draw his attention while another quietly reached down and triggered a round into the ceiling. At that point all hell would break loose, culminating in Fat Stuff beating the guard for having accidentally discharged his rifle inside the building.

One night a particularly offensive guard was on duty in the hallway opposite the stairwell. In the course of our confrontation, we decided that he was too alert and mean for us to attempt to carry our stunt to its usual conclusion. Sometime later, I was sitting on my bunk when the sound of his rifle firing nearly deafened me. Thinking that the fellow had stepped inside our room to fire at someone, I dove for the floor. Not hearing a second shot, but hearing the sounds of a scuffle going on outside our door, I charged into the hall and found Art in a life-or-death struggle with the guard over the possession of the rifle.

Art claimed that the guard had started the fracas. He'd been en route to the latrine when the guard refused to let him pass. The situation escalated immediately beyond mere words. When the guard lifted the rifle to point it at him, Art, remembering that it was ready

posted twenty-four kills in the air and four on the ground, it lost fourteen of its own. The loss of twenty-two P-38s on a single mission was a heavy price to pay, but it was the beginning of the end of the Romano-Americano refinery.

Of the pilots of the twenty-two aircraft lost, Hisey was one of six survivors. When the war ended, of the scores of fighter pilots shot down over Rumania there were only twenty-eight survivors in the camp. As low as the downed bomber crew survival rate was, the fighter pilot rate was even lower. The P-38 survival rate was the lowest of all, because of the unique bailout problems related to the P-38's twin-boom design. Not only was getting out of the aircraft difficult, it was extremely hazardous, particularly during combat. Most of those who survived did so by belly-landing their aircraft.

2. One of the more curious aspects of prisoner of war life is the tendency of some men to lose hope and will themselves to die. The phenomenon is believed to have occurred far more frequently among World War II prisoners held by Oriental captors than those held by European captors. It surfaced again among the prisoners held captive by the Chinese during the Korean War. Significantly, the phenomenon appears to be unique to Americans. No prisoners of other nationalities—British, Greek, etc.—are known to have willed themselves to die. In Korea, U. S. Army doctors, themselves prisoners of war, kept records which were subsequently the basis for exhaustive studies by U. S. Army and Air Force researchers. As could be expected, many perished in North Vietnamese camps from the same phenomenon.

to be fired, grasped the barrel to push it aside. In the process, the guard squeezed the trigger, firing a round that barely missed hitting Art in the left side. Disarmed and pressed on all sides by curious prisoners, the guard was frightened half out of his wits.

The Fat Man's squeal trumpeted his arrival and caused the guard's eyes to move wildly about, not so much in search of the direction from which the attack would come, but for a route, even the smallest rift in our ranks through which he could escape. But there was no escape. Fat Stuff arrived on the scene, saw Art in possession of the rifle, shifted into "maniac" gear, and beat the guard unmercifully.

The piglike sound of Fat Stuff's voice was always an occasion for laughter. When the Fat One squealed, everyone vied for a ringside seat. Our reactions to his sadistic acts were most curious, perhaps even a pagan phenomenon. We never had a valid reason to cause Ioanid to abuse a man as harshly as he was wont to do. Indeed, we held his cruel attitude toward his men in utter contempt. Yet, many of us enjoyed watching our chief jailer make a fool of himself, and gave little thought to the cruel consequences it meant for the guards.

While I was lounging on my bunk one morning, the quiet of the early hour was shattered by frantic squealing coming through the windows on the south wall of our room. There was an immediate dash for a position to watch Fat Stuff maim a guard. But the action wasn't visible from our room windows. We had to jimmy the lock on the south stage door and get to the rear stairwell window in order to see.

In many ways the brutal scene was worth the effort. To our shocked surprise, the sound wasn't coming from the fat colonel. The space between the rear of the gym and the large building next to the compound had been cordoned off as a hog pen. Two huge sows were in residence, awaiting Fat Stuff's insatiable appetite. The window at the stairwell landing was directly above the hog pen. André and four other Russians were slaughtering a sow. André had plunged a large butcher knife into the animal's heart and cut its throat with a second knife. He was standing quietly, the bloody knife held in his hand, amused by the other Russians' struggles to hang onto the hapless animal's thrashing legs as it squealed away the final tendrils of life.

In response to our calls, André looked up, smiled, pointed the bloody knife at the dying sow, and spoke.

"We do Fat Stuff when war over."

I was surprised at his having spoken even those few words of

English. The shock I felt at the thought of the cruel end they were contemplating for our chief jailor ruined my mood of amusement at being fooled into thinking Fat Stuff was beating one of the guards. When excited, not only did the man sound like a pig, he sounded like a dying pig. I wondered if he would squeal and thrash about as the sow had done. It was a gruesome thought, one about which I should have felt shame and horror. I did.

This was not the first time that the hog pen had been the source of a bit of bizarre humor. Prior to our arrival, three NCOs bent on escape had secreted themselves in the auditorium during one of the brief periods when the prisoners were allowed access to the piano. During the dead of night they lowered themselves out through the stage-stairwell window, only to drop uneremoniously into the hog pen. Suffice it to say, the swine squealed on them.

Several days after the butchering incident, a different kind of incident occurred, one that came perilously close to causing serious repercussions. The incident didn't just happen: we made it happen. During the morning, Ollie, Buck Jolley, and I and perhaps a dozen other prisoners were in the rear yard when the gates opened and a large truck with high sideboards drove into the compound and parked near the building. Someone on the stair landing shouted that the truck was full of flyers' clothing. The sudden movement of prisoners toward the truck brought an immediate and noisy reaction from the guards. Everyone stopped moving—that is, everyone but Ollie. He walked to the rear wheels of the truck, climbed up the side, reached over, then dropped back to the ground with a flying jacket clutched in his hand. Ollie had accomplished his maneuver with complete calm, as though the guard standing a few feet from him didn't exist.

But the guard *did* exist, and he was so enraged by Ollie's effrontery that he was on the verge of losing control of his anger. By the time Ollie dropped to the ground the man's dark-skinned face had become almost black from the blood surging through facial veins as he screamed and motioned wildly with his rifle for Ollie to return the jacket to the truck.

Ollie, continuing to ignore the man, calmly tried the jacket for fit.

The screaming guard noisily chambered a round into his rifle.

The jacket was too tight. Ollie took it off and climbed back up onto the side of the truck.

Ollie's replacing the jacket caused the guard to relax. When he dropped back to the ground with another jacket in his hand, the guard was dumbfounded just long enough for Ollie to slip the jacket on and disappear around the tail of the truck toward the entrance steps.

Attracted by the guard's shouts, Fat Stuff arrived on the landing at the same time as Ollie strolled unhurriedly past him and into the building. The guard, rounding the tail of the truck, stopped dead in his tracks at the sight of his feared commander. He then tried to snap to attention, change hands with the rifle and salute, all in one motion. He bungled the maneuver badly and would have suffered dire consequences at the hands of the fat man, had the gate not opened at that moment to allow a staff car to enter. I was already in motion toward the building entrance and caught only a glimpse of the car coming through the gate. I wanted to get upstairs where I'd have a better view of the contents of the truck.

Art met me at the stairwell and told me that some of the fellows were going to try to set fire to the truck. We hurried up to the second floor and joined the small group of would-be saboteurs at the window at the end of the hallway.

Looking down at the truck, I was amazed at the mass of American flyer clothing and parachutes that filled the large truck body. Of more interest was the small group of Rumanians standing on the sidewalk, in earnest conversation with Fat Stuff.

Everyone's attention was focused on the tall air force officer who, from the look of his ornate epaulets, was a general. His commanding look of calm, and quiet manner of speech, were in stark contrast to Fat Stuff's red face and sweating effort to hold his pear-shaped body at attention. Standing next to the general was another air force officer, probably a colonel. To their right and rear were two air force enlisted men. One, a sergeant, was holding onto a handsome briefcase. But the item that was causing all the excitement among us was the Norden bombsight, apparently intact in its unique carrying case, resting on the sidewalk in front of and between the general and the colonel.

Our group at the window was rapidly formulating plans to fire the truck, but above all to destroy the bombsight. They had acquired a large chunk of broken concrete (from only they and God knew where) and two fist-sized pieces, and were impatiently waiting for others to arrive with some benzine-soaked paper with which to wrap their missiles. The plan was to light the paper on all three rocks, toss the two smaller missiles onto the paraphernalia in the truck, and heave the large piece at the bombsight. Getting two smaller firebombs into the truck would be easy, but I doubted there was anyone in the camp strong enough to toss the large chunk of concrete and hit the bombsight. The distance was too far and the angle too difficult. Then there was the considerable problem of the barbed wire lacing the window. Indeed, all facts considered, the operation promised to be a total failure.

By the time the benzine paper arrived, the plan was finalized and set in motion. There was no problem with aiming or throwing the small stones, but not having any string with which to secure the paper to the missiles, we had great difficulty in wrapping the large piece so the newspaper would remain on during its flight to the ground. I couldn't see the value of the paper on the large piece. The metal sight wasn't going to burn. The highly flammable paper only made the impossible task more difficult. Nevertheless the missiles were wrapped, lit, and heaved.

The smaller fireballs found their mark but did no damage. They both landed on parachute material, which is difficult to burn. The large missile was a near-disaster.

I was standing to the right of the window where I had a good view of the general's party and the bombsight, when the three missileers set fire to their missiles and the two smaller ones were tossed, followed immediately by the large one. The need to get all three out of the window in minimum time undoubtedly made the large one more difficult to heave with any sort of accuracy. As it passed through the window, barbed wire ripped the burning paper free.

The large piece of concrete arced downward, leaving me momentarily frozen as my mind projected the trajectory arcing toward ornate epaulets. It was going to be close. The potentially deadly chunk of concrete missed the general by mere inches and crashed onto the sidewalk—at least four feet short of the bombsight. My last panicky impression of the scene was that of the general in midflight of a remarkable leap backward, and bursting bedlam. I bolted for the nearest door.

I didn't know whose bed it was that I'd commandeered for my feigned siesta but I was confident that he wouldn't mind. The ruse worked. Guards, pounding into the hall with much shouting, saw nothing and discovered nothing. After much talk and shuffling about, they left. I sauntered back to the gymnasium and my own bed. My appearance of casual sauntering was only that, appearance. Inside, my mind was churning with grave misgivings. It had been a damned fool stunt. Although it had been devised and perpetrated by old heads, I was as guilty as they. Fat Stuff, already under pressure from his superiors, had been put in an untenable position in the presence of a general. Beyond that consideration, the general had narrowly escaped serious injury, even death. The more I thought about it, the greater my alarm. We'd be lucky if someone were not shot. Perhaps the older prisoners were right after all. Well-intentioned acts of harassment can easily get out of hand and do great harm.

Whether it was politics, the politics of losing the war, or perhaps the general instinctively knowing we were aiming for the bombsight and in a way accepting our motive—whatever the reason, nothing came of the matter other than the word being passed that our own leaders were as embarrassed and angry as Fat Stuff. In my own mind I recognized that the time had come to settle down to pursuits more serious and productive than harassing the guards. The one bright aspect of the incident was my new appreciation of the old heads. Perhaps I'd judged them too harshly.

XVIII

During the night of July 26 the siren wailed us hurriedly into the basement. It was another false alarm. After several periods of sporadic antiaircraft fire, probably rounds sent in vain search of a too-distant bomber, I groped my way up dark stairs to see if I could catch a glimpse of the action. Again, there was no way of knowing the cause of the alert, but my guess was the British were sowing mines in the Danube. Planting mines from low-level at night, in a river, or any other place for that matter, exceeds my concept of excitement by a good measure. One had to admire the courage and skills of the men who flew such extraordinarily difficult and dangerous missions.

One of the most curious aspects of those Bucharest nights was the deathly quiet that seized the city during the endless moments between the final moan of the warning wail and the guns' commencing their terrifying fusillades. It was as though death hovered quietly, savoring the moment when it would seize its intended victims. Guards cowered in dread and made little effort to enforce the rules governing our movements. If they spoke, it was in low voices for fear that death, lingering amusedly in the shadows, had ears that were easily offended by loud voices. It occurred to me that the night raids and their stultifying effect on the guards offered interesting possibilities for escape.

It was a moonless night, but I could make out the group of prisoners crowding the open entrance at the end of the hall. Joining them at the door, I arrived in time to witness the final moments of a classic night air battle involving a South African B-24 trapped in the apex of several powerful searchlights.

Searching the sky immediately behind the bomber, I saw it, a German nightfighter making a pass on the bomber from six o'clock low. The distance from our vantage was too great for us to see the torrent of tracers from cannon and machine guns that characterize such ghostly duels. On the contrary, the weaving bomber and its trailing fighter were more like toy craft frolicking playfully, or moths flitting in a beam of light.

The stalking fighter, barely visible to us in scatter light, suddenly shone crystal clear as it entered a beam, then just as suddenly disappeared from view as it danced out of the light and the sight of the bomber's tail-gunner. Within moments, another appeared, wraithlike in a closing pass from the bomber's rear.

The advantage a fighter has over an illuminated target is great. Even when not caught in searchlights, a bomber's engine exhausts often disclose its position. Once the fighter pilot sights his quarry, it is usually only moments before the unwary bomber crew is trapped in a flaming coffin. Trapped as it was in multiple beams of light, we waited for what we were certain would be the tragic outcome.

I couldn't tell whether the first fighter had gotten in a telling blow or the bomber pilot had added yet another factor to his evasive maneuvering, but the bomber appeared to have suddenly entered into a shallow dive. Then, as if by magic, it disappeared. It didn't explode, nor did the lights pinioning it like deadly lances waver from their prey, yet the bomber vanished quickly as if someone had flicked a switch and erased it from the dramatic scene.

A sense of relaxation worked its way through our small group as the searchlights moved about in sweeping patterns, probing the blackness for the elusive craft. When it became apparent that the bomber had bested the lights and the fighters in the uneven contest, I felt myself relax and realized how tense I'd become. I'd seen enough of the engagement to know that I preferred the massive violence of day combat to the terror of those brilliant fingers of light that singled one out, as if to say, "This one. Now!"

To me, death in the lonesomeness of night-blackened skies is so impersonal it violates the rules of dying. Death should never be without meaning or purpose, or dignity. To disappear suddenly in the faceless void of night is to lose one's very existence, to become as an incomplete sentence.

Interestingly, the British viewed the night terror as the normal environment of the bomber, and thought us foolish for flying in daylight where enemy fighters could be massed against us. Each concept had its advantages and disadvantages. Our advantage, and it was an overriding one, was our ability to find the target and do precision bombing. Precision bombing at night, particularly on a mass scale, was beyond the state of the art.

July 27 dawned clear, but late in the afternoon grew leaden. The weather had been flawless, and I found the overcast sky a welcome change from the repetitiveness of each hated day. Another enticing aspect of the changed weather was the prospect of a respite from the frequent wailing of the air raid siren. Being jolted into action by the awful screaming was nerve-wracking, despite the fact that no bombs seemed to be falling on Bucharest. I believed that in time I would adjust to its harsh message, but for the present the sound bothered me more than I cared to admit, even to myself. Going through frequent dry raids was like watching a giant storm building in intensity, lightning flashing as it marshals its forces before loosing them in a final fury. Most of us felt that it was but a matter of time before the bolts struck home and ended our curiosity as to the nature of the air activity causing the alerts.

I'd spent the day trying to relax by lying on my bunk, letting short naps consume hated time. It was near midnight, and Pop Egles and I were deep in conversation. We were sitting on the top step in the stairwell when the siren sent the first wave of men scurrying for the dubious safety of our half-basement. Although nearly trampled in the rush, Pop, in characteristic style, hardly interrupted his speech. I fought the urge to follow the crowd but pride won out over discretion. Reluctantly I remained seated beside the unflappable Englishman.

We'd been discussing the courage and skill the South African pilot had displayed in escaping the searchlights and fighters, and the pros and cons of day versus night bombing. Pop explained that Pathfinder Radar operators were responsible for finding and lighting the target with flares. The bombers, flying in single file, would each try to aim their bombs on a specific point in the target area. If the flare ships were off the target, the bombers would often release their lethal cargo far from their target; that is, unless the flare ships (by means of radar) selected random aiming points within a city.

He had been on a flare ship the night he went down. His explanation of RAF target-marking procedures didn't bolster my confidence in their bombing accuracy, or my determination to remain on the stairs with him.

If the flare ships couldn't identify the primary target, he continued, they'd release yellow flares to let the bombers know that their illumination was not on the target. Nevertheless the bombers would use the flares as their aiming point. The next flare ship in the stream still had a chance to find and illuminate the correct target, to release its yellow flares on the same area as the previous ship, or to light another aiming point in hope of finding the target. If the target was hidden by clouds, as tonight, the illuminators would simply locate the city with radar, mark it with yellow flares, and try to achieve as much destruction as possible.

At that point in Pop's unnerving dissertation, a sudden explosion of antiaircraft gunfire almost sent me racing for the basement, but his loud "Blimey, they got one of the blokes!" froze me in the sitting position.

Beyond the wall of stairwell windowpanes, a glow of yellowish light intensified and spread through the clouds. I visualized the final terror of the crew as their flaming craft plummeted down.

"Oh my God! We're the bloody target!" Pop yelled as he catapulted upright, then down the steps, with remarkable agility and speed for a man of his size.

Dozens of yellow flares suspended beneath parachutes appeared ghostlike out of the clouds. Pop, his way lit by the bright flares, had reached the midlanding and turned down the final flight of stairs before I could get to my feet. So much for British stoicism and Yankee pride.

By the time I reached the doubtful sanctuary of the black at the foot of the stairs, I heard the first onrushing scream. The damned Limeys use screamers on their bombs! I thought. It wasn't enough to blow the enemy into oblivion, the British had to terrorize them with screamers that make each bomb sound as though it is right on top of you.

My sympathy for the enemy was lost in the onslaught of explosions as the stick of bombs approached, then passed by the schoolhouse.

The first string bracketed our building, missing to the east by mere yards. Seconds later the concerted screams of another stick of death hurtling downward approached with earsplitting accuracy. Again the building rocked from nearby explosions. The gathering storm had burst its bonds and struck with unprecedented fury.

Between bomb bursts, the cacophony of scores of men in earnest prayer made the dark even more threatening. Each of us, in an effort to be heard above the enormous sounds of battle, prayed louder than his neighbors. The rumble of bombs walking toward us, exploding buildings along the way, raised the level of prayer commensurately. Death and prayers for salvation were being orchestrated in waving crescendos by the fury of combat. Between strings of explosions, antiaircraft shells shredded the air overhead and added yet another measure of terror to the night.

Nearby explosions broke like waves on a stormy coast, then ceased. Fresh waves pounded a few blocks distant as a flare ship lit another aiming point. That illuminated area had no sooner died when the next Pathfinder ship flared an area nearer to us. Again the sound and intensity of prayer rivaled that of the marching bombs. It seemed the frightful experience would end at any moment in unparalleled violence suddenly suppressed by sweet eternity. I didn't know how much more I could stand before I . . . I didn't know what.

Muscles ached from the pressure as I squeezed my balled body into an ever smaller compaction. I couldn't fight. I couldn't die. Squeeze! Squeeze harder!

The sound of a dying aircraft crept through the din of battle as the whine of increasing airspeed built in pitch and volume to instant oblivion. I concentrated on listening for the explosion that would end their frightful pain, but it never came. The sound of the exploding ship, like the life it carried downward, was lost in the larger sound and fury of battle: a nothingness in the face of violence and carnage. I tried, but I couldn't feel anything for the men who'd just died, not even relief that they had passed their moment of ultimate terror. My own terror was still too much within me, magnified by the screams of shells and bombs. I only wanted it to end, with no thought or concern as to how. Whether I lived or died was unimportant.

But the terror didn't end. It stretched on and on to a fearful eternity. Eternity is forty-five minutes long. No more, no less. And after that, for many, there's another eternity, an endless aftermath of waiting for the next raid, the next dream. For some, there is but one escape.

Following the All Clear, the sounds of a deeply wounded city lit by numerous fires reflecting off a smoke-blackened overcast kept tensions at a high level. Few of us returned to our bunks on the floors above. After going to the gym just long enough to get my blanket and have a short look at the ongoing terror in the neighborhood, I joined the crowd on the cement floor of the dining hall. The floor was hard and uninviting, but since many of the older prisoners were convinced that the British would return before morning, "hard" was not a consideration.

Discomfort wasn't the only reason for my insomnia. I wanted to forget the lingering terror, but the sounds of battle were too fresh in my mind. My thoughts wrestled endlessly with the improbability of our having survived the raid. Lit as we were by the first, then later spreads of flares, it didn't seem possible that we hadn't been hit by one or more bombs. I finally concluded that the reason the schoolhouse wasn't hit was because of the height of the illuminated clouds above us. The bombardiers had nothing more than a dim patch of light glowing on the *top* of the clouds for an aiming point. Their attempts to compensate for the elevated aiming point would have been little more than guesses. Satisfied with the rationale, my tortured and weary mind was fading to blessed relief when I became aware of a strange pressure on my chest.

At first puzzled, I was startled by the realization that a large rat was standing on my chest. My thoughts raced for a way to get rid of the creature before it bit me.

The schoolhouse had a sizable population of rats. Until their ammunition ran out, or was confiscated by the guards, the older prisoners had amused themselves by throwing shards of window glass at the plentiful source of fresh protein.

But this fellow standing on my chest in the black dining hall was no game. I visualized its tiny eyes glaring at my throbbing throat. That the creature was looking at either my head or feet, I was certain. The pressure of its tiny feet told me the line of its orientation, but not which end its teeth were on. I hadn't heard of any prisoners being bitten by rats. Neither had I heard anyone complain about rats getting in bed with them. Mine, perhaps disoriented by the bombing, was, I was certain, capable of anything. Worse yet, the damned thing showed no intention of moving on.

Lying in blackness with my eyes squeezed firmly closed, I could see my plan clearly. I'd grab at where I visualized its back to be with my right hand and immediately fling the hateful creature away. If my sudden movement caused it to scurry off, that would be an adequate solution. If it didn't bite me and I was successuful in knocking or flinging it away, that, too, would be fine.

"One, two, three," I counted in my mind to set a cadence and start the action. I reached, grasped, and flung. I was surprised at the weight of the squealing rodent as I loosed it into the black of the room. Surprise gave way to fleeting regret at the sound of a frightened yell. In my haste to get rid of the rat I hadn't considered where it would land. My smile was lost in the restless dark as I contemplated where on the poor guy's body the scrambling critter had landed.

It was late the next day before I spotted him. I'd never met the fellow, and conscience wouldn't allow me to get close enough to his clawed face to ask how he'd acquired his unusual injury. It is best to let sleeping rats lie.

The next two days were particularly painful. The deep depression that had plagued me during my initial hours of captivity returned with a vengeance. I didn't want to talk to anyone or even go to the dining room for meals. One of the most curious aspects of captivity is the very deep sense of isolation that seizes one even in the midst of a crowd. It was as though the other prisoners didn't exist.

I tried reading the pocket Bible my mother had sent to me for Christmas. It had a metal plate covering the front cover. The publisher intended the Bible to be carried in one's breast pocket, over the heart. The gold-tinged metal plate had been inscribed, *May this keep you from harm.* I had dutifully carried it in the left breast pocket of my flying suit. For several days following the raid, whenever I found myself alone, I opened the Bible, vowing to read it from cover to cover. Try as I did, the small print and numerous interruptions, to say nothing of my mind's frequent return to the miseries of the British raid, meant that I never got beyond the seemingly endless "begatting" of Genesis.

At first my mind seemed frozen, unable to rationalize the fears that plagued me. The most persistent was that the schoolhouse would eventually be destroyed by our own bombs. Nevertheless a glimmer of rationality flickered hopefully within deep gloom, then grew to cogent thought. I was determined never again to allow an air raid to frighten me as had the British raid. Pop was right, I had to adopt the attitude of "Come again lads. Give 'em Bloody 'Ell."

By the morning of the thirtieth, the weather cleared and brought with it a welcome brightening of my own spirits. Shortly after breakfast, Art hurried back from the morning staff meeting and asked if I'd like to get out of the camp for a few hours. The reason—to attend a burial—did little to dampen my enthusiam. In order to go, we had to give our parole—promise not to attempt to escape. I found that a small price to pay for a few hours' relief from our boring routine. Unaware of the grisly experience that lay in wait, I eagerly agreed.

Our party was made up of Fat Stuff, Captain Cristi, who would serve as the interpreter, two guards, Art, myself, and one of the older prisoners, who'd assumed the duty of keeping up with the location and nationalities of those buried in a military cemetery. The old head believed that the Rumanians were lax in identifying the nationalities of the men they buried. He said that their usual procedure was to bury all bodies as American Unknown.

The trip to the cemetery was made by trolley car and was uneventful except for one incident. En route to the proper car line, we were walking along, admiring the beauty of the morning and the architecture of the lovely city, when Fat Stuff spied a Rumanian soldier approaching on the opposite side of the street. I saw nothing amiss in the man's manner of dress or deportment but our maniacal jailer had other views. Just prior to drawing abreast of the hapless soldier, Fat Stuff launched his ridiculous bulk off of our sidewalk and charged across the street screaming and flailing his arms in an effort to do the man maximum harm. The surprised victim ducked a wild right and sped off unharmed. Fat Stuff, defeated in purpose, screamed what I took to be obscenities at the retreating figure. Then just as suddenly, the irate colonel rejoined our party and stomped angrily on. His disgusting behavior cast a pall over our light spirits and ruined what I had hoped would be a pleasant outing.

Upon arriving at the cemetery, I was surprised to see the old priest who conducted mass at the camp. Dressed in black chasuble, potcap, and other vestments appropriate for the occasion, he was standing near two open graves with crosier in hand and looked as much the *grim reaper* as a priest. Perhaps it was due to the severe damage a British bomb had done to the rear of the Orthodox church across the street from the schoolhouse, or perhaps it was the nature of the duty that he was about to perform, but for whatever reason, he seemed to be angry and was in a hurry to start the service.[1]

Two plain wooden coffins were resting on sawhorses at the head of their open graves. After a short exchange between the priest and Fat

---

1. I later learned that the priest was from Giurgiu and that his belongings had been destroyed by our bombs the day I was shot down.

Stuff, Cristi asked if we wanted the coffins opened. The old head replied with an emphatic yes. This seemed to upset the priest, but he nodded to a soldier standing nearby.

Inserting the blade of the shovel into the joint between the top and sides of a body-shaped coffin, the soldier slowly worked his way around the box prying upward until all of the nails were released; then he and another guard lifted the top free.

From the moment the top had started to loosen, the smell of burned and rotting flesh spread around us. Once the top was free, numerous flies flew out of the opening then back inside. If the stench was nauseating, the contents of the coffin were infinitely more so. They left little to the imagination as to the violence of air combat.

There was no body as such in the rough box. The inside had been filled to capacity with various bits and hunks of burned and raw meat. Judging from the amount of material and fragments of blood-blackened clothing that could be seen, the coffin contained more than the equivalent of one man. Someone had thoughtfully placed a bare foot and a shoe at the foot of the mass, and a white and swollen hand at the left side where it would normally be. The cuff of a white woolen sweater ringed the wrist and obscured the awful sight of where the hand had been severed.

The old head immediately exclaimed, "See that sweater, that's a South African."

He then asked Cristi who the men were.

Cristi replied, "American."

The old head gave Cristi a venomous look and said, "The hell they are. You people don't care what nationality they are. They're South Africans."

Instead of arguing the point, Cristi asked if we wanted the other coffin opened.

"Damned right we do!" the old head replied.

Cristi, with his don't-give-a-damn attitude, was getting to the old head. In view of the tragedy and drama of the occasion, we were all very much on edge. I figured that it wouldn't take much more for the old head to lose control and slug Cristi.

The second overfilled coffin was a duplicate of the first except the only recognizable human parts were a rib cage and a full scalp resting on top of the meat at the head of the box. It lay there shining in the sunlight like fine copper. The foot and hand in the first coffin were body parts common to all men. As such, there was nothing personal about them. But this patch of flawless red hair lying neat and clean on rotting flesh was warmly human and personal.

When the first coffin was opened, I'd had to force myself to look at its contents. Perhaps, in my thoughts, I was merely trying to deny the inevitability of life, death, my own mortality. I found it difficult to admit that these piles of unidentifiable carnage had been men: husbands, brothers, perhaps fathers, lost forever to their families, their comrades. Their cause was precious, their rotting debris an abomination, not worthy of their courage and sacrifice. What had happened to their dignity, their spirit of life that made them what they had been?

Satisfied that each of the coffins contained the remains of more than one man, the old head told Cristi to close them. The guards banged the nails back in place as best they could with the flats of their shovels and lowered the boxes into the graves. The old priest intoned the service complete with censer and holy water. The ceremony had been strange to me, a Southern Baptist. It left me with a feeling of barren, depressing loneliness.

One by one we each picked up a handful of earth and trickled it onto the coffins, our simple farewell to the misfortune of valor. Perhaps it was best that their families would never know. Were it not for their unselfish sacrifice, what remained of a bomber crew would have to be counted a pitiful shame. We, who but for the grace of God would have already come to a similar end, understood their sacrifice. Another tragedy lay in the rapidity with which others would soon forget, perhaps even deny the meaning of their deaths.

While the soldiers were filling the graves, we wandered about the cemetery marveling at Rumanian grave markers. Almost every gravestone had a photograph of the deceased mounted in a glass-enclosed frame. Many of the markers had military medals hanging beneath the photographs. The graves of airmen were distinguishable by the miniature aircraft mounted on the tops of their headstones. The models were of aircraft of every description, many of which I didn't recognize. The Rumanians must have found it difficult to find models to display; two of those that I saw were models of American aircraft. One was a Douglas DC-3, or as we knew it in the army air force, a C-47, or Gooneybird.

The second American aircraft was a model of a P-38. I couldn't comprehend the use of a hated enemy fighter on a gravestone. Perhaps the man had been shot down by a P-38. But that too defied comprehension: that the man's family would mount a model of the aircraft that had shot him down. We didn't know it, but within hours the Luftwaffe (if they practiced such burial customs) would have need for many more such models.

It was late in the morning of the next day when the air raid siren sent us scurrying for the basement. We'd been huddled below for fifteen minutes or so, and had come to the conclusion that it was another false alarm, when the city's antiaircraft guns exploded in relentless fury. After a few minutes of mounting fear, I decided that the target was some distance from us and headed for the the upstairs hall and doorway where I could get a view of the action. It was a full-fledged raid on a target several miles from us. That had to be the Doicesti oil refinery on the southwest edge of the city. Black smoke boiling up from the target indicated that the B-24s ploughing through the pall of flak smoke were giving the refinery a first-class shellacking. But the action that drew everyone's attention was the fierce air battle taking place about 20,000 feet up and about a mile south of us. Twenty or so Messerschmitt 109s and Focke-Wulf 190s were in hand-to-hand combat with a much more powerful force of P-51s and P-38s.

The German fighters, hopelessly outnumbered, had drawn into a Lufberry Circle—a ring in which each aircraft is following close behind the ship ahead. It was a purely defensive manuever, designed to allow the ship behind a chance to get onto the tail of any enemy fighter that tries to come up behind the ship ahead. The maneuver had worked quite well in World War I when aircraft were much slower and more maneuverable. But on this thirty-first day of July, 1944, it was a useless defense that allowed the Americans a field day at the expense of the venerable Luftwaffe. The battle was brief but furious. And we had ringside seats.

When the Germans set up their Lufberry, the P-51s set up a larger Lufberry outside them, in the same direction. From their superior position, each time a German fighter moved into a position that made it vulnerable to a P-51, the American would dart in, deliver a stream of .50-calibers into the German, then dart back into position in his own circle. If the damaged German headed for the ground, the P-51 would pursue him to his demise. If a German pilot's nerve broke and he rolled into a dive to escape the fight, a P-38 would break from the

Lufberry circling above the battle and engage the escaping German.

I saw only one German try to escape. It was a 109. He'd no sooner rolled into his dive when a P-38 directly over him rolled to follow. Both aircraft were in near vertical dives with the pursuer gaining rapidly. We couldn't tell if the German pilot saw tracers passing by him, or if he saw the P-38 in his rearview mirror. Whatever the reason —perhaps the P-38 pilot had shot him dead—the 109 pilot made no attempt to pull out of the dive. One moment his little fighter was streaking straight at the ground, the next moment was punctuated by a large explosion with a ball of smoke puffing up from the point of impact. The P-38 pilot, pulling back on his control wheel with all his might, bottomed out of his dive mere feet above the smoke and debris of the exploded 109. Moments later, the German Lufberry broke as pilots dove to escape the fury of the American fighters. There were probably fewer than half of their original number remaining when they scattered from our sight, with P-51s and P-38s in deadly pursuit.

It was a fine show, perhaps a more fitting salute to the unknown South Africans we'd buried than are Mr. Kipling's timeless words:

O it's Tommy this, an' Tommy that, an' Tommy go away;
but it's "thank you Mr. Atkins" when the band begins to play.[2]

---

2. British army Lt. Col. J. P. Macdonald, a former defense attaché to Rumania, believes that the bodies could not have been South African. His on-site investigations of the losses of all Commonwealth aircraft over Rumania provide convincing evidence that the bodies may well have been those of Americans who were shot down on the July 28 raid on Ploesti. As to the probability of an American wearing a South African sweater, if indeed it was South African, that is easily accounted for by the American flyers' taste for wearing Commonwealth flying garb, as did Ralph Hisey and others. Lt. Col. Macdonald's research also indicates that the aircraft that we heard in its death dive was very likely a Messerschmitt-110 that was shot down that night by Commonwealth gunners.

XIX

Following our sobering experience at the cemetery, I resigned myself to what I believed would be endless days of boredom. However, two days after the funeral Art hurried back from the morning staff meeting with the news that he, Lt. Myron Dare, and I were being transferred to the NCOs' camp at the hospital. We would depart by truck shortly after breakfast in the morning. I was delighted. The transfer would allow me to check on the condition of my gunners.

According to Art, the NCOs were allowed to take two hot showers a week. Their bath house was located in the hospital complex adjacent to their compound and was operated by the hospital. Hospital personnel counted the number of showers taken by the POWs and charged the POW Administration a fee for each shower taken. The new commandant had noted that only 250 or so showers were being taken each week. If all prisoners took two baths each, over 800 should be taken weekly. The new commandant interpreted the low rate of shower usage as an indication of poor POW morale.[1]

"A new commandant?"

"Yeah," Art replied. "Fat Stuff's still in command here, but there's a new guy. A colonel has been put in charge of both camps."

That was great news. A new commandant, perhaps someone who'd actually be interested in our welfare. Art didn't know the new colonel's name but we figured we'd meet him while we were at the hospital.

Following breakfast, I gathered my few possessions and waited impatiently for the word to leave. The morning passed and lunchtime arrived: still no word to go. I was beginning to think the whole thing was a charade when Art returned to collect his belongings and inform Myron and me that it was time to leave. We went to the rear yard and climbed into the back of the waiting truck. Because we had given our

---

1. As it turned out, the shower situation was quite the opposite. The NCOs had been regularly denied the privilege of showers. Fat Stuff was suspected of falsifying the shower records and putting the money in his pocket.

parole not to try to escape while we were en route, there was only one guard in the rear of the truck.

The trip took longer than I'd expected, attesting to the size of the city. Despite all the furor of the last raid, I saw little bomb damage, and wondered how long Bucharest could go relatively unscathed by the war. The British raid had undoubtedly destroyed buildings, but we saw nothing that we could attribute to the bombing. Our route was in the opposite direction from the area where we believed that most of their bombs had hit. Surprisingly, even the area near the marshaling yards did not show excessive damage. This was probably owing to the Rumanians' clean-up activity, the fact that we approached the hospital from the side away from the marshaling yards, and the limitations placed on our view by the route our driver was taking.

Without warning the truck turned into a cindered alley and shortly thereafter slowed as it moved between two barbed wire fences. Art, rarely at a loss to find humor in a situation, grasped a carton of strawberry jam in each hand, held them over his head and shouted, "Staveley for President! Staveley for President!"

The broad alley separated the two compounds forming the camp. One of the single-story buildings in the left compound turned out to be the camp kitchen and dining room. The other housed guards and Russian POWs who served as camp cooks and dishwashers.

The compound to our right also contained two buildings. The first, a two-storied brick structure, formerly a hospital ward, served as the main barrack. The second, a long, one-story wooden structure, housed the camp sick bay, a small office, and the overflow of prisoners. Beyond the far fence to our right lay the buildings and grounds of the Regina Elizabeth Hospital. Aside from the barbed wire fences, the area was rather pleasing in that it afforded ample room for the prisoners to move about and enjoy the luxuries of exercise and fresh air. Trees lining both sides of the alley added a pleasant contrast to the otherwise barren appearance of the camp.

The parked truck drew a crowd of curious, bedraggled men who stared up in wonder at us. This was an unaccustomed experience, officers visiting the camp; were they bringing food? Art, still campaigning for votes, spotted several of his men and immediately engaged them in shouted conversation.

Taking advantage of our elevated position in the rear of the truck, I searched and searched again for the familiar faces of my crew. I was about to give up and climb down from the truck when I spotted them. Standing next to Leon Claverie, with a smile on his pink face, was Frank Lynch. It took a moment for me to realize and accept the fact that he wasn't dead. The more I shouted at him, the broader he grinned. Finally realizing that the compound gate was open, I dropped off of the truck and headed for my two crew members. By the time I reached them, all six had gathered. They'd all made it through the jump without serious injury and seemed in reasonably good health. Lynch had lost a considerable amount of skin from his face and body because of the blistering effects of 100-octane gasoline, but he professed to have suffered no other ill effects. He couldn't remember jumping, and was still puzzled as to what had happened to him between the time he'd gone back to his guns for another round of ammo and his awakening on the ground, surrounded by troops. Since Joe Ukish had jumped before Ollie and Willie pulled Frank out of the bomb bay, Joe hadn't been able to explain beyond what he could guess.

I explained that King and Willie had used one of the new static-line cables to drop him through the bomb bay, and let it go at that.

Matthews, the first to jump from the rear of the ship, had had a particularly trying time. At the first scent of gasoline he'd climbed out of his gun turret, snapped his parachute onto his harness, and dropped through the camera hatch. He landed on a hilltop near the target and, like Bill Snaith, had curled his body into the smallest possible size while hundreds of bombs rained down. His had been a ringside seat at the bomb impact area, a seat which he'd have gladly given to anyone for the asking. The last aircraft had hardly cleared the target when he was captured by Rumanian troops.

Chris Dittman had sustained the worst injury. He'd landed in a manner that put severe pressure on his toes. Following his capture, he'd been forced to march for several days with toes that were either broken or severely sprained. They were still tender and painful.

Leon Claverie was a sight: emaciated, shoeless, and wearing nothing but brief shorts that he'd fashioned from a piece of canvas. He'd gone through a harrowing bailout that was still punishing him in his dreams.

The moment gasoline sprayed his turret he knew that the ship was mortally damaged and in danger of blowing up. He rotated the turret and hoisted it back into the aircraft. After climbing out, he ordered the men in the rear to jump, then checked the bomb bay. He saw

Lynch lying in the fuel and tried to pull him onto the catwalk but was unable to do it alone. Believing that Lynch was dead, and with his mind fading from too much 100-octane and too little oxygen, he snapped his chest pack onto his harness and dropped through the camera hatch.

One of our premission activities had been the ritual of checking our parachutes. The most important part of the check was to unsnap the release-pin cover and insure that the pins were not bent and that they operated freely in the cover retaining studs. The pins were attached to the end of the D-ring cable. If even slightly bent they might not pull free of the studs and allow the canvas cover to open and release the parachute. More often than not the pin-cover snaps were difficult to unsnap. There was a trick to opening them, but it didn't always work. In Leon's case, the procedure hardly if ever worked. Consequently he couldn't always check the release pins. This happened to have been one of those days; and it was his first jump.

Outside the aircraft and having gone through the violent decelera-tion, he'd grabbed the D-ring and pulled. Nothing happened. Intent on pulling again, he realized there was nothing to pull. He was hold-ing the ring and release cable in his hand but the parachute was still in its pack.

Driven by panic, he clawed at the pin cover that had previously resisted his most earnest efforts while under the ideal conditions on the ground. Adrenalin gave his fingers the strength of ten. While prying and pulling at the stubborn snaps, he was constantly aware of the ground losing its distant appearance.

The last snap finally popped loose, and the flap fluttered open exposing a broken cable-pin lodged in the retaining stud. The pressure of bungee cords pulling the canvas cover tight against the stud made freeing the small pin all the more difficult. Having lost half his altitude, he clawed and pushed at the pin with fear-driven fingers. Suddenly, his world turned white as the pin came free and released the bundle of nylon into his face.

Just prior to landing, he tried to steer the parachute toward more open ground. The effort caused his body to oscillate. Swinging beneath the chute like a giant pendulum, he struck the ground very hard, and injured both knees and his right ankle.

Soldiers had seen him land and were moving up the hill toward him. Having been spotted by the enemy, there was no need to hide his parachute. Turning to move in a direction away from the approaching troops, he was confronted by a young boy brandishing a hoe. He then turned toward a patch of woods to his right only to see another youngster pointing a rifle at him. "Trapped by a couple of kids," he spat in telling the tale, Leon waited for the soldiers. The officer in charge of the group took his morphine and cigarette lighter, then struck him with his fist.

After marching for several days, he was accosted by a priest with a young boy at his side. The priest angrily pointed to a nearby building that had been struck by a bomb, then to the boy. Shouting in anger, the priest struck him several blows with his fist. He then repeated the pointing and blows until Leon, feigning an injury, dropped to the ground. The ruse worked.

For five days Leon was paraded with others through the countryside and villages until he arrived at the camp. When he'd jumped from the aircraft, there had been no time to remove his parachute harness and don his flight suit and boots. He had landed clad only in his fighting garb: electrically heated underwear and socks. Now, clad only in his crudely fashioned canvas shorts, he looked like a refugee from a desert island.

During the course of our reunion I spotted a familiar face, one I hadn't seen for several years. It couldn't be, I thought, but the moment he saw recognition on my face, his own countenance broke into a broad grin. The grin belonged to Charles Kourvellas, a schoolmate from back home. We traded gossip on mutual friends as our group walked toward the main building.

By the time we arrived, Art was in conversation with a senior NCO, Technical Sgt. Robert B. (Pop) Culver, Jr., and was negotiating for a place for us to stay. Pop gave us his room. It was a small room, possibly a utility closet, just inside the main entrance.

We spent the afternoon talking with the men about living conditions and the camp routines. There were the expected problems of poor diet and medical care, and the overriding problem of the camp's location so close to the marshaling yards. I was surprised by some NCOs' apparent lack of trust in us. We'd been warmly greeted by our own men, but many of those whom we didn't know were openly suspicious. There was also grumbling about the food at the officers' camp being better than theirs. I couldn't tell whether the problem stemmed from rumors planted by the Rumanians, or whether the men assumed that we ate better simply because we were officers. When all ranks were imprisoned together at the garrison and the schoolhouse, everyone ate the same food. I assumed that this was still true, but not having eaten in their mess I was at a loss to reply to their complaint. Certainly the strawberry jam we'd brought with us, and the promise that jam would henceforth be a regular item on the menu, indicated that there were at least some differences in the camps' fare. In any event, as we had our first meal, we'd know if there were major differences.

Medical care was such that the men were reluctant to ask for treatment when they became ill. Most injuries received less than expert care, if any at all. Prior to June, the wounded slept on the same rude bunks and burlap mattresses as did the rest of the prisoners. The single sheet was changed about once a month—sometimes. No medical staff was assigned to take care of the wounded, and bandages were changed at two-week intervals. What little sulfa was made available appeared to have come from our own confiscated first aid kits. Iodine was in plentiful supply and was the standard treatment for infections.

Initially, at the Royal Garrison, the wounded and ill were housed in four unlit rooms in the POW compound and were cared for by an American officer and several NCOs. If a patient needed surgery, he was carried by stretcher more than a half mile to a hospital operating room, then returned by the same means to the prison sick bay. Because of infrequent changes of dressings, the stench in the ward had been almost unbearable.

In June, the wounded were moved to the present hospital building and given half of the second floor for their ward. The other half of the floor was devoted to Rumanian patients with venereal diseases. At one point a Rumanian soldier with syphillis and a Russian soldier with rabies were bedded with the Americans. The only improvements the new ward brought were the regular beds and a Rumanian nurse who volunteered to assist in the care of the wounded during her time off from regular duties.

At least two men had died needlessly. One, a man with multiple wounds, was kept in a body cast that allowed access to only one of the wounds. He developed lockjaw, was removed from his room long enough to be cured, then died of unknown causes several days after being returned to the ward. No attempt was ever made to remove the cast so that all his wounds could be treated.

The second death occurred during surgery. Because of a neglected leg wound, the man had developed gangrene. During amputation, fluid was injected into his veins in a manner that allowed air to enter his circulatory system. He died shortly after the surgery.

The main problem with medical care appeared to stem from a lack of concern by people in authority, not necessarily the doctors. Indeed, the care of Rumanian patients was little, if any, different from that given the prisoners. On the positive side, several men who'd been burned told us that they'd had excellent care. I could only assume that the quality of care one received was yet another of those inexplicable paradoxes of war. If one had the right type of injury, he received reasonable treatment. Others were less fortunate.

The overriding problem was the camp's location, only a few hundred yards from the main marshaling yards. From our position on the ground, the red crosses painted on white backgrounds on the gabled roofs of the buildings were readily visible. Although the paint was faded, I was certain the markings would be visible on reconnaissance photos and to the eye from bombing altitude. It was highly unlikely that the area would be intentionally bombed during the day; night missions were another matter. But all the red crosses in the world wouldn't protect the buildings from stray bombs. In order to prosecute the air campaign against Rumanian rail transportation, the Bucharest marshaling yards would have to remain a major target.

Shelter from the raids was provided by the building's basement, two slit trenches for the prisoners, several foxholes for the duty guards, and one small underground bunker just outside the main building. The slit trenches were not deep enough to provide real protection. Should the brick building receive a direct hit, it would most likely collapse, burying those inside and in the basement. All in all, not only did the location of the camp and the amount of protection provided to the prisoners violate the Geneva Conventions, but the Rumanians didn't even seem concerned that they were exposing their own sick and wounded to stray bombs intended for the marshaling yards.

The first mission flown against Bucharest had been against the marshaling yards. There could be no doubt in Rumanian minds that the existence of the hospital would not keep us from bombing such a vital target. Indeed, the Rumanian government may have continued to use the hospital in hope that bombs would impact within its grounds. Such incidents could be used to rally civilian support for the war, and reinforce the government's propaganda regarding the criminality of American airmen. While our thoughts on the matter were pure speculation, continued use of the facility as a hospital and POW compound was only a mild instance of inhumanity when compared to other things happening in the war.

By dinnertime our physical activity during the day had left me ravenous. Regardless of how unsavory the food turned out to be, I was hungry enough to eat most anything. Seeing the crowd heading toward the gate we'd entered, we fell in with them, crossed the alleyway and entered into the other compound.

We were greeted at the dining hall door by a very large sergeant who glowered at us, pointed toward the rear of the room and said, "Your food is on the back table." The man was obviously angry, and we were at a loss as to why. Art led the way as we walked toward our table, to the accompaniment of loud mutterings and uncomplimentary remarks aimed at us from various places within the room. By the time we reached our table, anger was boiling within me. I had no idea what was wrong, unless the men simply resented our presence in their dining room.

As we neared the table, the cause of their displeasure became clear. Three plates of fine food were awaiting our pleasure. There were croquettes of some sort, vegetables, and rolls. We looked at each other in puzzlement and took our seats. None of us spoke. We simply stared in wonder at the food, at each other, and took note of the chatter and hooting which grew in volume and intensity as the men filled the room and heard about the food at our table.

"That the way they feed in the officers' camp?"

"You eat that way all the time?"

"Look what we have to eat!"

The more and the louder they shouted, the angrier I became. I was angered by their implied accusation that the officers would break faith with them, that we consciously accepted better food than they had. I thought about rising, trying to quiet them and explain that we ate the same soup that I could see sitting on their tables, but the large sergeant, now at the other end of the room, appeared to be shouting them to even higher levels of anger. The situation was rapidly taking on the aspects of a mutiny. Angered to the point of losing control, I did the most shameful thing I'd ever done in my life. I started eating.[2]

The food was enticing yet I couldn't taste it, at least not well enough to identify what it was that I was eating. It was by any standard a small meal, yet when I was halfway through it I could eat no more. To his credit and ever clear conscience, Lieutenant Dare never touched the food on his plate. Then it was almost as if nothing had happened. When Art and I started eating, the men settled down and paid us scant attention. A few continued their loud comments, but in my anger I was beyond hearing them. We sat at the table until the first men started to leave, then followed them back to the barrack compound.

In the seclusion of our room, we discussed a number of theories as to why we had been given the special food. None made sense. Certainly the Rumanians hadn't given us the food to cause dissension. We'd been sent to the camp to improve morale, not destroy it. That was a joke. Since our arrival, not only had a number of the NCOs shown distrust, but several had been openly hostile. After the fiasco in the dining room I doubted that we could gain their trust. As evening shadows darkened the room, I went in search of my men, to explain as best I could about the food. Hampered by the night, I didn't find a single one of them. That gave rise to an even deeper hurt. I wondered if they were avoiding me because of the incident in the mess hall.

I had just returned to our room when two guards entered and motioned for me to follow them. Both seemed to be upset. (I later learned that they had been looking for me while I was wandering about in search of my crew.) Wherever they were taking me, they were in a hurry to get there. The moment we were outside, the guard following me gave me a shove. The mild push angered me, but upon reflection I decided that his urging could have been more forceful; he could have used his bayonet or the butt of his rifle.

My puzzlement as to where we were going ended when it became

2. I have tried many times during the intervening years to rationalize my action. There were a number of options open to me. I could have offered the food to any of the men who'd trade with me. That would have been the best solution. Or I could have simply stood and walked out of the room. The latter occurred to me, but I knew that I could never have accepted the catcalls I'd have garnered in my defeat. Pride wouldn't let me walk out of the place, yet eating the food was a stupid act. It is a shame for which I have never forgiven myself.

apparent that we were heading for the one-story building that housed the camp office. The guards stopped at the door, knocked, and upon hearing a muffled response, opened the door and nudged me inside.

"Close the door and sit down."

Sitting behind an office table was Captain Cristi. Now what the hell does he want? I wondered.

The single bulb suspended from the ceiling cast a dingy glow about the sparsely furnished room. I was curious about the line voltage in this semibackward country. So far, except for the large bulbs in the gymnasium, every light I'd seen in Rumania was dim.

Cristi, growing impatient for me to sit, motioned emphatically for me to take the chair opposite him. I still couldn't put a mental finger on the cause but just looking at the guy irritated me, and I was too hungry and tired to play his stupid interrogation game. Before he could launch into one of his threatening tirades I picked up the pencil and interrogation form lying on the table and started filling in blocks.

Name, rank, and serial number. Religion? I penciled "SB" in the space and pushed the paper across the table.

Hardly glancing at it, he shouted, "Complete the form!"

I returned his stare and replied, "It is completed."

My insulting response brought blood to his pasty face.

"Answer all of the items!"

In response to my silence and my attempt to look disdainful, he shouted, "I could have you shot!"

It wasn't likely that he would, but it bothered me all the same. I sat frozen-faced and said nothing.

Turning the form so he could read it, he pointed to the religion block. "What does SB mean?"

The tone of genuine interest in his voice almost caused me to laugh.

"Southern Baptist."

He thought that over for a moment and decided that I was being insubordinate.

"If you don't complete the form," he threatened, "I'll report you to the Swiss Legation."

"For what?"

"For giving me information other than your name, rank, and serial number."

Cristi's stupidity was amazing. First he threatened to have me shot if I didn't complete the form. Now the dumb bastard was threatening to squeal on me for giving him too much information—*if* I didn't give him more information. The urge to laugh was almost overpowering, but laughing at the simple jerk was the last thing I wanted to do. I doubted that he could have me shot and I figured he hadn't the guts to shoot me, but he could sure as hell have me beaten. Prudence caused me to put on a poker face and wait. As the impasse lengthened, he angrily ordered me to return to my room.

Art and Myron hadn't warned me that I was about to be interrogated. They'd gone through his mock interrogation while I was looking for my men and decided, as a joke, to let me face the ludicrous captain unawares. I wished that they'd told me. I would have had time to make up a fine tale by the time I arrived at his table. Bone-weary, sleep came to me in infrequent patches.

Morning brought with it the first hot bath I'd had in a month. Shortly after breakfast, we gathered in formation and ambled through the hospital grounds to the shower house. I didn't count the number of men in the formation, but a rough estimate appeared to substantiate the claim that only two hundred or so were taking showers. Having already noted the general state of their cleanliness, I didn't find the two hundred–plus baths as anything out of the ordinary.

The feel of hot water and rough soap on my tense body was heavenly. For the first time since my brutal parachute landing, I felt rejuvenated. Because of the shower house's limited capacity, I had to leave long before I wanted to relinquish the feel of the soothing water. There were no towels, but that was a small inconvenience. Before leaving the place I vowed that on the next trip I'd wash my flying suit. I had taken advantage of this opportunity to wash my underclothes. Although clinging wet, they felt better.

At midmorning, we were summoned to the yard, where a Rumanian officer we'd never seen before introduced himself as Lieutenant Rudolph, and a most distinguished-looking officer, Colonel Ciacanescu, as the new commandant.

The colonel, tall, recruiting-poster–handsome, riding breeches tucked into fine, highly polished boots, exuded the confidence of an experienced and capable officer. I couldn't follow the conversation, which was in German, other than bits and pieces and what Art interpreted for us. In essence Colonel Ciacanescu wanted to know how we were faring, and what we needed to assist us in improving conditions in the camp.

It was the wrong question. Art was eloquent in rendering an interminable shopping list of fixes, foremost of which was moving the camp. The colonel listened patiently and with obvious concern on his face, then explained that he'd do what he could. His nonspecific response didn't mean much, but under the circumstances anything he could do would be a godsend. I was heartened by the points that Art interpreted for us. In my mind, Colonel Ciacanescu's goodwill and offer to alleviate the stresses of captivity were established when he allowed us to bring the strawberry jam into the camp. Toward the end of the conversation, he smiled while making a short remark and nodding at each of us. As Lieutenant Rudolph interpreted what the colonel had said, Art's face froze in disbelief. He turned to us and said, "Colonel Ciacanescu sent us the food. He paid for it out of his own pocket."

"If he does that again," I said, "we're liable to have a riot on our hands."

I watched attentively as Art explained to Rudolph, and Rudolph to the colonel. Our well-intentioned benefactor appeared embarrassed. By the time the conversation ended, I was convinced that the prisoners had a friend in the person of the new commandant. The man was obviously intelligent and interested in our welfare.

Shortly after Ciacanescu and Rudolph departed, a guard hurried into the compound carrying a large pitcher of beer and three paper cups. His excited jabbering was probably meant to convey to us the source of our unexpected treat, but no explanation was necessary. The beer was undoubtedly Colonel Ciacanescu's method of apologizing for the trouble he'd caused us.

"Beer Call!" Art shouted, as he filled the cups and passed the pitcher to an NCO. I took two sips of the warm but delicious brew and passed my cup to a panting sergeant who'd slid to a dusty stop. Within moments, the pitcher was empty and late arrivers were grumbling over their great misfortune. One of the older inmates opined that the beer was Bragadiru, a beer of fine quality brewed in the village of Bragadiru, located ten kilometers southwest of Bucharest.

Late in the afternoon, a commotion at the gate drew our attention. An elderly lady was being escorted into the compound by a Rumanian officer. Our curiosity changed to guarded interest when their attention and direction of travel focused on Art and myself where we stood chatting with several NCOs. Before coming to within earshot of our group, one of the NCOs whispered, "Here comes Princess Boteanu."[3]

During our stay at the schoolhouse, we'd heard several stories about visits from Rumanian royalty. There were differing, sometimes strong opinions expressed by the older prisoners as to the reasons for the visits. Most felt that the prisoners were being courted for future favors, for "good words" on behalf of those who helped us. Titled Rumanians knew beyond question that they would be brutalized by the Russians when the war was over. In view of the manner in which Marshal Antonescu had wrested the government from them, one could not truly look upon the royal and titled families as true enemies. Indeed, from a practical point of view Antonescu was more their enemy than were we. King Michael and Queen Mother Helena had tried to improve conditions within the camps, but they were blocked by Antonescu at every turn. In effect, Michael and his mother were almost as much prisoners as were we. Having never met a princess, I was at a loss as to how I should conduct myself. The dear lady solved that problem rather handily.

"How do you do? My name is Boteanu," she spoke in accented but perfect English.

Fiftyish and slight to the point of frailty, her small face reminded me of the Disney cartoon character Jiminy Cricket. However, her manner and speech bespoke a person of integrity and dignity. Although there was no place to sit, we went inside our building so she wouldn't have to stand in the August sun.

Surprised to see her smoke cigarettes, I was amused by her manner of disposing of the ashes. We were standing in the central hall of the building. Each time the ash grew on her cigarette, she carefully tapped it into the palm of her left hand. After several such deposits, she moved to a glassless window, thrust her arm through to the outside, and let the ashes drift down to the ground. Although the floor of the barren room was quite dirty, her integrity and manners wouldn't permit her to flick cigarette ashes onto it.

3. Princess, or Madame, Boteanu was a member of the Red Cross. We addressed her as Princess, and she never corrected us in our use of the title. Years later Princess Catherine Caradja explained that Madame Boteanu was the daughter of a highly respected general of World War I fame. Titled or not, she was a princess to us for the invaluable assistance she (and Princess Catherine) rendered in aiding our wounded and helping us in many ways.

The visit was short but productive. She wanted to know how she could help us. Art talked about food and moving the camp. She openly sympathized with our desire to move the camp, but professed to have little influence on those who made such decisions. Nevertheless, she was in frequent contact with important civilian members of the government and repeatedly appealed to them for better food and medical treatment for the prisoners. Hers was an indirect influence that had produced little, according to her, but she felt that she could be of some help. I seized the opportunity to ask for pencils and paper with which to publish a news bulletin, and colored pencils and a small map of Europe. I explained that I wanted to draw a map upon the wall of this room and post the war news we gathered from new prisoners. She smiled and said that such small things were possible.

Since she was so obviously intent on helping us in any way she could, I felt a bit guilty for having deceived her about our sources of information. In addition to incoming prisoners, the hospital camp was now receiving a fairly regular flow of news from two other sources. The alleyway separating the compounds was commonly used by civilians making their way to an air raid shelter nearby. One civilian, an interned English oilfield worker, had Jewish friends in the city who secretly listened on a small radio tuned to the BBC newscasts from London and passed war news to him. In turn he would pause while walking along the alley and chat with prisoners standing near the fence. If he didn't tarry too long, the guards ignored him.

Our second source stemmed from an amusing affair of the heart. One of the NCOs, nicknamed Frenchy, would stand at the wire during alerts and engage a young Rumanian woman in conversation, in French. Under the giggling guise of courtship, she'd pass information that not only corroborated that which we received from the Englishman, but often went beyond that. As to her source, who she was, and her reason for taking the risks of keeping us informed, we could only guess. So far as any of us knew, her reasons were related solely to her feelings for Frenchy. Whatever their reasons, the young lady and the Englishman performed a vital and much-appreciated service.

The following morning, Madame Boteanu returned with everything I'd requested. Within two days I had drawn a creditable map of Europe on the wall, posted our latest battle information, and tacked our first news bulletin to the wall. The information was probably two weeks old, but was of great interest to the prisoners and to Madame Boteanu in particular. On her first visit following the completion of the map, she spent the better part of an hour staring at it and lamenting the fate of her home and lands in Bessarabia.

That small country, at one time the Principality of the family Basarab, has over the centuries been part of Russia, Rumania, the Principality of Moldavia, and the Ottoman Empire. It lay to the east of the Carpathian Mountains, between the rivers Pruth and Dniester; in 1940—with the help of the German army—Rumania regained control of the country from the Soviet Union. Madame Boteanu knew what it was like being oppressed by both tzars and communists. At the moment the Russian army had regained the territory and was sitting poised on the west bank of the Pruth, gathering strength for the final offensive into Rumania. Boteanu was aware of these facts and was depressed. She spoke openly of her hope that Rumania would be occupied by American forces but knew that it would not happen. Open and honest in her desires to have us speak well of her when the war ended, that was not the only reason she defied Antonescu by helping us. The dear lady was an authenic humanitarian. Under the auspices of the Red Cross, both she and Princess Catherine worked tirelessly on behalf of Rumanian victims of the war as well as for us. At war's end, Princess Catherine had more than 3,000 orphans in her care.

We'd been in the camp for three days when the air raid siren sent everyone scrambling for the basement or other personal place of refuge. I was in the yard at the time and chose to stand near a slit trench. A few minutes after the wailing subsided, several flak batteries in the direction of the marshaling yards started blasting away at an unseen target. Since no bombs were falling, and the city's general defenses were not firing in full force, I decided that it was only a P-38 on a reconnaissance mission. I climbed out of the too-shallow trench and walked to where a guard was crouching in his hip-deep foxhole. He'd laid his rifle aside and was clutching his large shiny belt buckle with both hands. I pointed to his hands, then to the sky, held my hands to my face as though I were looking at him through binoculars, and made a long whistling sound which I punctuated at the end by a loud BOOM.

His knuckles whitened as he grasped the buckle even tighter and

looked up at me in fear. I couldn't tell whether he was silently pleading for me to stop the raid or simply go away. Seeing the depth of
the poor fellow's fright, I smiled reassuringly and walked into the
building.

Two days later God punished me for my cruel jest. I awakened
before daylight with a searing pain in my belly. Our building, designed
as a hospital ward, had a single, Western style toilet only a few feet
from our cubicle. I barely made it. Within thirty minutes I was again
perched on my porcelain throne, doubled over with pain. By the
middle of the afternoon I was so weak and dehydrated I had to crawl
to get to my treasured artifact of civilization. I couldn't eat, nor could
I get to the faucet at the washbasin to drink. By nightfall I abandoned
my bunk for the concrete floor next to the commode. I needed medical
help, but I was determined to tough it out alone. On the third morning
I tottered to the mess hall for much-needed food. The ailment had
left me weak and light-headed. The breakfast of stale bread and ersatz
tea did wonders for my shakes.

At midmorning I was sunning on the front steps of our building
when a commotion just inside the gate of the mess compound told
me that a grave situation had developed. Art, several NCOs, and a
Rumanian captain were in the throes of a violent argument. I got to
my feet and wobbled over to the group as fast as weakened legs would
allow. By the time I arrived the captain was in a fury and pointing his
pistol at one of the NCOs. Art was pleading, in German, for the
captain not to shoot the man.

The heated argument continued for some minutes until the captain,
somewhat mollified by Art's pleading, holstered his pistol and waved
us toward the main compound. The NCO, at Art's urging, led the
way. When he arrived at the gate to our compound, he stopped and
stood just inside the fence. As the captain walked through the gate,
the NCO muttered, "Son of a bitch!"

The captain whirled and drew his revolver. Art threw his arms
around the NCO, looked back over his shoulder at the captain and
pleaded with him. The captain, unable to motion Art aside, appeared
to be on the verge of shooting both of them.

At that point, I got into the fracas yelling, "Nui!" Art released the
NCO and joined my efforts.

The argument continued for another ten minutes or so with Art
and me seemingly getting nowhere with the captain except that he

hadn't yet shot anyone. At that point Captain Cristi arrived in the alley with Madame Boteanu. Cristi, we later learned, had telephoned Madame Boteanu shortly after the altercation began.

With the coolness of a patient parent talking to an offending youngster, she drew the captain aside, and entered into quiet discussion with him. After only a few minutes in which she spoke and he listened, attentively, he bowed and limped quietly out of the compound. Then, as though the incident had been no more than a trifle, she turned to us and announced that there'd be no more trouble. I couldn't imagine what she'd said to the man, but from the moment she'd arrived he'd become calm and most respectful.

It had been a narrow escape for all of us. Art later told me that the argument started when he was summoned to the camp kitchen to inspect meat that had blackened from spoilage. The captain, a combat veteran, bore his physical and mental scars of combat with intense anger. He was of the opinion that the food was good enough for gangsters and criminals. Art wasn't certain as to how the NCO had become involved, unless it was because of some scathing criticism he'd leveled at Art for starting a fracas and disrupting the status quo of the camp. The captain may have misread the NCO's intentions and considered the man guilty of insubordination to himself.

Perhaps it was because of the incident, but for whatever reason, we were told two days later to get ready to return to the schoolhouse. Before leaving, I assured my men that the war would soon end and that we'd be released. They were hollow words at best. I had no idea when the war would be over. Privately I expected it to last until winter but I had no basis other than hope for that vain speculation. The thing that bothered me most was the knowledge that our visit had been of little value. It was presumptuous of us to think that our presence in the camp would make any difference. Politics being what they are, the Rumanian government's reasons for locating the camp near the marshaling yards and starving us involved considerations beyond anything that Art and I could expect to influence. We were no more than despicable prisoners, subject to the whims of an enemy. Indeed, if our captors so chose, our conditions of captivity could be made markedly worse. As it was, barring stray bombs, we could last for a long time on the food we were receiving.

Since we had no power to influence the physical aspects of captivity, our ability to survive and the quality of that survival depended on our ingenuity in overcoming the psychological problems of captivity. Although we'd been in the camp for only a little more than a week, I'd seen many evidences of the NCOs' resourcefulness in coping with the pressures of being prisoners of war. The ways they kept themselves entertained and informed on the progress of the war were adequate for the time that they were likely to remain prisoners of war.

Their most serious problem, other than the possibility of being bombed, was in keeping mentally and physically busy. If they allowed themselves to become inactive in their social intercourse they would become psychologically immoblized and fall into a creeping state of helplessness. From there it would be a short journey to hopelessness and the destruction of the human spirit.

Perhaps it was the relatively good news regarding the progress of the war that had slowed their escape activities. It wouldn't be particularly difficult to escape from the camp, but once outside there remained the formidable problems of food and travel. During the early days, when they were at the Royal Garrison and the schoolhouse, the NCOs had been quite aggressive, only to have their escapes end in failure after a few days of freedom. Although we detected no specific plans for the near future, I was certain that if the war bogged down some of them were planning to go through the wire.

As to their ability to survive long-term captivity, the rigors of their existence had developed strong leadership in a selected few of them. Technical Sgt. John Chonka was perhaps the most valuable man in the camp. A quiet, introspective man, Sergeant Chonka spoke Rumanian. From the outset his utility as interpreter thrust him into a position of leadership. Beyond that, his steady temperament and desire to escape marked him a natural leader.

As the truck pulled through the gate, I spotted another of their leaders, the unique figure of Sgt. Leroy Drane. Leroy would stand out in any crowd, and not because of the utter lack of hair on his head or his manner of dress (he had only underwear when we arrived). Leroy's quiet steadiness was a pillar, a rallying point for many of the men. A sleight-of-hand artist, when not relieving others of their possessions in a poker game he often entertained them with his considerable deftness of hand. The most interesting thing about him was the way he hovered like a mother over the others, providing ready cash to any in need of toilet tissue, soap, et cetera. On at least one occasion Leroy bribed a guard to bring beer into the camp. The guard had no sooner arrived with a large pitcher of Bragadiru, however, than he was intercepted by our revered interrogator, Captain Cristi, who knocked the pitcher from the guard's hand and sent it crashing to the ground.

Leroy carried his poker winnings in a cigar box, his constant companion. It was more than just a box of money. It was more like a field marshal's baton, a symbol of power in this place of less than bare necessities.

I gained the impression that Leroy was often amused by our pitiable circumstances. Certainly Sgt. Eddy Lauary found humor in one of the more demoralizing aspects of captivity, that of being cut off from communications with our families. Sergeant Lauary appointed himself camp postman and inked his authority, "P.O.W. POSTMASTER," across the front of his cap. That few received mail was immaterial. He cheerfully waited each day for it. His optimistic cap provided the men yet another opportunity to make light of their condition.

Perhaps therein lay the source of our strength, our ability to laugh at ourselves: to find humor in grim, even deadly, circumstances. The thought eased my conscience for not having accomplished more during our stay.

As the compound disappeared from view I found myself relieved to be returning to the schoolhouse where I felt that I would have more freedom to react to our circumstances in such manner as I chose. I wondered about the consequences of my growing tendency to become a loner in an environment that seemed to foster unwanted loneliness. It troubled me to admit that my growing desire to be alone could become a self-fulfilling prophecy.

XX

Our return to the schoolhouse brought a marked change in my daily routine. During our absence the gym had filled to capacity. Having no place to sleep, I went in search of a bed, finally locating an empty bunk in one of the end rooms at the front of the building. It was a much better setup than the gym. The room had fewer men —only a dozen—and its windows offered a view of the street with the trolley tracks and the church. Art found a bunk on the second floor with the senior officers. His association with them, and my involvement with new friends, spelled the end of our plotting ways to harass our captors.

After lunch I sought out my officers and told them that Frank Lynch and the other NCOs were alive and well. Curious as to any changes that had taken place in the schoolhouse while we were away, I spent several hours listening to stories about the success of the variety show that was being rehearsed at the time we left, and other happenings within the camp. Ollie was silent on the outcome of his and Tichbourne's plans to escape so I didn't push the matter.

During our absence our original SAO was transferred to the low-altitude raiders' camp at Timisul. Their SAO, Maj. William Yeager and two others, in turn, transferred to our camp. Except for the two men accompanying Yeager, there was little profit in the trade from the viewpoint of either camp, except that we gained a different and most valuable asset. Yeager arrived with a small radio hidden in a sleeve of his coat.

The mere possession of the radio, being in touch with the outside world, was probably as important to morale as was the news it brought to us. Each night the radio was tuned to the BBC, then afterwards broken down into several pieces and hidden in a chimney. A map, similar to the one I'd made at the NCOs' camp, had been drawn on the wall of a second floor room and was being posted with battle information. A news bulletin was tacked beside the map. Rumanian officers often came to the room to stare at the battle lines and be briefed on whatever information we had.

It was a remarkable paradox: enemy officers relying on their captives for information about the progress of the war. Surely they realized that we had a radio, a contraband that under normal circumstances should have been taken from us with appropriate threats and fanfare. However, as long as it was kept from view, it appeared that neither Fat Stuff nor his officers would become openly curious and demand to know our source of information. It was better to ignore the obvious. The irony of the situation was not without humor.

Rumanians, other than those who covertly monitored BBC, knew little of what was happening in the war. Rear area army officers, except those on high-level staffs, appeared to be no better informed than was the populace. If they received any war news from Rumanian news broadcasts, it would be something like "There is fighting east of Galati,"[1] with no details given regarding the size or implications of the battle, or how many miles east of Galati the battle was taking place. Had our radio been confiscated they would have had no definitive idea as to how the war was progressing. Except for their obvious alarm over rumors of a build-up of Russian activity to the east they gave the impression that the war couldn't end soon enough for them.

August 14 brought with it another of our oversized jailer's attempts to count noses. The incident, as usual, had its elements of humor. Confident that he'd finally devised a foolproof method of counting us, without warning we were herded into the first floor hall and counted as we exited the door to the rear yard. It was Fat Stuff's intention to count us going out, then immediately re-count us as we moved back inside. It was not a bad plan, providing he didn't end up with an average that included a half-prisoner. Considering the old heads' abilities to foil his counts, some of the fellows living on the second floor would probably escape to the attic and lower the total.

As the guards crowded us into the rear yard, pressure, caused by the press of our bodies, developed against the wooden fence separating the yard from the street. Before the guards could react, several fence posts cracked and let the fence lean toward the street. There were a few tense moments as confused and frightened guards shouted threats,

1. A small Rumanian city near the Soviet border.

until the pressure changed direction away from the fence. No one was foolish enough to attempt an escape under such tense and open circumstances. On the contrary we made sport of the broken fence thereby confounding the guards even more. The count ended with Fat Stuff standing in our midst, fighting to hold back tears streaming from his eyes.

"If you escape they'll shoot me" the interpretation of his words went.

"Six men escaped. While I'm counting, four more escape. They'll shoot me."

The pitiful bastard was an emotional wreck. Self-pity turned into instant anger as he shouted for the guards to move us back inside, then walked somberly through the basement door to his quarters.

His impassioned comments were puzzling. I hadn't heard anything about an escape, but something was clearly afoot and his superiors were obviously angry with him. I couldn't blame them. They were probably tired of his inability to account for the number of prisoners he should have.

During our absence, Fat Stuff had given the prisoners permission to use the north courtyard for a few hours each day. Because of the aborted count, he withdrew our outside privileges for three days. I preferred the small north yard with its shaded coolness, but the loss of privilege didn't bother me. I had taken to sitting at a window for hours on end chatting with roommates and amusing myself by watching street traffic and trolley passengers staring at us. I tried to read their stares, to understand their feelings. Except for an occasional shout of "gangster" or "criminal" most passersby were merely curious or fearful, and when they caught me watching them they'd often turn their heads as though they were unaware of our presence.

Some faces seemed to register wonderment. Rumanians, much like my young guard the night of my capture, traditionally held Americans in high esteem. I believed that many of those whom I saw passing our windows had difficulty relating us to the "Americans" they visualized in their minds. I felt that they were confused by our appearance and friendliness vis-à-vis their government's propaganda and the fact that we had bombed and killed their friends and relatives.

During the period we were restricted from using the yards, an amusing incident occurred in the street in front of the tavern. We had gathered at the windows to listen to the sounds of an argument building in intensity inside the tavern. A man and a woman were at odds about something. A third participant, the authoritative voice of a man, could be heard in the background. The tower guard, the fellow with a bad temper, was showing signs of growing irritation as he divided his attention between the sounds of the argument and his efforts to warn us away from the windows.

Suddenly a man staggered through the tavern doorway and into the street. Close upon his heels, a woman, wielding her purse, was bent on pounding him through the pavement. Less drunk than he, she stopped swinging long enough to turn and smile acknowledgment at our appreciative cheers.

We had reason to cheer. The woman, handsome of face by any standard, was voluptuous, with a skin-tight black dress that left nothing to imagination. Its ripped bodice hung loosely, exposing remarkable breasts that quivered seductively with her every movement. Having been denied the intimate sight of femininity for so long, we shouted wildly for the action to continue. Encouraged by our enthusiasm the woman returned her attention to the man.

The guard, obviously embarrassed by the scene in the street, was furious. He pointed his rifle menacingly, then turned to berate the combatants. The moment he turned away, we returned to the windows. Despite his threats, our new wave of cheers caused the woman to attack her victim with renewed vigor. The poor fellow seemed incapable of defense, other than by ducking and trying to ward off her blows with his hands and arms.

The guard, now black with rage, whirled in his tower and jacked a round into the chamber of his rifle. The time had come for us to duck.

Before he could pull the trigger, the woman, who had paused to again accept our appreciation, started shouting and flailing away at the man in earnest. I peeked over the windowsill just in time to see the guard take aim and fire a round into the street, a few feet from the scuffling pair. The loud crack of the rifle and echoing whine of the bullet ricocheting along the street ended the affair, but not before the curvaceous woman turned to us, smiled, and took a deep breath that all but freed her remarkable breasts from the straining cloth. It had been quite a show, one that was related, with appropriate embellishments, to breathless, disappointed inmates crowding into our room too late for the action.

The fracas brought welcome relief from the tensions that had gripped the camp during the past two days. There had been a week's relief from air raids, during which time we received the electrifying news that American and French forces had landed in southern France. With the invasion came hope; a major step had been taken toward ending the war. There were the usual speculations as our "barbed-wire strategists" modified timetables and made new predictions as to our release date. By the week's end, however, the siren had sent us dashing for the basement on succeeding mornings. No bombs fell on Bucharest; nevertheless, we were ravaged by the unfailing effects of alerts on our nerves.

It was a curious phenomenon, our reaction to the wailing siren. Not unlike Pavlov's experiments with the dogs, the sound produced instant reactions, powerful responses beyond the physical act of seeking immediate shelter. I, like most of the others, would be seized by an instant coldness that left me feeling hollow and momentarily numb. I was making progress toward controlling my reactions, but I was still inwardly embarrassed.

During combat I'd experienced fear, but not hate for the black puffs of smoke that signaled the presence of instant destruction and death. Even the swift fighters boring in at us did not produce unreasoned fear. I believed that through skill and luck we'd survive enemy fire.

Whether we were flying the aircraft or firing our guns, our thoughts and actions were objectified in terms of putting bombs on a target or defeating the enemy in an aerial duel. Fear was a constant companion in battle that took the form of great body tension, heightened reflexes, and an acute sense of awareness of events occurring around us. Once the battle subsided we could escape our circumstance of fear and prepare for the next engagement. But here in the camp, we couldn't fight, and there was no place of safety to which we could escape. Fear for our survival too often crystalized as our objective. One would think that the desire to survive would be sufficient, but such was not the case. Indeed, the desire to survive may well have been what fueled the fear that the siren inevitably triggered.

The sound couldn't kill or maim us, nor did we know whether it signaled a raid on Bucharest or on some distant target. Located as we were in the south-central part of the city, away from any known target, we should have had little to fear. In the case of the NCOs, their probability of being bombed was quite another matter. When the siren sounded, theirs were well-founded concerns. Regardless of probabilities, the near misses that both camps had experienced were a stark reason to relate the sound to violent death. I was learning with every pore to hate the screaming demon. Professor Pavlov would have found the laboratory aspects of the camps intriguing.

Lying on my rude bunk, enjoying the peace of deepening dusk, I was curious about my ability to think in such a clinical manner, and wondered why it was that when the time came and the siren started its fateful moan, I couldn't react with equal detachment. And why did the sound of the "All Clear" produce the same feelings of hate as did the warning signal?

Adrenalin seeped from its containing glands, and tightened my stomach and back muscles. It took a moment to recognize the clattering roar of Messerschmitt engines. The hawks were gathering. Dusk had darkened to near night. I couldn't see them, but I could hear the faint sound of idling engines as pilots throttled back to land. Others in the room had heard them and were murmuring my own thoughts.

The raids of the past two days, judging from the length of the alerts here in Bucharest, had been major strikes. Air activity observed far to the north indicated that Ploesti was the target. If events followed past patterns, assembling fighters meant that our turn could come tomorrow.

Fitful sleep gave way to another sparkling morning. Invigorating air suggested that a dry cool front had passed during the night. I regretted that my tensions on waking robbed the morning of its refreshment. Breakfast passed in relative silence. Few had the desire for their usual banter. The word had been passed regarding the fighter fly-in. Silent in private thought, we waited for the hated scream of the siren. At midmorning, the banshee's wail energized us to instant response. Because I lived so far from the stairwell, the small area beneath the stairs was filled to overflowing long before I came to a breathless stop. Finding no room, I stepped around the corner and sandwiched my body between two other tense figures.

The waiting was interminable. Why weren't guns firing? Where was the rumbling thunder of walking bombs shaking the earth with their every step?

The quiet was disturbed only by nervous breathing. After several minutes of tense anticipation, choked murmurs of light banter were followed by body movements as some stood to go above, while others shuffled well-worn decks and invited partners to "sit in" until the "All Clear" sounded.

Curious as to what the target could be, I returned to my room where I could watch for action to the north. I saw nothing, not even our fighters sweeping the heavens for a sight of the enemy. The "All Clear" released my tensions and I was lying on my bunk anticipating bitter salad and cabbage soup, when I was disturbed by suddenly fading light and a rush of excited voices moving toward the windows. An overcast of oily blackness was drawing an impenetrable curtain beneath the sky. The entire northern horizon was black.

Men crowded the windows. Others stood in the front yard talking quietly as they stared at the ominous overcast some two thousand feet above. The tough tower-guard and several passersby were also staring upward, their frightened faces registering something akin to superstition. Accustomed as they were to the smoke of battle, this pall was unlike anything they'd experienced. It was unlike anything any of us had seen.

Within minutes the last vestige of blue disappeared. The sun, eclipsed by the canopied residue of war, was lost in a universe of black sludge. As in a total eclipse, the level of light fell rapidly to an eerie glow. While the phenomenon frightened Rumanians, its cause was readily apparent to us. A layer of warm air, overlaying cooler air next to the earth's surface, had created a temperature inversion that trapped the smoke as would the ceiling of a room. To me the real marvel of the phenomenon was the vast amount of smoke.

As one would expect, the oily overcast dominated our conversation throughout the day. By nightfall it had disappeared as rapidly as it had appeared. By then there was common agreement that the remaining oil facilities at Ploesti had been severely damaged. None ventured to conclude that that most vital and feared target had been destroyed. It was sufficient to assume that the bombers had returned Ploesti's hell in full measure.[2]

---

2. Unknown to us, this was the twentieth and final raid by Fifteenth Air Force against Ploesti. On the nineteenth of August, formations of B-17s crossed and recrossed the huge Romana Americana plant, the only refinery still in operation. Directed by P-38 reconnaissance aircraft circling overhead, the bombers were able to line up with sufficient accuracy to cause severe damage to the plant and its tank farms hidden beneath the covering smoke screen. Where the missions of the seventeenth and eighteenth had cost the raiders twenty-two of their aircraft, there were no losses on this final day. The Luftwaffe, severely battered during the previous raids, did not respond. Finally, after one of the most intense and costly air campaigns of the war, the Ploesti nightmare came to an end.

The morning of the twentieth brought relief from the pressure of raids. It was Sunday and the old priest was on hand to hold mass. Bill Rittenhouse passed the word that he'd hold a Protestant service following the mass. The day had dawned lazily bright and I opted to skip the service and spend my Sunday in quiet conversation and lounging on my lumpy bunk. The day was filled with boredom and a longing to be elsewhere. Evening brought no particular news on the radio, so I retired with the sun.

The following morning was somehow different. I couldn't put my finger on the cause, unless it had something to do with the number of Rumanian officers standing at our map, engaging each other in long and furtive conversation. The BBC hadn't carried any news out of the ordinary, but something had certainly caught their attention.

By nightfall, word spread that the Russian army was on the offensive. No one had any details, nor was anything posted on the bulletin board about unusual activity. I ignored the rumor and passed it off as hopeful speculation. I was much more interested in the large number of prisoners that had been brought in during the past two days. They were the survivors of the Ploesti raids of the seventeenth and eighteenth. Fresh from the trauma of having been shot down, many were still ravaged by thir first loneliness. The school was being packed to its rafters. Pretty soon we'd have to either assemble double bunks, or sleep in shifts. Despite the good news of the past two weeks, we felt that our condition could be on the verge of becoming worse, perhaps much worse. Consequently, one and all were taken by surprise when on the twenty-third we were assembled to receive our first Red Cross package.

Until now, each time we asked Fat Stuff why we hadn't received Red Cross packages, his stock answer had been, "The packages arrived but were destroyed during the last air raid." No one believed the thin lie, but there was nothing that we could do about it. Shortly after our arrival in July, an official from the International Red Cross, a Swiss with detectable German leanings, visited the camp. When asked about packages, he'd admitted they'd been shipped but could tell us nothing more. Those who spoke to him called it a waste of time.

Consequently, we had been surprised when the day after we had arrived at the NCO camp, Tony Polink showed up with a truckload of new American uniforms. I hadn't needed clothing. Although in need of a good laundering, my flying suit was in fine shape. Nevertheless, I had joined others in making humorous comments as we watched those dressed only in underwear, or striped prisoner garb, searching through stacks of shirts and trousers to find a set that hadn't been cut to fit King Kong.

The uniforms had been provided by our government and forwarded through the International Red Cross. An American flag accompanied the shipment, but Fat Stuff refused to let us have it. Indeed, we were surprised that the Rumanians let us have the clothing. Some read our captors' unaccountable generosity as an omen that we would be prisoners into the winter. But now, only a few weeks after receiving the uniforms, without any indication or pressure on our part, it was Christmas in August. We each received one of the treasured boxes.

Prior to their being distributed, packets of soluble coffee, the canned goods—spam and corned beef—and powdered milk had been removed and stored in the kitchen for communal use. The remaining largesse, five packs of Old Gold cigarettes, a bar of Tasmanian chocolate, cheese, hardtack crackers, raisins, and other edibles were left in the boxes for our individual consumption.

The Old Golds were disappointing. After smoking dry skinny Nationals, the fat American cigarettes tasted strange and much too wet. My initial disappointment passed when I estimated the amount of money the Old Golds would bring on the black market. We'd have no trouble getting a guard to perform that service for us.

Our captors' reason for not giving us the packages sooner remained a mystery until we heard the story about how they arrived in camp. On August 3, Tony Polink had been given a truck and a Rumanian driver and told to go to a certain place in the marshaling yard and return with the uniforms. He'd done so without incident. This morning, when directed to return to the marshaling yard for the Red Cross packages, he'd found the two rail cars containing the packages guarded by German soldiers. Upon showing them the papers he had been given, the soldiers broke the seals on the car doors and allowed Tony and the driver to unload the parcels without incident. The story had fascinating implications.

In April, when the air campaign against Rumania started, there had been difficulties with the Germans. They had wanted to ship all American prisoners to Germany. Premier Antonescu, possibly because of pressure from the King and the titled, insisted that the Americans were prisoners of Rumania. The Germans had given in on the point, but to reaffirm their dominant position they had not only insisted upon the right to interrogate us, but they had obviously taken control of the Red Cross packages and clothing when they arrived. Small wonder the Rumanians never admitted that the items were available. They would have been much too embarrassed to disclose their subservient position. This was only speculation, but it made sense.

At the moment we weren't interested in the political infighting between Rumania and Germany. Perhaps we should have been. The future would soon disclose that we prisoners would be very much a part of Germany's forthcoming actions in the war.

Fat with our unexpected largesse, and a bit queasy from over-indulging in the chocolate, we found the day had been almost enjoyable. All anyone could talk about was when we would be getting out of the place. Certain in my own predictions, I wagered two hundred dollars against Lt. Irving Fox's estimate that we'd be out of Rumania by Thanksgiving.

The night had grown black. Tired of the day's banter I was trying to get settled on my bunk when the sound of hurried footsteps and voices yelling in the hallway claimed everyone's attention.

"Everybody go to the auditorium! Everybody upstairs! Move it!"

"What the hell's this all about?" someone spoke in the dark.

"I'll bet Fat Stuff's pulling another damned head count," someone ventured.

"I don't think so," another voice chimed in as we moved toward the stairwell. "If it's a head count, he'd have sent guards."

Our puzzlement ended abruptly when we squeezed into the packed auditorium. Standing at the front and center of the stage, Major Yeager's face grew dark from his effort to shout the unruly prisoners to silence.

"What the hell's that guy doing up there?" someone nearby murmured.

It wasn't a question. The speaker was echoing my own objection to the major's authoritative presence. Behind him, standing at the rear of the stage, an unusual collection of luminaries was patiently waiting: Fat Stuff, Bill Snaith, an American lieutenant colonel whom I'd never seen before, Colonel Ciacanescu, a chunky general and his frowsy daughter (known to us as Miss Bucharest), and an older man—a civilian—dressed in a business suit. Miss Bucharest, her large breasts challenging the strength of her dress, as usual was smiling as her eyes swept the audience, mentally raping each of us in the swift course of her glance. She was the subject of most of the conversation I could hear from those nearby.

As the crowd quieted, Yeager's loud voice continued.

"I have an announcement. Anybody makes a sound, I'll take him outside and whip his ass!"

Before any of us could accept his challenge, he shouted: *"The war's over! Rumania has capitulated!"*

His last word was almost lost in the deafening roar. Men screamed, whistled, and pounded each other; and there were tears. It was finally over. We were free. *Free!*

Shouting us into submission, he explained. "King Michael has arrested Antonescu and taken control of the government!"

Again we roared our approval. The general smiled and waved a fat hand. Miss Bucharest almost cracked the thick layer of makeup plastering her leering face. Fat Stuff's grim countenance looked to be on the edge of tears.

Yeager continued, "Rumania has declared war on Germany and given them forty-eight hours to withdraw their forces. You're to remain in the camp until we can figure out what to do."

The babble of loud speculation drowned out his next words. None believed that the Germans would withdraw. They were locked in battle with the Russian army. There was no way the Russians were going to allow them to turn their backs and walk away. With the return of order, Yeager continued, "The general has something to say."

No one was interested in anything that fat bastard had to say. We were convinced that he had something to do with our conditions of incarceration and was responsible for the camps being located as they were. He walked to the front of the stage, smiled, raised an arm, and spoke. "Rumania is finally on the right side of the war."

The room was silent as over eight hundred, hate-filled eyes glared at him. He was the wrong one to make that statement to us. I felt like throwing up. If I could have done it on him, I expect I would have.

Sensing an imminent disaster, Yeager shouted, *"Dismissed!"*

His command brought instant bedlam as men yelled and bolted from the room. Being near the door, I was one of the first into the hall. To avoid the stampede on the stairs I moved in the opposite direction, and was immediately grabbed by a guard who shook my arm as he gleefully shouted, *"Pace! Pace!"* Then he loosed his hold to grab another prisoner and repeat his *"Pace! Pace!"*

I didn't need an interpreter. They, too, had heard the news. Understanding was immediate. The old farmer was saying "Peace! Peace!"

Other guards were in the hallway. Some, still on duty with their rifles, seemed at a loss as to what to do with the weapons. Others, unarmed, had come in from their barrack in the rear yard to join in our celebration. All were shouting, *"Pace! Pace!"*

By the time I made it to the first floor, I too was shouting, *"Pace! Pace!"* The stairwell guard grinned and returned my shout. Thoroughly imbued with *Pace*, I dug my hand into a pocket and handed him a fresh pack of Old Golds. The little fellow, a man with whom I'd had some difficulty in the past, was overwhelmed by my generosity. He had such a grasp on my arm that I feared I'd have to take him all the way back to the States to have him surgically removed.

After charging out of the auditorium, most of the prisoners didn't go to their rooms. Their purpose was almost universal: walk out that back gate. By the time I arrived at the landing, scores of men were in the street, whooping like Indians attacking a wagon train. One enterprising group was trying mightily to tear the fence down and push it into the street. The gate guard seemed to be trying to decide if he should join the effort. The fence no longer had any meaning to me, so I stepped through the skewed gate opening and added my rebel yell to those in the street.

For a half-hour or so, we had the street to ourselves. We'd been told about the capitulation before the news was released to the public.

First there were two or three of them, then more and more civilians joined us shouting *"Pace!"* and *"Peace!"* Many invited individual prisoners to come with them. Some did, and were filled beyond their capacities with food and wine, and beer, and tuica, *ad infinitum.*

Tiring of the noise and weary from spent adrenalin, I returned to the building and went in search of my officers. I found only King, so the two of us joined others discussing our good fortune and what we should do next. There were at least three hundred miles of land, and the Adriatic Sea as well, between us and Italy, not to mention thousands of German soldiers along the way. Scattering was the worst thing that we could do. Our best course of action, most agreed, was to remain at the schoolhouse and wait for developments. I wondered if the NCOs had heard the news. I could imagine the wild celebration going on at their camp.

Going to bed was out of the question. We were bent on taking advantage of every moment of our new freedom, with minds and senses that reveled in the very thought of being free. As soon as the visiting dignitaries left, Fat Stuff, his record of inhumanity to the Russian prisoners foremost in his mind, returned to his quarters. Painfully aware of his Russian charges' threats, he called the senior Americans to his room to discuss the situation. He wanted four American majors, armed with .45 automatics from the salvage room, to guard him day and night. As the story we heard went, after thoughtful consideration, he relented. With tears rolling down his fat cheeks, he said something like, "No, If they're going to kill me, they will kill me."

Hearing the story momentarily robbed me of the fine edge of joy, but my compassion for the pitiful bastard was short-lived. I was certain that he deserved whatever would happen to him. I'd seen his bestiality to his own men and despised him for it. Yet I had to respect him for his attitude at the moment he decided to accept his fate. At that moment he was probably as human as a man can be.[3]

Around two in the morning, word passed that breakfast was being served. Perhaps it was the pause in celebration wherein the flow of vital juices is interrupted long enough to allow recuperative functions to take charge; whatever the reason, following a snack of bread, jam, and coffee, I dragged my weary body upstairs and collapsed on my bunk.

I awakened to the sound of cheering coming from outside. Stepping into the hall, I fell in with an excited group of ex-prisoners hurrying toward the rear entrance. Joining the crowd in the yard, I followed their silent gazes upward to see the most beautiful sight in the world. The Stars and Stripes, draped in all its magnificience against the blue sky, was fluttering in the morning breeze. A half-dozen men had climbed onto the roof, raised the flag, and were now watching its slow, colorful movement with unbounded pride. It was a picture, a moment that would endure in all who watched.

3. Years later, Princess Catherine disclosed that Russian troops tied Fat Stuff, the captain who'd almost shot Art at the NCOs' compound, and Stinky—an abusive lieutenant not otherwise mentioned herein—to a tree and shot them.

Following breakfast, Ollie and I decided to explore the neighbor-hoods nearby. I had visions of the lovely park and boulevard only a few blocks distant. Turning the corner at the trolley tracks, I noticed that the Leica camera I'd been admiring in the shop window across the street from my new room had disappeared. I wondered who had made off with it, or if the shopkeeper had hidden it for safekeeping.

It was a magnificient morning for a stroll. Buildings along the street basked in the early light and gleamed invitingly, but the invitation seemed hollow. It took a few moments for the reason to register.

Where were all the people?

There was no one on our street, which had been the site of many celebrations during the night. Ahead, where our street met the boulevard and its tree-lined esplanade, I spotted several townsfolk hurrying along. Normally at this time of the morning there should have been many people on their way to work, out buying food for the day, moving about for many reasons. I had expected to see crowds of people celebrating their joining our side of the war. Instead, the city had come to a virtual standstill.

Moments later the cause of the abandoned streets came faintly on the sound of distant gunfire. The chattering machine gun was not challenging us. It was too far away to be of any danger.

When we reached the boulevard, we turned right to follow its inviting path. Buildings were of much the same architecture and purpose as those across from the school, but nicer. There were shops of all sorts at the street level, and doorways to apartments above. We'd walked no farther than half of a long block when sudden gunfire almost dumped the war smack in our laps. We couldn't see where it was coming from or who was being shot at, but it was no more than a block or so away, and it was all we needed to reverse our direction and run like hell.

Gaining the cover of our street, we hurried to the sidestreet and the tenuous safety of the schoolhouse. The gunfire sounded more distant now, but I knew better. It was only three or four blocks away. Others had heard the shooting and were having thoughts not unlike my own.

Bright smiles of freedom gave way to expressions of deep concern. The prisoners had just learned that the Germans would make an attempt to recapture us. The sound of gunfire lent truth to the rumor and emphasized the fragility of our new freedom. The Rumanian government had given assurances that tanks and troops would cordon off our area and defend it to the death.

I wasn't impressed. I knew nothing about the quality of Rumanian troops, other than what I'd surmised of the men who'd marched us from the military compound to the school. I had to admit that they'd had the look of capable fighters. One way or the other, we were trapped and helpless; that is, unless we could arm ourselves or slip away to safety should our situation become untenable. No matter how we dissected our situation, all of us arrived at a common conclusion. The war was far from over for us.

XXI

T he sounds of battle grew slowly. Fire fights broke out in several
directions within hearing. First there was the scattered crackling
of rifle fire, then the chatter of machine guns, occasionally the muffled
whump of a mortar or the sharper sound of a grenade. I listened
intently to determine the locations and progress of the battles. Fear
mounted with each increase in the level of fighting. There was no
fighting nearby, but the noise of battle captured the thoughts and
imaginations of airmen who knew little of the realities of ground
warfare and feared the worst.

With each renewed burst of fighting I recalled newsreel shots of
street-fighting as I tried to get a "feel" for the problems we faced. At
some point, I thought, we might have to find weapons to protect
ourselves and move to a quieter area of the city. The risks involved in
a group of our size trying to move through an unknown battle situation
without guides would be very high. If necessary I would escape on
my own, or in the company of only two or three others. Rumanian
divisions were undoubtedly allowing Russian forces to maneuver at
will. The German army would have to give ground in order to shrink
and consolidate its dispositions and lines of communications and
supply. If we had to leave the city, I intended to opt for a place to dig
in and let the fighting pass me by. In the meantime, I would sweat it
out with the rest here at the schoolhouse. All in all I was not impressed
with my ability to rationalize our situation. To sit it out and see what
developed seemed the best course of action, at least at the moment.

So intent in such thought and conversation were we that when the
screaming whistle of a bomb froze our distracted minds, it was a long
moment before we realized what was happening.

At the hospital, many of the former prisoners had abandoned prison
for the luxuries offered by civilian goodwill; many were drinking and
dining in private homes and apartments, or at fashionable restaurants

and pubs. Leon Claverie was in the compound behind the main building, talking with others about the sounds of gunfire, wondering what it meant, what they should do. Looking upward to locate the drone of engines, he was startled to see a formation of what at first he thought were American B-25 bombers approaching. Simultaneously with the release of their bombs, someone yelled, "Heinkels!"

Men dived for the safety of slit trenches. Some charged into the familiar basement of the barrack. Others ran for the distant safety of an unfinished office building—a skeleton of reinforced concrete some fifteen stories tall, and probably the finest and most heavily-used air raid shelter in the city. It was toward this shelter, roughly two hundred yards away, that Leon fled with most of the ex-prisoners.

Tony Polink had wandered onto the street in front of the schoolhouse and was chatting with a group of civilians when the bomb started its chilling scream. The group crowded onto a sidewalk elevator and lowered itself to the safety of the cellar below. While bombs exploded above, Tony enjoyed the safety and bounty of the cellar: bread, wine, and salami.

Inside the schoolhouse, realization turned to near panic as the approaching bomb screamed louder and louder, falling directly at us. I dived for the floor and scrambled for the doubtful safety of the underside of my bunk. Others charged into the hallway and dashed for the stairs.

A second bomb was already screaming its approach when the first bomb exploded a short distance away. Frozen beneath the bunk and confused by this new sound of battle, I was at a loss to understand what was taking place. They weren't British bombs. The British didn't drop one bomb at a time. It had to be a German dive-bomber. The bastards were trying to kill us!

My outcry was lost in the sound of the siren. Hurriedly backing out from underneath the bunk, I lifted my head too soon and struck it against the rough edge of the sideboard. It hurt like hell, but the sharp pain that brought tears to my eyes was the least of my concerns. Approaching bombs and the wailing siren vied for the position of being the driving force in my record speed down the hallway.

The second bomb, sounding as if it would hit the schoolhouse, exploded some distance away. That momentary knowledge did nothing to slow my flight for the basement. Despite the unceasing wail of the siren, I could hear other bombs starting their unnerving sound. The ragged explosions of uncertain antiaircraft fire were just starting when I leaped the final steps, landed on the concrete floor, and dropped next to the basement wall.

The men huddled there were more tense and confused than usual. The screaming bombs and unending siren knotted muscles and froze minds in a vacuum of fear. Sporadic antiaircraft fire gave us little comfort. Heretofore, flak batteries had been manned by German gunners who were both accomplished and relentless in their craft. The few guns that were now firing were probably manned by Rumanians, and I had no confidence in their ability to operate the guns.

At the hospital camp, following the passage of the Heinkels, JU-88 dive-bombers appeared overhead and pushed over into screaming dives, aiming directly at the huge air raid shelter and the hospital. Later in the day 109s came in low and tried to skip-bomb their lethal cargoes into the open sides of the shelter. The men on the lower floors were well protected from all but the bombs that were skipped. Those remaining at the compound were vulnerable to every type of bombing and strafing attack. There was no reason for the Luftwaffe's selection of such targets other than revenge—to kill as many people as possible.

By the time the second raid was over, at least one hospital building was in flames. Many others were severely damaged. Between raids, those still at the compound fled to the large shelter or elsewhere.

The raids throughout the city were staggered in such a manner that one could not rely on the siren. After a while it was impossible to tell which signal was being given. The moment it appeared there was an All Clear, Messerschmitts, JU-88s, or high-flying Heinkels would loose their bombs or drop down to building level and strafe.

Taking advantage of a break in the action, Leon and another NCO returned to the compound for bread. They never got to the mess hall. Inside the compound, his back propped against a tree, an NCO lay dead, robbed of life in a blinding instant by a massive head wound. Beyond his torn body, flames were working their way through the building containing our wounded. Losing all thought of hunger, the two men ran to the burning building.

There were no litters to be found. Desperate for a means of carrying the wounded they ripped a door from its hinges and started transporting helpless men the long distance to shelter in the unfinished building. On their third trip Frank Lynch, Charles Kourvellas, and others joined them, ripping doors loose and carrying the wounded men the two hundred yards or so to the multistoried shelter.

During the course of the evacuation the hospital again came under dive-bombing and strafing attacks, but the evacuation teams, true to their mission of mercy, carried on until all thirty-nine of the wounded were safely inside the shelter.

Assuming the raid was over, I walked to the rear yard. Large fires were burning to the north. We judged them to be near the center of the city. While no one with whom I spoke had seen anything, we were certain that the attackers were German. Within moments lingering doubts were fully erased. A formation of six Heinkels appeared to the south of us, heading in a northeasterly direction. Bursting antiaircraft shells dotted the sky at odd altitudes and places. The closest shells missed the formation by at least a quarter-mile. The scene would have been laughable, were the guns not on our side. As it was, there was no time to laugh at the inept gunnery; the wailing siren sent us skipping back inside the building. Within moments more bombs screamed.

Having learned the lesson the hard way in previous raids, I remained at the cellar entrance where I could watch the flight of the bombs and not worry needlessly. The tactic failed miserably. I could not see them, but I could sure as hell hear them; they were right on top of us. I dove for the safety inside.

I heard their explosions but felt nothing. Again I'd been fooled. Apparently the bombs were small, perhaps two-hundred-and-fifty-pounders. But they were powerful enough to demolish this old stone building. Since I hadn't been successful in spotting the bombs, I thought it best to remain inside and worry.

A much closer explosion blew my level of worry to near panic as I awaited the next blast. The plaintive sound of men at prayer didn't help. Their supplications seemed to bring impending doom to the edge of reality. I wished they would shut up and pray quietly, as I was doing.

As the day wore on, the attacks would start suddenly, then just as suddenly be over. I gave up relying on the siren for warning. It accomplished little, other than to heighten tensions and irritate frayed nerves. The pressure of unrelenting tension left me feverish and half-numb. I wasn't hungry. Eating anything substantial was out of the question, but it didn't matter. We'd lost our water pressure because of a severed main or some other cause. Without water it was almost impossible to prepare a meal. While the water lasted I had drunk my share and then some. I had learned early on that tension on the ground is as thirst-producing as its high-flying counterpart.

Night brought no relief. The Luftwaffe was intent on destroying as much of the city as possible. Prisoners who'd left the schoolhouse during the day drifted back with stories of widespread destruction and civilian casualties. The palace had been severely damaged, as had other government buildings and private residences.

Rumors were rife. The enemy was bent on recapturing or, if necessary, killing the Americans. The most devastating rumor of all was that the enemy had seized pumping stations ringing the city and poisoned the water supply with cyanide. I didn't believe either rumor, but a queasy feeling in my tight stomach weakened my disbelief. Others who did believe the rumor became intensely frightened.

Sleeping in my bed was foolhardy. We had crowded into the basement all day, and it appeared that we would be wise to remain there. I opted for a patch of concrete on the dining hall floor, but uninterrupted sleep was impossible. Sporadic raids continued throughout the night by both Heinkels and dive-bombers. Antiaircraft fire was totally ineffective, seldom heard. The screamers had been frightening enough during the day. Now the night magnified the terror. Each bomb seemed to be coming directly at us. Such was the nature of the sound pattern. If we were within the cone of sound, the bomb promised our senses that we were the target. Realizing that such rationalizations didn't help, we waited, tightened muscles, prayed, and sweated.

Early morning brought enemy bombers back in force. This time, the bombs were closer, much closer. The moment the raid started I crowded in with a group at the foot of the stairs. I had never heard such intense prayers, not even on the night of the British raid. Nearby, a major, one of the new prisoners I had not yet met, was immersed in deep terror.

"I'm dying! I drank some water. I've been poisoned!"

Over and over he repeated the words. Each repetition was louder, as though the words proved his self-diagnosis. The poor bastard was crying, then screaming: "I'm dying! I've been poisoned!"

"Somebody make that son of a bitch shut up!"

I didn't know who'd said it, but I agreed with the sentiment. The man's wailing was getting to me. He hadn't been poisoned any more than the rest of us, but damned if he wasn't starting to show the symptoms. He did not appear to be frightened by the bombs; indeed, so overcome was he with the thought that he was dying of cyanide poisoning that he seemed oblivious to the raid. I doubted that he could even hear the bombs. I was so intent on the dark color he was developing that I too forgot about the raid.

Moment by moment his complexion darkened. Suddenly his gasping breath stopped altogther. Someone started pounding his back and shoving on his chest to get him breathing again. Within moments I could hear his strangled breath and moaning. Then came convulsions and uncontrolled sobbing. By the time the raid ended he had calmed to a dejected hulk of humanity, barely able to stagger away from this place of dark terror. I never saw him again.

The raid had barely ended when the roar of engines overhead sent me crouching against the basement wall again. One of the most curious aspects of our fear was the way we bunched together in tight knots of torsos and extremities. I didn't know why. One body offered little or no protection to the next body. Perhaps by bunching so closely we offered a smaller target. By occupying a tiny place, there would be less damage than if we were spread out.

Ridiculous thought? Not when one of those huddled bodies is you, when real bombs sound like they are going to explode directly on *you*.

The raids, the loss of water and food, the lack of reliable information and meaningful direction made the place a living hell. We were existing on the last crumbs from our Red Cross packages, but the need for water was paramount. The latter problem came to a sudden and happy end when Tony Polink drove into the yard with a tank truck. He'd filled the tank at the hospital compound.

Tony reported the death of the sergeant. The hospital and compound had been severely damaged by bombs. That ended all doubt that the enemy was trying to kill us. Tony had no specifics about individuals, other than that the wounded had been evacuated to shelter and were being cared for by NCOs.

The day wore hard, as raid after raid loosed screaming death on the city. During the morning a request was passed for volunteers to assist Rumanian crews on the antiaircraft guns. The gunners needed help in identifying friendly aircraft. The request was laughable. I figured that neither friendly nor enemy pilots had anything to fear from Rumanian gunners. But accurate or not, they were trying. The volume of antiaircraft fire became noticeably greater as the day wore on.

Another amusing request was passed at the same time. Someone wanted to organize fighting units to take on the German army. If the time came to defend ourselves, I thought, that would be a different matter. But to go looking for a fight was sheer folly.

Late in the afternoon, I went in search of a better air raid shelter. Some of the prisoners were using Fat Stuff's covered bunker in the rear yard. No one knew where the "human pear" had disappeared to. I had not seen him since the night of the twenty-third.

Weary of the crowded basement, Ollie had discovered a much better shelter: the bottom of the rear stairwell at the left side of the stage. We were there with several others for the balance of the afternoon and most of the next day. I spent the night on my favorite spot on the mess hall floor. Again sleep was all but impossible. The sounds of street-fighting and brief air raids were too threatening to ignore.

August 26 started as had the previous two days. The bombers and fighters were back, but in lesser numbers. The Rumanian air force had collected its own meager resources and some captured German fighters, and was taking on the Luftwaffe with intense vigor.

Early in the morning, Major Yeager arrived back at the schoolhouse riding a black BMW motorcycle. The man was obviously fatigued and very dirty, his clothing covered with masonry dust. On the morning of the twenty-fourth, he had left the camp in search of a radio transmitter powerful enough to make contact with Allied forces, to tell them of our plight. He had ended up with a radio set up in the basement of a bank. The bank, unfortunately, was located in the area hardest hit by the Luftwaffe. He had stayed at the radio night and day, until German bombs severely damaged the bank and ruined the set. He believed that he had established contact with a British station, but the signal was so weak that he couldn't be certain about that.[1]

---

1. His transmissions were received by a British station in Cairo, but it was days before the message was forwarded to Allied headquarters in England.

Late in the morning the air raid siren sent us hurrying inside. Several minutes later someone standing in the yard shouted, "B-24s!" It was hard to believe. B-24s bombing Bucharest? Our situation was bad enough with the enemy bombing us night and day. Surely Fifteenth Air Force had gotten the word that Rumania was now on our side. The temptation to see what was going on was too much. I stepped outside.

It was a remarkable sight. Group after group of B-24s rained bombs on a target to the north of us and not a puff of flak smoke was to be seen. We had no idea as to what their target was, but I sensed a universal prayer that it be the German airfield from which our tormentors were flying. Indeed it was. There were two targets: a large enemy barrack area at the northern edge of the city, and nearby Otopeni Airdrome.

There was no way of knowing whether it was because of the B-24 strike, or because the enemy had run out of bombs, or for some other reason, but by nightfall the bombing stopped. Nevertheless I spent another night on the dining hall floor. And I slept.

Major Yeager's return to the schoolhouse unearthed a subject that I hadn't thought of until he walked through the gate and haggard men gathered around him. Where were the camp's senior officers? What were they doing while we huddled inside what we thought was an enemy target?

Following the announcement of the war's end, I had learned that the unidentified lieutenant colonel on the stage was our new SAO, Lt. Col. James A. Gunn. He had been in the camp for three days, but that was the first time that I'd seen him, and I hadn't seen him since. Neither had I seen Bill Snaith. I had no idea who was in charge, or what if anything was being done to get us out of the city and the country. Until today, the twenty-sixth, we had drifted in limbo, enduring the air raids as best we could. As the day progressed and no bombs fell, hope glowed and grew with each passing hour. The sounds of fire fights persisted, but seemed more distant. To the north, perhaps beyond the city's edge, the dull boom of artillery was distinct. The day the bombing started I had heard the rumble of tanks several blocks away, but no major battle had erupted. At the moment our position seemed safe enough, but that was hardly reassuring. Still shaken by the relentless bombing, it was impossible to relax and make any kind of plans, but the rumor mill was running full force.

Sometime during the day I heard that we would move to a new location. I wanted to believe it, but since there had been no official announcement the rumor only depressed me.

It wasn't rumor. Small buses were parked alongside the building and prisoners were already in the street, waiting to board the buses and leave this place of morbid memories. There were not enough buses to carry the more than four hundred of us in one trip, so I waited for them to return. It was a long wait. They didn't return until morning.

Our new home was a barracks area about five miles south of the city. It lay in open country, among large fields patched with wooded areas. What appeared to be a very large parade ground could easily serve, too, as a landing field for light aircraft. By the time we arrived those who had traveled on the first convoy were upset and wondering what to do. The camp had been buzzed by ME-109s, and I couldn't get the straight story. Some claimed that the Messerschmitts had strafed. Others said that they'd merely been buzzed. The conflicting stories were typical of the reactions of men under stress.

Delighted to be out of the city, I reveled in the freshness of the air and the quiet of the surrounding countryside. Inside the barrack I chose a real cot with a real mattress, luxuries I hadn't enjoyed for months. Sleep came early and deep.

Following a breakfast feast of scrambled eggs, fried spam, and coffee, Art and I returned to the schoolhouse to pick up .50-caliber machine guns and a load of ammunition. Lugging the heavy guns and ammunition from the schoolhouse basement to the truck was a waste of effort. We worked all day trying to anchor the guns so they could be fired. We tried fastening a gun to a wooden post set in the ground near the parade field. The moment the gun was fired, the post leaned backward. We finally gave up on the project and left the guns and ammo for others to puzzle over. Perhaps a suitable mount could be had from the Rumanian army.

Men arrived throughout the day. Most of the NCOs from the air raid shelter came by bus convoy. Many arrived in small groups, some as single passengers in civilian autos. The latter were the result of

Rumanian radio broadcasts and notices in the newspaper. The highlight of the day was the arrival of the low-altitude men from Timisul. After being released from their camp, they had holed up in the small village of Pitrositza. Immobilized by large numbers of German troops retreating through the area, and having no idea of where to go or how to get there, they had wisely waited until someone came for them. Princess Catherine commandeered five trucks, hid the hundred men underneath blankets, and bluffed her way through German lines with the ruse, "We're going to pick up German civilians trapped in Bucharest."

By evening, August 29, there were over one thousand of us in the camp. A handful of NCOs had remained with the wounded at the air raid shelter. Others had gone underground and were enjoying the delights of the city. Eventually, twenty men, caught up in the revelry of townfolk, had to be ordered to report to Popesti Airdrome.

By evening, the camp was humming with the latest and finest rumor yet heard. In the morning, we were going to be bussed to Popesti Airdrome and be flown back to Italy.

No one knew how it would be done. No one cared. The only thing that mattered was that we were leaving Rumania.

XXII

When Lt. Col. James A. Gunn III, the new SAO, awakened on the morning of August 24, he faced the task of protecting and arranging for the evacuation of more than eleven hundred half-starved, widely scattered ex-prisoners of war to Italy or any other place of safety. By noon the combat situation in the city and the nonstop bombing made his task seemingly impossible. During the past week he had been caught up in a whirlwind of events that demanded more of his courage and leadership at every turn.

As commander of the 454th Bombardment Group he had led the group on the August 17 mission against Ploesti. A last-minute radar malfunction forced him to change his position in the formation and to allow Capt. John E. Porter to take the lead. On the bomb run, four of the eight aircraft in the lead squadron, including his, were shot down by flak. It was three days before he arrived at the schoolhouse to take command of the prisoners. Three days later, in hardly enough time to adjust to the tenuous nature of his new command, Rumania quit the war and Germany appeared determined to punish its former ally. Gunn found himself faced with grave responsibilities without either authority or means to accomplish the tasks the situation demanded of him—to insure that the ex-prisoners of war were not slaughtered or recaptured by German forces, and to arrange for their return to Allied control.

Colonel Ciacanescu and Fat Stuff had disappeared, and the Bucharest telephone exchange and most radio stations had been either destroyed or damaged beyond use. The Rumanian government was in fully as much disarray as the prisoners. Without communications or responsible Rumanian authorities to work with, Gunn realized that he had little other than his own ingenuity and that of others to extricate the Americans from these difficult circumstances.

As the day wore on, with no letup in the bombing, the situation grew more desperate. He visited the NCOs' camp at the hospital and found the situation under control but fraught with potential adversities. There was no room at the school for the NCOs, nor any means to move them. Advising the NCOs to stay put at the air raid shelter until he could make arrangements to move them out of the city, he left in search of the means to do so. He soon discovered that the bombing and fire fights within the city had caused so much damage and confusion that buildings where one would expect to find persons in authority were no longer usable. Leaders had fled to unknown locations.

The night brought no relief from the bombing or progress toward contacting Rumanian officials. Gunn rationalized the situation as best he could, and by morning he knew the course of action he would take.

He called the senior officers together and dispatched Major Yeager to search for a means of communicating with Italy or Cairo. Bill Snaith was given the task of making contact with the Red Cross. Maj. Haas would take over the administration of the camp, while Gunn himself attempted to establish personal contact with the Rumanian government.

Before he could leave, two Palestinians arrived. They were Rumanian Jews who'd escaped the country before the war, only to return by parachute as British agents a few months prior to Rumania's capitulation. They had been hiding in Bucharest, and had surfaced now to carry on a new mission. They wanted Gunn to gather the Americans and join with them in forming a guerrilla force. Knowing that the physically weakened ex-prisoners, untrained in methods of ground warfare, would suffer excessive casualties in a fire fight, Gunn refused; but he said their suggestion to reconnoiter Bucharest for gaps in German dispositions was well taken, though not possible at the moment. Their request refused, the Palestinians left, accompanied by Snaith.

Gunn's first stroke of good fortune occurred with the arrival of Sergeant Dali. After talking with Gunn at some length, Dali departed on his motorcycle. Leaving the schoolhouse, Dali went in search of Colonel Silescu, the general staff officer responsible for all prisoner of war camps in Rumania. Sympathetic to the plight of his ex-charges, Silescu made arrangements for Gunn to meet with Lieutenant General Racovita, minister of war. Unaware of Dali's success and the fact that Colonel Silescu had set in motion a vital course of events, Gunn spent the night of the twenty-fourth in dismay over his apparent lack of progress.

The next morning, a Rumanian lieutenant arrived at the schoolhouse in a 1938 Buick provided for Gunn's use by the general staff. In excellent English he informed Gunn that later in the day he would be taken to the War Department where he'd meet with the minister. Where moments before he had been in the depths of frustration and despair, Gunn was now revitalized with hope. In the meantime he decided to use the automobile to reconnoiter the city. The reconnaissance would be done by majors Haas, Call, Ferguson, and the Rumanian lieutenant. The party left, then returned an hour later to report that with the exception of a few barricaded buildings, the southwest area of the city was free of enemy troops.

Later in the day Colonel Ciacanescu arrived to accompany Gunn and the lieutenant to meet with the minister of war. The War Department buildings in Bucharest had been so heavily damaged by the bombing that temporary headquarters had been set up in a complex of recreational buildings in a woods several miles outside the city. It was a quiet ride, one that allowed Gunn time to collect his thoughts as to what he'd say to the minister.

Gunn waited only a few minutes before being ushered into a room and introduced to Lieutenant General Racovita and his wife. The Racovitas were friendly and gracious.

Upon hearing the plight of the prisoners, the general said he'd make immediate arrangements to move them out of the city. When he promised to move them the following day, Gunn revealed his plan to fly to Italy personally in a borrowed aircraft and arrange for the ex-prisoners' rescue.

Upon hearing the plan, the heretofore friendly General became unsure, or else suspicious. However, when Gunn suggested that his return to Italy would result in the Americans at once mounting a bombing mission against Banasea Airdrome, the field that most German bombers were using to bomb the city, Racovita's attitude changed. He made no commitment, but his manner and words contained hope.

At this point Gunn took out a pack of Lucky Strikes from his flying suit and offered one to Mrs. Racovita. Noting her pleasure he insisted that she take the remainder of the pack. Diplomacy takes many, often unconventional avenues in its delicate course.

Shortly after Lt. General Racovita left the room, Mr. Rico Georgescu, secretary of state and economic minister, entered and offered Gunn the hospitality of his home. The offer resulted in wine and a steak dinner in a fine restaurant in the downtown area, and was accompanied by the sounds of bombing and spirited fire fights in many directions.

Having been assured by Lt. General Racovita that the Americans would be moved to a safer camp, Gunn approached his host with his proposal to fly to Italy. Unlike General Racovita, Georgescu was receptive to the idea.

Upon returning home, the Minister made numerous calls by means of a field phone. During this time several visitors arrived to discuss the proposed flight. The discussions and phone calls continued until 4:00 A.M., at which time the exhausted Gunn went to bed. Early the next morning—the twenty-sixth—Georgescu took Gunn to another location, where he was introduced to the minister of the Rumanian air force. Through an interpreter, Gunn was told that arrangements were set for him to be flown to Italy. Within minutes, he and Georgescu were on their way to Popesti Airdrome, a few miles outside the city.

Disappointment lay heavy on Gunn as he stared at the ancient Savoy-Marchetti, a twin-engine relic of the Italian air force. A Rumanian pilot and two armed soldiers were standing by. None of them could speak English. Worse yet, they appeared to be frightened of him. It was as though they thought once they were airborne he might try to kill the pilot and take control of the airplane.

Twenty minutes after takeoff Gunn's spirits sank as the pilot banked the aircraft and rolled out on a course back to Popesti. He indicated that he was having engine trouble, but Gunn couldn't hear or see anything wrong with the engines. The pilot was either too frightened to fly the mission, or he'd been ordered—via his radio—to return to the airdrome. Dismayed by the turn of events, Gunn stepped down from the aircraft when it landed deep in thought as to what he should do next.

Waiting for him was Prince Constantin Cantacuzene, a Captain in the Rumanian air force.[1] In excellent English, Cantacuzene said, "If you will ride with me in the belly of my 109, I will take you to Italy."

---

1. Cantacuzene, cousin to Princess Catherine Caradja, was a flyer's flyer. During the years before the war, he was chief pilot of Rumania National Air Lines, and a stunt pilot with few peers. At the time of these events he commanded the Ninth Pursuit Group. With fifty-four victories—four of which were against his former ally as they bombed Bucharest —he was Rumania's leading ace.

It was an astonishing proposal, one that appeared to the dismayed Gunn to have an excellent chance for success. Despite the many and grave risks he would be taking in flying inside the small fighter's fuselage, he accepted without hesitation.

Perhaps Cantacuzene wanted to allay any doubts Gunn may have had regarding his piloting skills, or he may have just wanted to show off, but after Gunn made his decision, the daredevil prince took off in his personal acrobatic ship, an old biplane particularly suited for stunt flying. Those present were treated with a spectacular exhibition of low-altitude aerobatics, "the likes of which I'd never seen," as Gunn later exclaimed.

After wringing out the biplane, the two of them left the airfield and drove to Minister Georgescu's home where they spent the evening dining and discussing the strategy and details of their upcoming historical flight. The next morning—the twenty-seventh—they returned to Popesti to check the work being done on Cantacuzene's Messerschmitt and to make their final navigation plans. Major Yeager arrived during the morning, to suggest to Gunn that he could escape to Turkey by train and effect the ex-prisoners' rescue from there. Having committed himself to the flight, Gunn declined the proposal. Yeager returned to the schoolhouse, but told only a few of Gunn's intentions. Shortly thereafter Minister Georgescu arrived and told Gunn that Dr. Maniu, the interim president of Rumania, wished to speak with him.

Through an interpreter, Dr. Maniu pleaded with Gunn to deliver a formal request that Rumania be occupied by British or American forces. Dr. Maniu's impassioned plea testified to Rumanian fears of Russian occupation, a fear that had frequently surfaced during Gunn's conversations with other officials. Gunn promised the distraught man that he would relay the request.

Blessed in his undertaking by the highest authority, Gunn was impatient to be on his way. Cantacuzene, who wanted to plan the flight down to the smallest detail, reminded Gunn that should anything go wrong, he would be trapped in the belly of the little fighter with no chance of survival. They would have to penetrate three hundred miles of enemy airspace, then another hundred miles of American-controlled territory and antiaircraft gun placements, and land on an American base in an enemy fighter. To make matters worse, there was not a single map of Italy to be found in the Popesti Airdrome files.

Thoroughly familiar with the landmarks leading to Cerignola and San Giovanni, his base, Gunn drew a map of Italy on a piece of cardboard and briefed Cantacuzene on details of making the landfall and navigating to the airfield. He then drew a smaller sketch on cardboard, including details of antiaircraft gun positions, barrage balloon dispositions, and prominent landmarks. Cantacuzene would carry this second sketch in the cockpit.

Now there was disagreement between the two. Gunn wanted to avoid detection on American radars by going in low and landing before the American and British air defenses could react. Cantacuzene reasoned that it would be more prudent to fly high, in plain view of the searching radars, and if intercepted to lower his landing gear in surrender.

Having agreed to follow Cantacuzene's strategy, there still remained the problem of flight altitude. Gunn would be without oxygen, and could conceivably die en route if they flew too high for too long. They decided to fly at 6,500 meters—approximately 19,000 feet—until midway across the Adriatic. At that point they'd keep engine power high and utilize a shallow nose-down angle to maintain a high airspeed, thereby limiting the time available for American and British fighters to react. At this point only two other details needed to be accomplished. The radios had to be removed from the small fighter to make room for Gunn, and an American flag needed to be painted on each side of the ship's fuselage.

While this work was being done, Cantacuzene drew Gunn aside and explained that far too many people knew of the plan. He noted the politics prevailing in his country, and feared that someone had let the plan be known to the Germans. If the Luftwaffe knew of the flight an attempt could be made to shoot them down. The wise thing to do was to let it be known that they would take off early in the morning of the twenty-eighth. Then, as soon as the aircraft was ready on the twenty-seventh, they would devise a ruse to enter the aircraft, then take off.

After they made their decision, Cantacuzene telephoned Georgescu and the minister of the air force and explained the new plan. Both agreed that it was the proper thing to do.

With the painting of the flags almost complete, Gunn was outfitted with heavy leather flying clothing. Under the pretext of checking to see if he would fit inside the small space, Gunn was helped through the eighteen-inch opening and the cover plate was fastened into place. Under the ruse of wanting to check his engine, Cantacuzene climbed into the cockpit, started the engine, and taxied away from the small group of puzzled workmen and onlookers.

The takeoff went well with no aircraft weight or balance problems evident. It was very cold in the cramped space strung with control cables, and the lack of oxygen and space limited Gunn's physical movements. The lesser air density of their high altitude added to his breathing problems and to the dizzying effect (hypoxia) of being without oxygen.

Well into the flight Gunn discovered a small, spring-loaded plate hinged to the side of the fuselage. It was the step plate the pilot used in climbing into the aircraft. Swinging the plate in and down, he created a peephole that gave him a limited view out of the left side of the aircraft. Sometime later the increasing pressure against his eardrums told him that they were beginning the long descent. Opening his peephole he watched as the Italian coast came into view, then the river and other familiar landmarks that Cantacuzene was following so unerringly. Within minutes, providing that flak or a hungry fighter pilot didn't blow them out of the sky, they would land at San Giovanni.

Before takeoff, they had agreed that upon approaching the field Cantacuzene would extend his gear and wing flaps, and rock his wings while making a straight-in approach to the runway. They reached the final checkpoint, and turned to a heading of 340 degrees. The banking aircraft told Gunn that they were on the approach and would be on the ground within minutes. However, the weather failed to cooperate; the wind was blowing from the wrong direction.

Not wanting to make a downwind landing, Cantacuzene entered the traffic pattern on the downwind leg. Flying slowly with his gear and flaps down, he rocked his wings in an exaggerated manner to assure those below that he had no intention of attacking the installation. British gunners, astounded at the sight of an enemy fighter with an American flag on its side, tracked them with 40mm antiaircraft guns until Cantacuzene greased the fighter onto the runway.

Cutting his engine on the parking ramp, the flamboyant captain opened his cockpit canopy, smiled at the gathering crowd of open-mouthed GIs, and spoke.

"If I may have a screwdriver, I have someone inside you may be happy to see."

After removing the access plate, he stood aside to give the growing crowd a clear view of their missing commander emerging, GI boots first. Gunn stood uncertainly while he regained his equilibrium and cleared the effects of hypoxia from his brain. It was now August 27, 7:40 P.M., and there was still much to be done.

General Nathan Twining, commander of Fifteenth Air Force, was not at his headquarters when Gunn telephoned that he had returned. Consequently Brigadier General Charles Born, chief of operations for Fifteenth Air Force, instructed him to report to Mediterranean Allied Air Forces (MAAF) headquarters, where Born would join him.

After a quick meal Gunn and Cantacuzene went to the MAAF, where they briefed General Sir Henry Maitland on the situation in Rumania, the need to evacuate the Americans as soon possible, and Dr. Maniu's message. Before releasing the weary Gunn for a much-needed rest, General Born assured him that strikes would be made against German-occupied airdromes in Rumania until all of the missing airmen were returned. As to the rescue operation, that would require many hours of detailed planning and preparatory work before an acceptable plan could be devised and excuted.

Two days later, on August 29, at 8:00 A.M., Captain Cantacuzene opened the throttle on the P-51 he now was to fly and accelerated down the runway. Following him were two more P-51s piloted by Americans. It was a tenuous beginning, but Operation Gunn, the preparatory phase of Operation Reunion, was under way. Everything now depended upon the trustworthiness of Cantacuzene and the situation at Popesti Airdrome.

If the plan were to have any chance of success, contact had to be made with the men in Rumania. Cantacuzene was the logical—the only—emissary at hand for that task, but getting him back to Bucharest posed a problem. The fuel in his 109 had been exhausted and there was no time to locate proper fuel. The perfect solution, however, lay ready at hand. On the twenty-eighth, Cantacuzene had been briefed by Lt. Col. William A. Daniel on the engine operation and flying characteristics of the P-51, larger and nearly two thousand pounds heavier than the Messerschmitt. The talented captain had

had no difficulty flying the speedy fighter. Now, the following morning, he was leading Operation Gunn, the pathfinder mission, back to Bucharest. Unknown to him, should he try to break away from the formation or do anything suspicious, his American wingmen, both of them aces, were under orders to shoot him down.

Their mission was straightforward. Cantacuzene would land at Popesti and determine that it was still in Rumanian hands. His American escort would circle overhead, waiting for his signal that all was well. Upon seeing a double yellow star that Cantacuzene would fire from a Very pistol, his escort would broadcast the All Clear to another fighter circling at altitude, midway between Bucharest and Italy. The relay aircraft would then pass the signal to Bari, where two B-17s loaded with an Office of Strategic Services (OSS) team and equipment were waiting to take off.

Finding the field secure, Cantacuzene fired the double star, and the second phase of Operation Gunn was under way.

At 12:15 P.M., the B-17s, with thirty-two fighters in escort, took off for Popesti Airdrome. Onboard the bombers were twelve men, most of them from the Office of Strategic Services—forerunner of today's Central Intelligence Agency—and 250 gallons of 100-octane fuel for Cantacuzene's P-51. In command was Col. George Kraiger.

During recent months Colonel Kraiger had been working with Chetnik guerrillas in Yugoslavia, retrieving downed airmen who had evaded capture. A commanding and resourceful officer, Kraiger was a fine choice to head the advance party.

The task force encountered no opposition en route. As fighters circled overhead, the B-17s set down on the airdrome, discharged their passengers and equipment, then immediately took off for the return trip to Italy.

Colonel Kraiger and his party were greeted by Mr. Georgescu, who escorted them to the home of Demeter Bragadiru. (He was the Bragadiru of the brewery family, and son-in-law of Princess Catherine Caradja.) There, the OSS communicators set up two radio sets and attempted to contact Bari. The team would continue to operate the radios for several days without success.

In the party that greeted Kraiger was Major Yeager, our own inveterate communicator. Yeager accompanied Kraiger and briefed him on the status of the ex-prisoners. At this point Kraiger was faced with the seemingly insurmountable problem of rounding up hundreds of celebrating ex-prisoners, transporting them to Popesti Airdrome at the proper time, and establishing contact with Bari. Faced with so complex a problem he concluded that gathering the prisoners and finding transportation to move them to the airfield would be his first priority. Communicating with Bari would be handled in time.

The following afternoon, the thirtieth, radio communication with Bari still had not been established. Desperate to inform Fifteenth Air Force that all would be ready for the transporting bombers by August 31, Kraiger dispatched Cantacuzene in the refueled P-51, with a letter addressed to General Twining.

The indispensible captain had the wheels of his P-51 in their wells by 5:15 P.M. and arrived in Bari two hours later. Again the Americans had been forced to place their trust and the lives of many men in the goodwill of a former enemy who, until a few days before, had been fighting against them with great fury and success.[2]

Upon receiving Colonel Kraiger's report, General Twining made the final decision. Operation Reunion would launch in the morning.

The first of thirty-six B-17s of the Second and Ninety-seventh groups, with newly installed plywood flooring in their bomb bays, would start their takeoff rolls at 8:00 A.M. They would leave in groups of twelve aircraft, with one-hour intervals between groups. Heavy escorts of P-51s and P-38s would accompany the bombers while others swept the skies north of their route. It was a daring plan. The flight would be made at medium altitude, 12,000 feet. The ships would carry minimum ammunition, crews of only five men, and *no parachutes*. The distance to Bucharest and return, and the intervening landing and takeoff, would require so much fuel that the weight of the bombers had to be lowered to provide for the extra weight. The combined heft of a full crew, twenty passengers, parachutes, and full ammunition would have added several thousand pounds to the gross weight of the aircraft. More bombers could have been used in the operation and fewer passengers carried on each ship, but that would have meant

2. After the war, Cantacuzene escaped from Rumania to western Europe. For years he tried unsuccessfully to get a visa to come to the United States. Denied at every hand by an ill-informed and uncaring bureaucracy, a fine man who could have made valuable contributions to our burgeoning civil aviation industry died brokenhearted and impoverished in Spain from peritonitis, following surgery for an ulcer.

still more bombers and escorting fighters, consumed more time, and created higher risks because of the numbers involved. The planners believed that flak could be avoided and that the escorting fighters were adequate protection.

Despite these unusual and risky conditions, the Second and Ninety-seventh bomb groups were inundated with volunteers to fly the mission.

XXIII

The prospects of getting out of Rumania left us with little desire to sleep. As the evening wore on, a story came around that we would fly back to Italy in B-17s. It was a fascinating idea—B-17s carrying men in place of bombs. It was a revolutionary concept, and it kept many American ex-POWs awake throughout the night speculating about this trail-blazing event.

Awakened at 5:00 A.M., we had breakfast, boarded waiting buses, and headed for Popesti Airdrome. Again I had to wait for the buses to return from delivering their first load. Being the second group to arrive at Popesti also meant that I would have to wait for the second wave of bombers to arrive.

Popesti Airdrome was a beehive. Messerschmitt 109s, Focke-Wulf 190s, G-50s, and a host of other aircraft crowded the field's limited parking areas. The north side of the field was barren in preparation for the arrival of the B-17s. A bird-colonel—Colonel Kraiger, a man whom I'd never seen before—was waiting to give us instructions. We were to gather in groups of twenty, with 150 feet separating the groups alongside the field. When a B-17 stopped in front of a group and killed its engines, we were to enter the aircraft without delay and take seats in the bomb bay for an immediate takeoff.

I wondered about the instruction "take a seat in the bomb bay." The hinged, electrically operated doors of the B-17 are much stronger than the sliding doors of the B-24, but to put the weight of twenty men on them would be unthinkable. However, I would worry about that later. The carnivallike atmosphere at the field was too interesting to worry about bomb bay doors.

Rumanian troops stood guard as scores of civilians, some accompanied by ex–prisoners of war, arrived in automobiles. Happy ex-prisoners milled about, smiling, and as Americans are wont to do, traded articles of clothing and insignia for Rumanian memorabilia. Unbeknownst to me, a First Combat Camera Unit crew, armed with a 16mm motion picture camera, photographed the "grand farewell."[1]

Most of the Rumanian soldiers were content to stand and smile at hundreds of happy, friendly Americans who only a few days before had been considered gangsters and criminals. Their own friendliness belied any such lasting beliefs. With the war against us over, it was as though not a hostile shot had been fired. Other Rumanian soldiers seemed confused, unable to comprehend the remarkable turn of events.

A mixed formation of armed army and air force enlisted men were standing near our group. I assumed that they, like many other such groups of soldiers disposed throughout the area, were there to protect us should German troops make a sudden appearance. Their fixed bayonets also suggested concern that angry civilians could cause problems. I wasn't worried about civilians or a ground attack, nor did an air attack seem likely—that is, unless some of the many 109s and 190s flying overhead turned out to be German. The Rumanian air force was out in force to ward off the possibility of German attack.

A Rumanian captain and a lieutenant who appeared to be in charge of our guard had been watching us, obviously enjoying our outward manifestations of happiness. Catching my eye, the captain approached me and pointed to my silver wings. Without hesitation I removed the wings and handed them to him. Grinning like the fabled Cheshire cat, he unpinned his wings and pinned them on my flight suit. Not to be outdone, the lieutenant removed his rank insignia and slipped them onto the epaulets of my flight suit. It was turning out to be quite a ceremony.

A Rumanian army NCO removed his belt, hung with a fine German bayonet, and presented it to me. The solemn manner in which he presented the bayonet made me think of Lee surrendering his saber to Grant (even though I knew he never actually did that). I tried to return the bayonet to him, but he wouldn't have it. I had nothing to offer in return but a smile and handshake. That brought a smile and an animated speech as he explained something to the formation of troops. Whatever it was, they and the two officers laughed.[2]

1. Thirty-eight years passed before I learned of and saw the film, which showed the first large-scale air rescue in history.

2. Following the exchange of insignia, and my acceptance of the formal surrender of the Rumanian Air Force, one of the ex-POWs (I regret that I cannot now remember who) photographed me in front of the Rumanian troop formation with a camera he acquired

Our first indication that the bombers were approaching the field was a single P-51 making a low pass down the runway. Approximately fifty feet above the ground, and at midfield, the pilot executed a beautiful aileron roll, then chandelled up into a left turn, dropped his gear, held a tight pattern, and greased the ship onto the grass field. Within moments, formation after formation of P-51s made low, high-speed passes across the field—as knights of the air charging with the unique violence that only great speed can impart. The roar of engines was all but lost in the sound of voices cheering, driven beyond exhilaration by the thrilling sight. I almost missed seeing the pilot of the ship that made the daring low-altitude roll kill his engine and climb out. It was Cantacuzene.

Approaching the field, fighter-escort pilots were intrigued by the forty or fifty 109s and 190s, with their newly painted Rumanian insignia barely covering black crosses, flying helter-skelter all over the place. Capt. Leland Molland, an ace who would finish the war with eleven victories, pulled up beside a 109 and waggled his wings in friendship. The Rumanian returned Molland's salute. Both men realized that only a week before, sighting one another would have resulted in a deadly duel. When his aircraft arrived over the field, Molland's first instinct was disappointment that he couldn't take his squadron down to strafe the dozens of 109s and 190s stacked up so invitingly on the ground.

Our first sight of the big birds drew another cheer as B-17s peeled out of formation and circled to land. As a bomber pulled up in front of its group of twenty, the mass of eager men seemed to shift in concert, then fragment as they dashed wildly to be on board and off the ground. I found myself waving good-bye to those who made the first flight. An interminable hour would pass before I could board a ship in the second wave.

The smell of raw metal and zinc oxide paint brought·back familiar memories as I bent over to climb through the entrance door of the ship. Waving with a thankful smile at the grinning engineer who stood

---

following our release from the camp. Lt. Sherwood A. (Woody) Mark, a combat cameraman of the First Combat Camera Unit and attached to the Ninety-eighth Bomb Group, traded his expensive wristwatch for a relatively inexpensive Voigtlander camera. He took many memorable pictures in Bucharest and at Popesti Airdrome. Woody was shot down on his first mission.

ready to call the pilot and tell him we were aboard, I made my way forward to the bomb bay. Men crouched on plywood flooring and muttered about the absence of parachutes. With few exceptions, they had all experienced the irreplaceable value of those once-feared bundles of nylon. Before being shot down they had viewed the cumbersome devices as undesirable necessities that one had to put up with. Now, faced with a four-hundred-mile flight, most of which would be over enemy territory, flying without a parachute brought back fearful memories.

I had barely dropped to the plywood flooring and tested it for strength when an engine on the right wing coughed to life and awakened the waiting craft. Idling engines roared as the pilot let the B-17 trundle from its parking place. Moments before, we'd been laughing and congratulating each other as only men who have found release from imminent danger can. Each of us had tasted the bitterness of defeat, yet ours was the ultimate victory. We had survived and were starting the long journey home.

As the heavy bomber taxied into takeoff position, the gaunt men now huddling on the makeshift floor in the bomb bay grew silent —some in prayer, others caught in a vise of old fears. Each of us had known the terror of an emergency parachute jump, or the trauma of a crash landing. Now, on our final flight over hundreds of miles of enemy territory, the spectre that this flight would end as had our last brought back deep, unwanted fears.

Engines strained against their mounts until the pilot released his brakes and let the big ship lumber forward. We could sense the increase in ground speed by the sound of engines and the propellers biting ever more easily into the air. The tail lifted and gave us a more horizontal floor to sit on. Moments later the ship lifted into the air, lifting tense bodies and spirits as we realized we were airborne and on our way—not for home, but away from this place of unwanted memories, hunger, and terror.

The men began to move about in the aircraft, but the pilot asked that we limit our movements. Too many of us moving about at the same time would make the ship more difficult to handle. I appreciated his problem and recalled times when my crew, in order to punish me for some real or imagined error, had moved forward and aft in the rear of our craft and kept me constantly on the elevator trim wheel.

As men returned to the bomb bay, others left to visit the cockpit or chat with the crew. Some crew! There were only five of them including the two pilots. We'd also gotten the word about our light supply of machine-gun ammo, and that the crew was also flying without parachutes.

It had been almost a year since I'd flown a B-17, yet the cockpit was still as familiar as that of the B-24. I chatted with the pilot for a while and came close to asking him if I could fly the bird. But being in formation with the lead aircraft, I didn't want to embarrass myself trying to hold formation in the heavy-handed bird at only 9,000 feet.

Damn! Nine thousand feet. At this altitude, I thought, if we wandered over a flak site, as often happened in combat, we would be sitting ducks for the 88s and even for the rapid-firing 40mm guns. It was something to *not* think about.

It bothered me when I discovered that the waist guns had been removed and there was no belly-gunner in the turret. Looking through the waist windows, I'd never seen so many fighters. P-38s were flying lazy S's high above, and much nearer P-51s were flying similar patterns. Miles to the north, I saw another flight of what I hoped to be P-51s flying as outriders, should the Luftwaffe come diving in from that most likely direction.[3]

Tension grew, subsided, and returned as we droned our way over Yugoslavia. Once we cleared the coast, it would be downhill the rest of the way. Twice I left the bomb bay to peer through the waist windows for sight of the Adriatic. I was in the bomb bay, about two snores from a sound sleep, when someone poked his head through the front entrance and shouted that the Adriatic was in sight.

It had not occurred to me that others had been holding the same thoughts. We all knew instinctively that our rescue meant little until we were safely above that lovely sea. I had to restrain myself to keep from springing up, along with too many others, for sight of that longed-for blue. Many minutes passed before the first group returned from their prayer-fulfilling examination of the water below.

When it came my turn I went to the right waist window and drank in the sight of azure water. The feeling of peace transcended any I

3. During the daring airlift, a brief battle was indeed fought some miles north of the withdrawal route. One P-38, and one—possibly two—German Messerschmitts went down.

Ploesti POW Life Described By Rescued 450th Operations Officer

Was Blown From B-24 Over Target; Tells Of Liberation

By 1st Lt. JOHN A. STEVENSON

47th Wing (PRO) — "So much happened so damned fast those last few days, I am sure I couldn't have lived another week under that pressure," said Lt Col William G. Snaith, senior commanding officer of the AAF aircrew prisoner of war compounds at Bucharest, on arrival here after evacuation with the last contingent. He was describing those last hectic days between the capitulation of Rumania and the beginning of the mass aerial evacuation of the 1,000 odd survivors of the terrific battles in the sky over the Ploesti refineries.

Incredible Tale

His is the kind of a story that makes the press correspondent froth at the mouth at the thought of word economies required by cable restrictions and writhe at every stroke of the press censor's blue pencil. It begins with a miraculous escape when his B-24 was blown apart over Ploesti, gives the world one of its first glimpses of the operation and administration of an American prisoner of war camp, and reaches its striking climax with the daring flight of heavy bombers into Bucharest to snatch the liberated airmen right from under the nose of the enemy.

On July 15, 1944 Col Snaith, operations officer of the 450th Gp, led the entire 47th Wing in an attack on Ploesti. As the formation went into the bomb run, it was immediately wrapped in the smashing flak barrage always put up at this heaviest defended of all 15th Air Force targets. Col Snaith had just had the "Bombs Away" signal and was turning off the target when it happened.

Ship In Flames

"Someone called, 'We've been hit!' over the interphone," he remembers. "I barely had time to turn my head and look back to see the bomb bay enveloped in flames when the cockpit itself blossomed out with fire. I tried desparately to control the ship, but it nosed over and the dive angle kept getting steeper. Then self preservation took over. I tried to get out of the seat, couldn't—tried opening the window and failed, then cupped my hands in my face thinking, 'this must be it'. Then I was in midair, on my back, looking up at the burning plane some 200 feet above me.

"It was a strange sensation. I seemed to have all the time in the world. I calmly looked over my shoulder to estimate the altitude and then back to see if the damned ship was going to fall on me. Then I guess I must have pulled the rip cord."

Tells Of Prison Life

Lt Col William G. Snaith (left) being Interrogated by Lt Col Jack E. Thomas, 47th Wing A-2, at Wing Headquarters.

had experienced returning from previous missions. It was strange how the sight of the Adriatic, like the sound of the siren, could trigger such powerful responses within me.

Relief, the relief from danger, had always come each time I'd crossed that friendly sea. It was like adding up the score: one more victory, one step closer to the end. I remained at the window until the cliffs of Manfredonia appeared on the horizon. I hadn't seen the cliffs the night we'd stepped off the PT boat, but I had known they were there. Having seen them so many times while en route to or from targets, I had wanted a closer view of them from the ground. That seemed so long ago. Then, when we had finally gotten a closer look on the day we dead-sticked onto the British field, I had wished they were more distant. That had been a close one. In one way or another, all of our missions had had their elements of danger. Now, the cliffs having been spotted, this last half of my sixteenth mission became a joyride.

Except for the curious who'd gathered following the return of the first twelve aircraft, our arrival at Bari was without fanfare. There were only eleven ships in our flight. One aircraft had blown a tire when landing at Popesti. I stepped onto Italian soil, grinning through a small unspoken prayer. Some dropped to their knees and touched or kissed the ground. General Twining had been on hand to greet the first group, then had returned to his headquarters, but I was quite satisfied by the presence of General Born. Generals didn't concern me, but the call to mount waiting trucks and get a hot shower and clean clothing was tantamount to an engraved invitation from God Almighty.

It wasn't just a shower. We were taken to a remote open area and told to take off all our clothing and pile it on the ground. Our unwanted hitchhikers were finally going to get their due. Our clothing would be burned.

I'd never seen so many bare asses, skinny legs, and rib cages as those in the line of men stepping up to the medics, who doused our heads and other hairy parts with delousing powder. I hated to part with my flight suit, but I tossed it onto the growing pile of uniform parts, underwear, and socks—not, however, before removing my newly acquired Rumanian pilot wings, the lieutenant's insignia, and the Luftwaffe Eagle I'd bribed a guard to buy for me to aid me in escaping. I'd fought in that suit, I'd jumped in it twice and had lived through days of terror and privation, wearing it with pride and loving care. As with our worn flags, perhaps a funeral pyre was its fitting end.

New underwear, khaki shirt and trousers were soothing to skin scrubbed tender in a luxurious shower. I had forgotten how good it was to feel truly clean. The only item of clothing we retained was our shoes. With new socks on our feet, the old boots felt better than would new ones. I was most surprised at my size 28 trousers. Until now I hadn't realized how much weight I'd lost: some forty-odd pounds.

The GI food, of which I'd grown so tired before that last mission, didn't really taste any better than before—but there was plenty of it. The coffee and buttered bread could only be described as wonderful. I was so stuffed that I passed up the beer tent that had been set up in our area. Most of us chose to sit on canvas cots in our tents and to reflect on the past, savor the future, and dream of our coming return to families and friends. Thoughts of war, even the terrors of the camps, were put aside. One moment we'd been in Bucharest, with all its possibilities of sudden and violent death. Now, hardly more than moments later, we were noncombatants, with the promise of joyous lives extending for years into an enticing future. As I lay comfortably on the cot, sleep came—then exploded in the sudden boom of artillery and the hated wailing of a siren.

Not fully awake, I was aware of the sound of 90mm guns, interspersed with that of rapid-firing Bofors. I felt pain in my wrists, my knees; and what the hell was wrong with my nose and forehead? Something was smashing my face and head. The noise sounded as though a thousand guns were firing, lighting the night with each violent flash.

Realization licked my mind in gentle waves, then broke to full awareness: I'm in Bari. There's no war here!

The hell there isn't! The flak guns are still firing, and that damned siren isn't screaming for nothing.

I moved to get off the cot, and was momentarily confused by the position of my body. I wasn't on the cot. I was on my elbows and knees with my face jammed into the cross-legs that formed the center support of the folding cot. The pain was from various extremities I'd scraped against the wooden floor of the tent frame, or on the legs of the cot. The moment the siren, or the guns, had made their hateful sounds, I had reverted to my Pavlovian instincts by rolling onto the floor and trying to crawl beneath my cot.[4]

The sound of nervous voices drew me outside the tent. It looked like a Fourth of July celebration. A black sky was rent by hundreds of streaking tracers, weaving their colorful webs, seeking to ensnare and destroy the unseen intruder. It was a hell of a show but the target, most likely a German reconnaissance bird, appeared to have escaped unscathed.

The show was over and the siren had quieted, but I was too jittery and wet with sweat to go back to bed. The once-lonely beer tent could barely be seen within the press of anxious bodies. The time for thoughtful reflection was over. It was time to have a party.

My breakfast coffee wasn't on the best of terms with the aftermath of the beer I had guzzled following the alert. The beer hadn't helped the sweating, but after several cans of the warm brew I'd hardly noticed any trembling in myself or my cohorts. I hadn't consumed that much beer, I thought, but something was creating a nagging feeling within me.

Standing in the hot sun, hour after hour, waiting for bombers from our outfits to take us back to our bases was becoming a chore. No one knew when we'd be leaving Italy. For now we were returning to our respective groups for much-needed physical examinations, decoration ceremonies, and administrative processing. As soon as transportation could be arranged, we would be flown to a port of embarkation, where we would board a ship and join a convoy for the trip across the Atlantic. At the moment I was wondering why 450th aircraft hadn't arrived to retrieve their errant sons.

All morning aircraft from other groups had been arriving and departing with their celebrated cargos. I enjoyed the drama of several reunions as crews arrived and discovered missing comrades among the crowd of survivors. It was a particularly touching scene when an arriving crew discovered one of us, presumed to have perished, waiting patiently instead for a ride home. I might have enjoyed the drama much more had it not been for a 376th pilot who kept needling me about the failure of the Cottontails to reclaim their own. I'd pointed

4. Twenty-five years later, when enemy rockets exploded without warning in Saigon and on Thon Son Nhut Air Base, I was delighted to find my responses still in fine tune. Even in these late years, given a proper stimulus, I expect I could still awaken beneath my bed.

out to him that, carrying only ten passengers in each plane, the 450th would have had to send one-third of its aircraft to pick us up. Despite the constant needling we received in the camps, men from other units appeared shocked when all of the 450th men gathered in a group on the ramp, thus disclosing how many of us there actually were. And we weren't all there. There hadn't been enough B-17s to bring everyone back on the first day. Three-hundred and ninety-three more men would be flown back from Rumania today.

It was nearing noon, and only we and the 376th men hadn't been picked up. Suddenly a dozen B-24s in a formation of V's in trail, their bellies almost scraping the ground, streaked down the runway and fanned up and outward in a fighter approach and landing. It was pretty —and illegal. Someone would catch hell for that buzz job.

With pride, I turned to my tormentor. "See that, you bastard? There's the Cottontails."

"Bullshit! Where're the white tails?"

I looked at the bombers peeling up off the runway, and at those turning sharply onto the downwind leg behind me. There wasn't a white tail in the entire gaggle.

The heat of embarrassment flooded my face, but I held my ground. "I don't know where the white tails are, but that's the 450th."

"Shiiit," he drawled. "What makes you think that?"

"I can tell by the way they fly."

Who else but pilots of an outfit with so little chance of survival as the Cottontails would have had the audacity to pull a buzz job at Bari, right there at Fifteenth Air Force Headquarters?

The words hadn't mattered. It was his tone of voice that had gotten to me. He could have made the remark in jest. Instead he'd chosen to insult me. I made up my mind. Comrade or not, if he opens his mouth again I'll deck the son of a bitch. Luckily for both of us, he didn't.

Several minutes later revenge arrived with the sweetness of a spring freshet.

I watched, dumbfounded, as the lead aircraft made its awkward turn to taxi up and brake to a halt in front of us. Its nose art was a large black keyhole. Bending forward on shapely legs, peering through the keyhole, saucy derrière peeking provocatively from beneath a tiny skirt, was a fine feminine form. Painted above the figure were the words, PEEKIN THRU. In front of the art were the numbers 5 1 1.

EXTRA!

COTTONTALES

VOL. II. NO. 10   Saturday, April 7, 1945   ITALY

450th RECEIVES 2nd CITATION

General Twining Present At Ceremonies Here; Group Cited For Historic Ploesti Mission

At 3 P.M. this afternoon, Maj. Gen Nathan F. Twining, Commanding General of the 15th Air Force, presented the 450th Bomb Group with a cluster to the Distinguished Unit Citation. Earlier this week, it was disclosed that the award had been granted, in recognition of the group's successful leadership and outstanding performance of duty in opening the Ploesti Campaign last April 5th.

A year ago at this time, the Ploesti Marshalling Yards, key transportation hub for supplying petroleum to the still powerful Nazi forces on the eastern Front, was ablaze from an incendiary attack paced by the Cottontails. It was the first in a series of incessant blows that were to materially weaken the Wehrmacht and subsequently pave the way for the Red Army's conquest of the Balkans.

The 450th was in the vanguard of this initial, April 5th assault. Forty of its planes were dispatched to this "most highly defended target in the world" without the support of fighter cover. The Luftwaffe, a redoubtable force at the time, was sent up to challenge the formation and thwart it objective. Twenty five minutes before target time, a dozen ME 109s dove out of the clouds, and attacking aggressively, shot down three bombers from the leading box.

(Continued on page four)

General Twining

"Five One One!" There was only one B-24 in the Army Air Force with that nose number. My plane! The *Swashbuckler!*

"You son of a bitch!" I shouted at my tormentor. "That's not only the 450th, that's my airplane!"

The pilot was leaning out of his window, a broad grin painting his familiar face. It was a guy I'd checked out when he arrived at

Manduria, the same one who'd broken formation to bomb the round-house in northern Italy.

I was embarrassed. For the life of me, I couldn't remember his name. But he remembered mine.

"Get in, Cub! Let's go home."

I walked to the nose of the ship to inspect the new art. Etched in the pores of the shiny metal, a shadow of the old *Swashbuckler* emblem was visible beyond the edges of the new painting. The ship had been retrieved from its ungainly ending in the olive grove and had undergone extensive repairs. The white rudders had been painted silver and the lower front portion of the vertical stabilizers had been painted with vertical stripes. The old girl looked to be as good as new.

"What'd you do to my plane?" I shouted up at him.

"Your plane?" he answered with a grin. "It's mine now!"

I returned his smile and headed for the camera hatch. Inside, I grinned my pleasure at my crew and worked my way through the bomb bay to the cockpit. Sitting on the flight deck, rocking in rhythm with the ship's taxiing motion, I listened to the familiar sound of the Pratt & Whitneys and wondered if number-three would cough on takeoff.

FIFTEENTH AIR FORCE
Office of the Commanding General
A. P. O. 520

4 September 1944

2nd Lt. William R. Cubbins
Hq. Fifteenth Air Force
APO 520, U. S. Army

Dear Lt. Cubbins:

You are going home. With you will go the thanks and
admiration of the Fifteenth Air Force for a superb
and heroic performance. You are the returning heroes
of the Battle of Ploesti. You will be greeted and
treated as such by your loved ones, and by a grateful American public. They are proud of you.

Your safe return to my command marked the culmina-
tion of an outstanding campaign in the annals of
American military history. The German war machines'
disintegration on all fronts is being caused, to a
large extent, by their lack of oil - oil that you
took from them.

I have only one regret on this jubilant occasion.
I wish it had been possible to bring out of Roumania
every officer and man who went down in that battle.
Unfortunately there are some who will never return.
The memory of their sacrifice is an inspiration to
the all of us.

One of the memories of my life will be the thrill I
experienced as the B-17s came into view, circled,
landed, and I saw you unloading. It was impossible
for me to greet each of you and it will be impossible
for me to say "Good-bye" to each of you before you
return to the States. However, I do want you to
know my thoughts and those of your fellow soldiers
are with you.

Best of luck and Godspeed.

N. F. TWINING
Major General, USA
Commanding

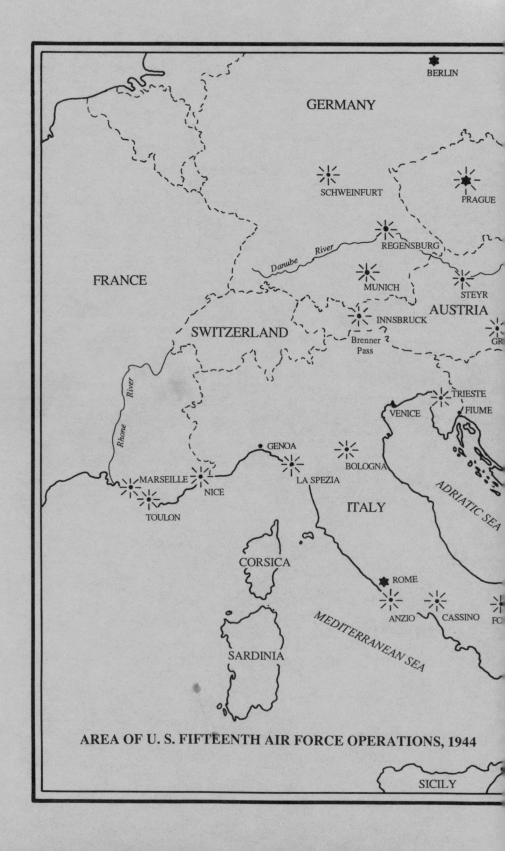

AREA OF U. S. FIFTEENTH AIR FORCE OPERATIONS, 1944